Law Across Borders

Law Across Borders examines the applicati
law to people and circumstances outside
analyses which have focused on a single a
examines the fields of criminal and hum
private law applied across borders – in a
in context before being thoroughly descri
surveys historical practice, describes cu
enforcement. The author's analysis incl
criminalisation of sex tourism, the extra
the application of human rights law to
intervention in the region. The book go
development of the extraterritorial appl
which greater coherence can be achieved.

Law Across Borders will be of particular i
scholars of international law, human rig
in its ambition to offer a comprehensive
territorial application of UK human rig
text.

Paul Arnell is a Reader in Law and Pos
University, Aberdeen, Scotland. His ar
application of law. He has published wid
International and Comparative Law Quarter
Law Journal.

Law Across Borders

The Extraterritorial Application of United Kingdom Law

Paul Arnell

Routledge
Taylor & Francis Group
LONDON AND NEW YORK

First published 2012
by Routledge
2 Park Square, Milton Park, Abingdon, Oxon OX14 4RN

Simultaneously published in the USA and Canada
by Routledge
711 Third Avenue, New York, NY 10017

Routledge is an imprint of the Taylor & Francis Group, an informa business

British Library Cataloguing in Publication Data
A catalogue record for this book is available from the British Library

Library of Congress Cataloguing in Publication Data
Arnell, Paul.
Law across borders : the extraterritorial application of United Kingdom law / Paul Arnell.
p. cm.
Includes bibliographical references and index.
1. Exterritoriality. 2. Conflict of laws—Jurisdiction—Great Britain.
3. Criminal law—Great Britain. 4. Human rights—Great Britain.
I. Title.
KD680.A97 2012
340.90941—dc23 2011023211

ISBN 978–0–415–55861–7 (hbk)
ISBN 978–0–203–15334–5 (ebk)

Typeset in Garamond
by Keystroke, Station Road, Codsall, Wolverhampton

For: Sarah, James and Alice

Contents

Table of cases

United Kingdom

Other jurisdictions

Canada

European Court of Human Rights

International Court of Justice

Israel

Permanent Court of International Justice

United Nations Committee on Human Rights

United States

Al-Skeini and others v the United Kingdom Application No. 55721/07, 7 July 2011

Subsequent to the submission of the manuscript of *Law Across Borders* the Grand Chamber of the European Court of Human Rights, on 7 July 2011, published its decision in *Al-Skeini and others v the United Kingdom*. This significant judgement must be noted as it directly and importantly relates to the subject matter of the book.

The facts and jurisprudence leading up to the decision are discussed in Chapter 4. Here it is sufficient to discuss the judgement. The crux of the issue was whether the relatives of the applicants, who were killed in the area of southern Iraq over which the UK exercised authority for the maintenance of security following the invasion in 2003, were within the jurisdiction of the UK under Article 1 of the Convention. The House of Lords had held that they were not, with Lords Rodger and Carswell explicitly stating that the UK was not in effective control of Basrah City at the relevant time.[1] Further, the House of Lords considered and rejected 'state agent authority' as an independent basis upon which jurisdiction could be founded.

Following the decision of the House of Lords the six applicants lodged an application against the UK on 11 December 2007 alleging that their relatives fell within UK jurisdiction when killed and that there had been no effective investigation into the deaths, in breach of Article 2 of the Convention.

The Grand Chamber unanimously held, in contrast to the decision of the House of Lords, that all the applicants were within the jurisdiction of the UK for the purposes of Article 1 of the Convention.[2] It stated that whilst jurisdiction is primarily territorial it can exceptionally extend to outside a State Party's territorial boundaries. The Grand Chamber held it can do so under two heads 'state agent authority and control' and 'effective control of an area'. The former was held to create a 'jurisdictional link' between

1 *R (on the application of Al-Skeini) v Secretary of State for Defence*, [2007] UKHL 26 at paras 83 and 97.

2 The UK was ordered to pay 17,000 euros in damages to each of the five applicants in regard to whom the UK contested jurisdiction.

the relatives of the applicants and the UK. The Court stated '. . . the United Kingdom, through its soldiers engaged in security operations in Basrah during the period in question, exercised authority and control over individuals killed in the course of such security operations, so as to establish a jurisdictional link between the deceased and the United Kingdom for the purposes of Article 1 of the Convention'.[3]

Al-Skeini and others v the United Kingdom is a significant judgement for several reasons. Most obviously it sheds considerable light on the nature of the application of the Convention across borders. Whilst emphasising the territorial nature of jurisdiction the Court clearly provides that it can exceptionally extend under two heads. Within UK jurisprudence and indeed the case law of the European Court of Human Rights itself the existence and nature of 'state agent authority' had been unclear. Secondly, the Court accepted that it is possible that the rights protected under the Convention may be 'divided and tailored'.[4] Hitherto, and supported by the previously leading case of *Bankovic v Belgium et al*,[5] the law provided that the Convention had to apply *in toto*, or not at all. This is a notable development, and only time will tell how exactly the protections under the Convention may be divided and tailored. The Court merely provides that where state agents exercise control and authority over an individual, the particular state is obliged to secure rights and freedoms that are 'relevant to the situation of the individual'.[6]

The usage of the term 'jurisdictional link' in the *Al-Skeini v the United Kingdom* judgement is in itself a notable aspect of it. As will be explained in Chapters 1 and 5, a theme emerging from the application of law across borders is a proper law approach. In essence this provides that the law will only be extended and applied in the presence of a sufficient connection or link between the state and the subject of the application of the law. The term jurisdiction link provides some support to this theme. Up to this point the term was rarely used. Finally, a point in the separate concurring opinion of Judge Bonello should be mentioned. This relates to the arguments made by the United Kingdom that to extend the application of the Convention as argued by the applicants would amount to 'human rights imperialism'. This is a point the present author puts forward in Chapter 5 as militating against the application of human rights law across borders. Judge Bonello dismisses it summarily. He states: 'For my part, I believe that those who export war ought to see to the parallel export of guarantees against the atrocities of war. And then, if necessary, bear with some fortitude the opprobrium of being labelled human rights imperialists'.[7]

3 At para 149.
4 At para 137.
5 (2001) 11 BHRC 435 at para 75.
6 Supra note 3.
7 At para 39. On the same day that the Al-Skeini judgment was published was that of *Al-Jeddah v the UK*, Application Number 27021/08. Whilst the UK Government had conceded that Article 5 applied to his incarceration in Iraq it, and the House of Lords, were of the view that UN Security Council Resolution 1546 in essence displaced its operation. The Grand Chamber disagreed and held that the Resolution could and should be interpreted in harmony with the Convention.

1 Introduction

Introduction

Increased international intercourse by persons and states has given rise to an enhanced desire to apply law across borders. The United Kingdom is amongst the states acting on this desire. UK law is increasingly applied to persons and circumstances that in some way exist or occur outside its territory. Not only does it occur more frequently than in the past, but it also relates to a wider range of legal fields. Traditionally, the criminal law was the sole field of non-private law that was applied across borders. Today, human rights law is also not uncommonly considered to relate to persons or circumstances outside the UK. The position is complicated further by distinct institutions and component parts of the UK acting in the area, with the UK and Scottish Parliaments, domestic and European courts and the UK executive all playing a part. The increased frequency of law being applied across borders, human rights law joining the criminal law in being applied in this way and the number of actors involved heightens the necessity for clarity and consistency. This is in part because those possibly subject to UK law whilst outside it, be that a criminal sanction or human rights protection, deserve to be aware of that fact. Indeed, those persons possibly subject to the criminal law whilst outside the UK may have their right to be free from the non-retroactivity of the criminal law violated where the law is unclear.[1] Further, the need for consistency and clarity results from the degree of commonality between the criminal law and human rights law to the extent that they are being related to persons and events outside the UK. It is desirable that where the law operates in a similar way in different fields, it does so, as far as possible, in a kindred manner based upon common principles. Where the law does not apply in a like manner, this should be for clear and defensible reasons. There is undoubtedly a need for principle to run through the application of all UK law applied across borders. The law should as far as possible be predictable. Finally, clarity and consistency are called for because in most cases the locus of

1 Found in Art 7 of the European Convention for the Protection of Human Rights and Fundamental Freedoms 1950 (hereinafter 'the Convention').

the person or circumstance to which UK law is applied across borders is within a third state. That state will almost certainly be entitled under international law to apply its own law in the circumstances, and so the issue of concurrent jurisdiction arises. A clear, consistent and principled approach within UK law can assist it not only in deciding whether to proceed and apply its law, but can also be used in coming to a decision as to where proceedings should take place in the face of concurrent jurisdiction. The factors supporting clarity and consistency in the law will become further evident throughout this book.

Investigation into the application of UK law across borders serves to meet the demand for clarity and consistency. In addition, it addresses the basic question of why it is felt necessary by the UK Parliament, courts or executive to apply the law across borders in the first instance. Related to this is why a line is drawn at any particular point and why the UK does not take a more expansive approach than it does at present. The answer to these questions is found in the notion of the national interest. The UK largely applies its law across its borders in an effort to protect or secure its interests. As Jennings noted over half a century ago in regard to why states act and the limits of international law:

> States claim extraterritorial jurisdiction in cases where they believe their legitimate interests to be concerned; whether that assumption be rationalized and expressed by means of the nationality claim, the objective territorial claim, the security claim, the passive personality claim or the universality claim. It is reasonable to say, therefore, that international law will permit a State to exercise extraterritorial jurisdiction provided that State's legitimate interests (legitimate that is to say by tests accepted in the common practice of States) are involved . . . [A] State has a right to extraterritorial jurisdiction where its legitimate interests are concerned . . .[2]

A related comment is that the application of law across borders is 'as a matter of law . . . presented as an issue of jurisdiction, the underlying problem is one of State interests'.[3] Whilst this simple fact – that the UK applies its law across borders where it deems that its national interest requires it to do so – may seem axiomatic, there are instances where the law is applied in the absence of readily apparent interests. Indeed, it may at times be thought that the application of law is inimical to such interests. Examples here include the crime of torture abroad by non-UK nationals and residents under section 134 of the Criminal Justice Act 1988, the criminalisation of various child-sex offences committed abroad under the Sex Offenders Act 1997 and the application of Article 2 of the Convention to the death in Iraq of an Iraqi national.[4] In these instances it

2 Jennings, R.Y., 'Extraterritorial Jurisdiction and U.S. Antitrust Laws' (1957) 33 BYIL 146 at pp 152–3.

3 Roth, P.M., 'Reasonable Extraterritoriality: Correcting the "Balance of Interests"' [1992] ICLQ 245 at p 273. The statement is made in the context of competition law.

4 *Al-Skeini and others v Secretary of State for Defence* [2007] UKHL 26.

is not wholly unreasonable to argue that the application of UK law is at odds with its national interest for reasons including that the victims are almost certainly non-nationals, the *locus delicti* or human rights violation was outside the UK, and that to do so would entail a not-insubstantial financial cost.

Discussion of the question of why the UK does not take an even more expansive approach to the application of its law across borders is perhaps even more illuminating than why it does so in specific cases. The answer is found in the interests of, and limits imposed by, international law and third states and practical difficulties. Public international law, whilst arguably vague and lacking in the provision of a clear and immediate legal deterrent, places limits on the range and nature of the applicability of domestic law. Related to the fact that the practice of states gives rise to rules of public international law is that the UK is one of approximately 200 equal and sovereign states. In order to be able to legitimately defend its own sovereignty and lawful ability to apply its law within and exceptionally outside its territory, it must act in a relatively limited and restrained manner. Perhaps as effective in limiting the scope of UK law is the fact that the enforcement of law across borders is inherently problematic. Procedural and evidential difficulties often conspire to affect its enforcement. Indeed, there exist indubitable legal and practical barriers to the application of UK law across borders The law applied in too wide a sense, even if lawful, may be ineffective and prohibitively expensive. These limitations on the application of UK law across borders raise an important underlying point. This is that the application of law across borders is and should be exceptional. The UK has traditionally and correctly taken a relatively narrow and conservative approach – generally applying its law only where there are material links between it and the crime, the criminal, the human rights victim or the violation. As will be argued in Chapter 5, there are strong and numerous reasons why this approach should be retained.

The fact that the application of UK law has been noteworthy in recent times because of its increasing frequency and breadth should not be construed to suggest that the phenomenon is novel. Indeed, the application of law across borders is almost as old as law itself. For example, the law has been applied across UK borders for as long as there have been diplomacy and piracy. The application of UK law to diplomats abroad – a concomitant of their immunity to host state jurisdiction – dates from 1698–9. An Act to Punish Governors of Plantations in this Kingdom for Crimes by them Committed in the Plantations extended the reach of English criminal law to Crown servants abroad.[5] Today, section 31(1) of the Criminal Justice Act 1948 provides for the extension of the criminal law to Crown servants abroad. Article 31(4) of the Vienna Convention on Diplomatic Relations 1961 confirms the legality of such practice, providing that 'The immunity of a diplomatic agent from the jurisdiction of the receiving State does not exempt him from the jurisdiction of the sending State'. In regard

5 11 Will.3, c.12.

to piracy, in *In Re Piracy Jure Gentium* Viscount Sankey begins his narrative of the crime with the Act of Henry VIII enacted in 1536, entitled 'An Act for the punishment of pirates and robbers of the sea', after noting the previous deficiencies in the law as applied to pirates.[6] Law and society, in many senses, have evolved considerably since 1536 – although piracy and diplomacy remain relevant subjects in the area. Over the centuries the state has chosen to regulate an ever-wider range of behaviour, and individuals have become considerably more active in a number of diverse ways internationally. Recent examples of situations in regard to which UK law has been applied include a meeting of representatives of private companies in Houston, Texas,[7] a murder in Guyana 20 years after it was committed,[8] and an individual's possible medical treatment in Estonia.[9] As these different examples illustrate, the historical scope of the law applied across borders has been widened considerably.

General subject matter

The subject matter of this book is UK non-private law applied across borders. In broad terms, this entails the UK executive, legislature or judiciary acting in regard to, providing for or taking cognisance of a person, event or circumstance occurring at least in part outside UK territory. It is here useful to give several concrete examples. 'Acting in regard to' can include treatment meted out, or possibly meted out, by those acting on behalf of the UK, as in the case of *R v Secretary of State for the Foreign and Commonwealth Office ex p B and others*.[10] Here the question was whether human rights law applied to the behaviour of consular officials in Australia. 'Providing for' denotes the enactment or issuance of legislative rules. Amongst the numerous examples in the criminal law are those crimes created under the International Criminal Court Act 2001 and the International Criminal Court (Scotland) Act 2001. Section 51(2)(b) of the International Criminal Court Act 2001 extends the application of the crimes of genocide, war crimes and crimes against humanity to acts committed 'outside the United Kingdom by a United Kingdom national, a United Kingdom resident or a person subject to UK service jurisdiction'. A further example is the Export Control Order 2008, which prescribes the shipment of a number of weapons and other goods between two states outside the United Kingdom, where done by 'United Kingdom persons'.[11] 'Taking cognisance of' signifies

6 [1934] AC 586 at 589.

7 The so-called Dunlop Three were sentenced on 10 June 2008 for an offence under the Enterprise Act 2002.

8 Michael Cheong was convicted under s 10 of the Offences Against the Person Act 1861 at the Old Bailey on 8 August 2005 for a murder committed in Guyana in 1982, see http://news.bbc.co.uk/1/hi/uk/4132374.stm, accessed 20 May 2011.

9 *Wright v Scottish Ministers (No 2)* 2005 1 SC 453.

10 [2004] EWCA 1344, [2005] QB 643.

11 SI 2008/3231. 'United Kingdom person' is defined as a UK national, a Scottish partnership or a body incorporated under the law of any part of the United Kingdom by s 11(1) of the Export Control Act 2002.

instances where courts or tribunals within the UK recognise and consider persons, events or circumstances not wholly within it. An example of this is the conviction and sentence in Southwark Crown Court of the 'Dunlop Three' for offences under section 188 of the Enterprise Act 2002, in part for cartel-related activity in the United States.[12] The provision giving the court ability to act was section 190(3), which states: 'No proceedings may be brought for an offence under section 188 in respect of an agreement outside the United Kingdom, unless it has been implemented in whole or in part in the United Kingdom'.[13] All of these examples are instances where UK law has been applied in some sense across its border. An important preliminary point to note is that in these cases the law has been extended geographically. This is distinct from the question of whether a court has the lawful ability to take cognisance of the person, event or circumstance. This distinction is described by Hirst as being between the ambit of the law and the jurisdiction of courts.[14]

Law Across Borders is not immediately and generally concerned with the lawful ability of a court (or the executive or legislature) to act in regard to a person or circumstance abroad according to UK law. Instead, its focus is upon the geographical scope or range of the law as applied to persons or circumstances in whole or part outside the UK. The two subjects, however, cannot be fully isolated from each other. They are often conflated by academic writers and courts, with the question of whether a court can lawfully take cognisance of an issue being indistinct from the question of whether the law applies at all. Part of the explanation for the confusion over this basic point is the usage of the term 'jurisdiction' to denote both subjects, and indeed more. 'Jurisdiction' is used in the sense of the lawful ability of a court to act, in regard to the Crown Court, by section 46(2) of the Senior Courts Act 1981, which provides:

> The jurisdiction of the Crown Court with respect to proceedings on indictment shall include jurisdiction in proceedings on indictment for offences wherever committed, and in particular proceedings on indictment for offences within the jurisdiction of the Admiralty of England.

'Jurisdiction' here denotes a lawful ability, competence or power. Indeed, section 151 of the Senior Courts Act 1981 states that 'jurisdiction' includes 'powers'. The second main meaning of jurisdiction relates to the geographical or territorial range of the law. This sense, more often than not, includes the legislature and executive and indeed the UK as a state itself, as well as courts.

12 See Office of Fair Trading Press Release, 11 June 2008, at http://www.oft.gov.uk/news-and-updates/press/2008/72-08, accessed 20 May 2011, and Lucraft, M., *et al*, The Dunlop Three – the Cartel Offence Makes its Debut (2009) *Archbold News* 7.

13 See MacCulloch, A., 'The Cartel Offence and the Criminalisation of United Kingdom Competition Law' [2003] *Journal of Business Law* 616.

14 Hirst, H., *Jurisdiction and the Ambit of the Criminal Law*, Oxford University Press, Oxford, 2003, Ch. 1, esp. pp 9–15.

It originates and still largely remains in the realm of public international law. As will be discussed in Chapter 2 there is a somewhat well-developed body of rules which govern the application of a state's law to persons and circumstances outside its territory. This issue is often phrased in terms of whether the UK has 'jurisdiction' over a certain situation, for example torture committed by a foreign national on the high seas. The word 'jurisdiction' in Article 1 of the Convention appears to have this sense. Article 1 provides that 'The High Contracting Parties shall secure to everyone within their jurisdiction the rights and freedoms defined in Section I of this Convention'. Because of the different meanings of 'jurisdiction', *Law Across Borders* generally eschews the word. Instead, 'application' is used. This more accurately describes the subject matter of the book – UK criminal and human rights law related to persons and circumstances in some sense outside the UK border.

Exclusions

The subject of this book is the application of UK law across borders. In particular, this book addresses the criminal law and human rights law. Excluded – at least directly – is private law. There are two reasons for this. The first is that non-private law applied across borders itself merits examination and analysis. Whilst there have been a number of works looking at the criminal law and human rights law in isolation, there is not a single source which examines them together and searches for commonalities between them. There is a gap in the literature in this regard. The second reason is that private law is fundamentally different from non-private law, both in general and in its application across borders. Private law applied across borders by and large fails to engender the same basic concerns and issues as the application of non-private law. Private law axiomatically directly affects natural and legal persons in areas that are not public. Here the state itself has relatively little direct and tangible interest. For example, the content of a standard UK private international law text covers the law of obligations, family law and property law.[15] A contractual dispute between two parties domiciled in different countries, for example, is not necessarily in the immediate interest of either state. The difference between private and non-private law in regard to the interest and role of the state is significant. It underlines the logic of separate analysis. For example, questions relating to state sovereignty are not central to the application of private law across borders whilst they relate to non-private law. It must be noted, however, that the exclusion of private international law from direct exposition in this book does not mean that it is not discussed. As will be seen below, one of the recurring themes in *Law Across Borders* is that a proper law approach is emerging and discernable where the criminal law and human rights law are applied across borders. The proper law approach has its origins in private

15 Fawcett, J. and Carruthers, J.M., *Cheshire, North and Fawcett Private International Law*, 14th edn, Oxford University Press, Oxford, 2008.

international law. It is argued below that this private international law doctrine is beginning to play a role, and rightfully so, in the application of UK non-private law across borders.

Forms of application – judicial, legislative and executive

The application of law across borders can be carried out by different arms of the UK – the judiciary, the legislature and the executive. In some cases one of these will act alone and in others two or even all three will jointly apply the law. A well-known example where the law is applied across borders by the judiciary, legislature and executive in regard to the same situation is found in the case of Baha Mousa. Judicially, the case at its most authoritative level to date is found in the House of Lords decision of *R (Al-Skeini) v Secretary of State for Defence*.[16] The main issue here was whether the human rights of the father of Baha Mousa were violated following the death of his son in the course of being restrained in Iraq by British soldiers. Legislatively, it was argued, and in part accepted, by the Secretary of State that the Human Rights Act 1998 (HRA) applied to the locus of the incident, with the question also being whether the circumstances of the death were 'within the jurisdiction' of the UK under the Convention. The executive branch of the UK was centrally involved in the case in the form of its armed forces acting within Iraq and exercising therein a degree of control and being responsible for the death of Mousa. As a result of differing arms of the UK being involved in the application of the law across borders it is necessary to discuss how in fact the law is so applied.

The different forms of the application of UK law across borders can be described and analysed in a number of ways. Most analyses come from the perspective of public international law. One well-known statement on the subject is found in the *Restatement of the Law (Third), Foreign Relations Law of the United States*.[17] Section 402, entitled 'Categories of Jurisdiction', states:

> Under International law, a state is subject to limitations on
> (a) jurisdiction to prescribe, i.e., to make its law applicable to the activities, relations, or status of persons, or the interests of persons in things, whether by legislation, by executive act or order, by administrative rule or regulation, or by determination of a court;
> (b) jurisdiction to adjudicate, i.e., to subject persons or things to the process of its courts or administrative tribunals, whether in civil or in criminal proceedings, whether or not the state is a party to those proceedings;

16 [2007] UKHL 26, [2008] 1 AC 153. A decision of the European Court of Human Rights in the case is pending. The case in general is discussed further below.

17 American Law Institute, *Restatement of the Law (Third), The Foreign Relations Law of the United States*, American Law Institute Publishers, St Paul Minn., 1987.

(c) jurisdiction to enforce, i.e., to induce or compel compliance or punish non-compliance with its laws or regulations, whether through the courts or by use of executive, administrative, police, or other non-judicial action.[18]

This iteration does two things. It illustrates the different ways in which law can be applied across borders and it provides authority for the point that international law places limits on that application – something discussed in Chapter 2.

In line with the American Law Institute in identifying three distinct areas of state competence is Akehurst, who designated them legislative, judicial and executive jurisdiction, defined as the 'power of a State to apply its laws to cases involving a foreign element', 'power of a State's courts to try cases involving a foreign element' and 'power of one State to perform acts in the territory of another State' respectively.[19] Brownlie, in contrast, proffered only two areas, stating that 'Distinct from the power to make decisions or rules (the prescriptive or legislative jurisdiction) is the power to take executive action in pursuance of or consequent on the making of decisions or rules (the enforcement or prerogative jurisdiction)'.[20] This approach is logical in that the legislative and judicial application of the law can sit together, with the enforcement of that law remaining apart. This follows the simple fact that the UK can, in the first instance, freely enact law and apply it judicially within its borders in regard to persons or circumstances outside it, but cannot enforce that law in the territory of another state without that state's consent. In regard to the criminal law, for example, the UK cannot generally arrest, try or imprison a person outside its territory. The presence of the accused within its territory is required. The executive enforcement of the criminal law outside the UK, i.e. the exercise of UK power in regard to criminal matters within the area of legitimate territorial control of another state without its consent is unanimously regarded as contrary to international law.[21] Conflating the application of the law legislatively and

18 Ibid at p 232.

19 Akehurst, M., 'Jurisdiction in International Law' (1972–73) 43 BYIL 145 at p 145.

20 Brownlie, I., *Principles of Public International Law*, 4th edn, Clarendon Press, Oxford, 1991 at p 298. This distinction is followed by both Jennings, R.Y., 'The Limits of State Jurisdiction' (1962) 32 NTIR 209 at p 212, and Mann, F.A., 'The Doctrine of Jurisdiction in International Law' (1964-I) RdC 1 at p 13–14. The *Restatement* (Third) (n 17 above), in its Introductory Note, states that 'it has become clear that the identification of prescription with legislation and of enforcement with adjudication is too simple', at p 230. It argues that substantive regulation (prescription) and enforcement are carried out by means additional to legislation and adjudication, such as administrative rules and executive acts in regard to both regulation and enforcement.

21 The European Committee on Crime Problems states 'it is widely agreed that in the context of enforcement the sovereign powers of the state may not be exercised within the territory of another state, save with its consent', in European Committee on Crime Problems, *Extraterritorial Criminal Jurisdiction*, Council of Europe, Strasbourg, 1990, at p 25.

judicially in no way suggests that they are in fact one and the same. Clearly they are not. As noted, Hirst distinguishes between 'jurisdiction' and the 'ambit' of the law because of the very fact that they are different. Hirst's view is that:

> [J]urisdiction is procedural, relating to the powers vested in the criminal courts, whereas ambit is substantive, an integral element of the *actus reus* of an offence. In other words, whatever the courts' competence, there can be no offence under English law unless the impugned acts take place within the ambit, or geographical scope of application, of that law to begin with.[22]

Practically, however, in most cases where the law is extended beyond the UK border legislatively that statute will have included a provision that allows courts to act in regard to it. For example, section 3(6) of the Landmines Act 1998 provides that in regard to the offences contained in section 2: 'Proceedings for an offence under section 2 committed outside the United Kingdom may be taken, and the offence may for incidental purposes be treated as having been committed, in any place in the United Kingdom'.

Here the law is extended legislatively, and, as a necessary concomitant, courts are enabled to deem the conduct outside the UK as having occurred within it. As noted above, it is the extension of UK law across borders that forms the main subject matter of this book – not the lawful ability of courts within the UK to take cognisance of a crime or human rights violation. However, it is necessary to comprehend the different ways in which the law can be applied, and the relationship between them. This latter point comes to the fore in particular, but not exclusively, in the area of human rights, where the application of law judicially and legislatively in some cases requires prior executive action. Indeed, in certain cases executive action is a *sine qua non* of the application of the other forms of UK law.

The largely unified or singular examination of 'UK law' applied across borders – legislative, judicial and executive are referred to jointly – must not detract from the relationship between them. Helpful here is the position in public international law. The *Restatement* (Third) stated in regard to the relationship:

> These categories of jurisdiction are often interdependent, and their scope and limitations are shaped by similar considerations. Jurisdiction to prescribe may be more acceptable where jurisdiction to adjudicate or enforce is plainly available; jurisdiction to adjudicate may be more acceptable where the state of the forum also has jurisdiction to prescribe by virtue of its links to the persons, interests, relations or activities involved. However, the purposes and consequences of the different categories of jurisdiction are

22 O'Keefe, R., 'Review of Hirst, M., Jurisdiction and the Ambit of English Criminal Law' [2004] *Criminal Law Review* 869 at p 869.

> not necessarily congruent, and balancing the competing interests in the different contexts can lead to different results.[23]

Brownlie suggested that there was not a significant distinction between them, writing that there:

> is no essential distinction between the legal bases for and limits upon substantive (or legislative) jurisdiction, on the one hand, and, on the other, enforcement (or personal, or prerogative) jurisdiction. The one is a function of the other. If the substantive jurisdiction is beyond lawful limits, then any consequent enforcement jurisdiction is unlawful.[24]

Bowett took a largely similar view, averring that there were two forms of law applied across borders and that:

> The relationship between the two kinds of jurisdiction is reasonably clear. There can be no enforcement jurisdiction unless there is prescriptive jurisdiction; yet there may be a prescriptive jurisdiction without the possibility of an enforcement jurisdiction, as, for example, where the accused is outside the territory of the prescribing State and not amenable to extradition.[25]

He then states that 'jurisdiction hinges, fundamentally, on the power to prescribe'.[26] From a different perspective Lowe notes that discussion of the forms of law being applied extraterritorially:

> draws attention to the underlying policy issue. Extraterritorial claims are more likely to be acceptable when used in service of legislation upholding generally-held values, such as personal safety and perhaps the prevention of corrupt practices, than when used to advance more parochial policies, as is the case in much competition, tax and export administration legislation.[27]

This brings to the fore the important point of the motivation for the application of the law – in whatever form – in the first instance.

Substance of application – criminal and human rights law

Two areas or fields of UK law comprise the central focus of this book – criminal law and human rights law. They are, of course, very different in nature and

23 *Restatement* (Third) (n 17 above), at p 231.
24 Brownlie (n 20 above), at p 310.
25 Bowett, D.W., 'Jurisdiction: Changing Patterns of Authority over Activities and Resources' (1982) 53 BYIL 1, , at p 1.
26 Ibid.
27 Lowe, A.V., 'The Problems of Extraterritorial Jurisdiction: Economic Sovereignty and the Search for a Solution' (1985) 34 ICLQ 734.

function. They are similar however in the important respect of being applied across the UK border. An underlying theme of this book is that a degree of commonality can be identified in the manner in which they are applied to persons and circumstances outside the UK. In order to set the stage, as it were, for the description and analysis below, the criminal law and human rights law must briefly be explained in terms of their nature and function – it is beyond the scope of this book to do more. Prior to this, however, it is interesting to note that the criminal law and human rights law are not uncommonly applied across borders jointly. In *HMA v Vervuren*,[28] for example, the accused had been charged with the importation and supply of amphetamines from Portugal to Scotland. His extradition was sought from Portugal. He argued, *inter alia*, that an irregularity in his extradition from Portugal should vitiate the case against him on the basis of a breach of his human rights.[29] The case, therefore, entailed the application of both the criminal law and human rights law across borders in that the crimes he was charged with commenced in Portugal and the alleged violation of human rights included his removal therefrom. A further example applying the criminal law (including the criminal aspects of competition law) and human rights law to a single incident are the cases involving Ian Norris, the former chief executive officer of the Morgan Crucible group of companies. In *Norris v Government of the United States of America*[30] the House of Lords held that Norris could not be extradited to the United States for criminal cartel-related offences occurring from 1989 to 2000 because at that time the acts were not criminal in England. Norris had argued that the double criminality requirement in section 137(3) of the Extradition Act 2003 was not met. Section 137(3) and (4) entail, in effect, the application of UK criminal law across borders in a hypothetical sense because they provide that the double criminality requirement can be met in regard to extraterritorial offences where UK criminal law is applied in such a way. In a later case, *Norris v Government of the United States of America*,[31] it was argued that the extradition of Norris would give rise to an unjustified interference with his Article 8 right to family life. He was unsuccessful and was extradited, tried and sentenced to 18 months' imprisonment in the United States.[32]

28 2002 SLT 555, [2002] SCCR 481.

29 See Arnell, P., 'Male Captus Bene Detentus in Scotland' [2004] *Juridical Review* 252.

30 [2008] UKHL 16, [2008] 1 AC 920.

31 [2010] UKSC 9.

32 It should be noted that the human rights argument was 'domestic' in that Norris' rights enjoyed within the UK would be unjustifiably infringed; this contrasts with 'foreign' cases where the argument is that a human rights violation will take place in the third state. Only the latter entail the application of UK law across borders. See further Chapter 4.

Criminal law – nature and function

The criminal law within the jurisdictions of the UK is, almost exclusively, prosecuted by public agencies,[33] be it the Crown Prosecution Service in England, the Crown Office and Procurator Fiscals Service in Scotland or the Public Prosecution Service in Northern Ireland. This prosecution entails the imposition of coercive rules upon legal persons by these agencies where it is considered that a rule has been broken and it is appropriate to do so. It is, in its simplest form, the forcible, vertical application of law by the state upon legal persons. Whilst general and basic, this definition of the criminal law, referring to the procedure under which it is applied, is the best to adopt. Other possible criteria upon which to centre a definition, such as the morality of the act in question and the nature or level of harm done, raise more questions than they answer. As Glanville Williams concluded on the point: 'a crime is an act capable of being followed by criminal proceedings having a criminal outcome, and a proceeding or outcome is criminal if it has certain characteristics which mark it as criminal'.[34] As alluded to above, in addition to imposing rules upon legal persons the criminal justice systems within the UK provide for the lawful ability of courts to take cognisance of certain acts, generally on the basis of the geography and seriousness of the offence. Geographically, this power is normally exercised territorially. Indeed, courts lower down the judicial hierarchy – where crimes are tried summarily – act on a territorial basis alone. More senior courts have a wider range of competence. As noted, the Crown Court in England and Wales is competent to hear cases proceeding on indictment, under section 46(2) of the Supreme Court Act 1981, wherever committed. That noted, the geographical extension of the criminal law to areas outside the UK is clearly exceptional. As Viscount Simons stated in *Cox v Army Council*: 'apart from those exceptional cases in which specific provision is made in regard to acts committed abroad, the whole body of the criminal law of England deals only with acts committed in England'.[35] O'Brien has stated that:

> The United Kingdom has, from the 19th century, been a strong supporter of the territorial system: (a) because in criminal law matters it is for the people of the relevant territory to determine the rules they wish to live under; (b) it is practical in that English criminal procedure places con-

33 Private criminal prosecution, for our purposes, can be ignored. Whilst, in England, it has been protected by s 6(1) of the Prosecution of Offences Act 1985 it is unlikely to take place in regard to most crimes applied across borders on the account of a specific consent requirement on the part of the Attorney General. In regard to torture, for example, this requirement is found in s 135 of the Criminal Justice Act 1988. For our purposes it is generally sufficient to refer to 'UK criminal law', although this is generally inaccurate. This follows the extent of the criminal law within the UK's jurisdictions being similar.

34 Williams, G., 'The Definition of Crime' [1955] *Current Legal Problems* 107.

35 [1967] AC 48 at 67.

> siderable reliance on the testing of oral testimony by cross-examination. That is best achieved in the relevant territory.[36]

From a different perspective Lew writes that the criminal law's historical link to territory 'was based on the fiction that innocence or guilt was determined by the empanelment of a jury who had personal knowledge of the accused and his culpability',[37] and that over the years the connection has become 'justified on the grounds of convenience of the forum and the presumed involvement of the interests where the crime is committed'.[38]

Reference to the 'presumed involvement of the interests where the crime is committed' as a justification for the application of the law, the last point mentioned by Lew, raises the simple yet almost intractable issue of the function or purpose of the criminal law. It is necessary to broach this subject, however, even if in general and basic terms, in order to understand why the criminal law is applied across borders. The motivations for the application of the law in this manner can in turn be used to begin to develop a framework for understanding – including comprehension of the interests served by the law and its reliance on particular connections between the UK and the crime or criminal as justifying and limiting that application. Commonly cited in discussions of the functions of the criminal law is the American Law Institute's Model Penal Code. It provides that the purposes of the substantive criminal law are:

> (a) to forbid and prevent conduct that unjustifiably and inexcusably inflicts or threatens substantial harm to individual or public interests;
> (b) to subject to public control persons whose conduct indicates that they are disposed to commit crimes;
> (c) to safeguard conduct that is without fault from condemnation as criminal;
> (d) to give fair warning of the nature of the conduct declared to be an offense;
> (e) to differentiate on reasonable grounds between serious and minor offences.[39]

The Labour Government's White Paper, *Justice for All*, published in 2002, provides that the purpose of the criminal justice system – indivisible from the substantive criminal law for our present purposes – is 'fighting and reducing crime and delivering justice on behalf of victims, defendants and the community'.[40] The Crown Office and Procurator Fiscal Service's Prosecution Code provides that the purpose of the criminal justice system in Scotland is the

36 O'Brien, J., *International Law*, Cavendish Publishing Limited, London, 2001, at p 237.
37 Lew, J.D.M., 'The Extraterritorial Criminal Jurisdiction of English Courts' (1978) 27 ICLQ 168 at p 168, citing Lord Diplock in *Treacy v DPP* [1971] 1 All ER 110 at 119.
38 Ibid, citing Brownlie, I., *General Principles of Public International Law*, 2nd edn, Oxford University Press, Oxford, 1973, at p 293.
39 American Law Institute, *Model Penal Code*, American Law Institute Publishers, St Paul Minn., 1962, Art 1, 1.02 (1).
40 Cm 5563, 2002, at p 13.

maintenance of the security and confidence of Scots by providing a just and effective means by which crimes may be investigated and offenders brought to justice.[41] The reforms made to the criminal law over the past several years have been criticised, in part, because they appear to fail to consider the nature of, and limitation to, the criminal law thoroughly. Ashworth writes of reform of the criminal law in England and Wales:

> Searching questions need to be asked rather than avoided. What is the nature of the threat to public safety presented by crime? . . . If it is the Government's task to increase public protection, are its policies directed at the most appropriate ways of doing this? . . . Should there be any limitations on the measures that the Government may properly take in the name of public protection, or is the situation so urgent that human rights considerations should be set on one side?[42]

Explicit or implicit in these and other discussions of the function of the criminal law is that the prevention of harm and 'public protection' are central. This is not to exclude as other purposes of the criminal law that of upholding morality and fairness, retribution and rehabilitation. All of these various functions of the criminal law are either prospective or retrospective. As Cryer notes, there are two broad approaches to justifying punishment – those which look forward (termed 'teleological') aiming at protection and deterrence, etc. and those which look back, focusing on the crime itself (termed 'deontological').[43]

Whilst academic analysis of the criminal law and criminal justice system undoubtedly assist in the process of coming to an understanding of the function and purpose of the criminal law, more authoritative is judicial dicta. In a relatively early leading case on the application of the law to circumstances abroad under the Theft Act 1968, *Treacy v DPP*, Lord Diplock stated 'criminal law is about the right of the state to punish persons for their conduct – generally where that conduct is undertaken with a wicked intent or without justifactory excuse'. He continued: '[T]he state is under a correlative duty to those who owe obedience to its laws to protect their interests and one of the purposes of criminal law is to afford such protection by deterring by threat of punishment conduct by other persons which is calculated to harm those interests'.[44] In *Board of Trade v Owen* Lord Tucker stated in regard to the crime of conspiracy: 'it is necessary

41 May 2001, cited at http://www.copfs.gov.uk/publications/2001/05/prosecutioncode, accessed 20 May 2011.

42 Ashworth, A., 'Criminal Justice Act 2003 Part 2: Criminal Justice Reform – Principles, Human Rights and Public Protection' [2004] *Criminal Law Review* 516 at p 517.

43 Cryer, R., *et al* (eds), *International Criminal Law and Procedure*, 2nd edn, Cambridge University Press, Cambridge, 2010 at p 23. Cryer refers to Garland, D. and Duff, A., *A Reader on Punishment*, Oxford University Press, Oxford, 1994 and Hart, H.L.A., *Punishment and Responsibility*, Oxford University Press, Oxford, 1968.

44 [1971] AC 537 at 560–2.

to recognize the offence to aid in the preservation of the Queen's peace and the maintenance of law and order within the realm with which, generally speaking, the criminal law is alone concerned'.[45] A leading modern statement upon the function of the criminal law and its application outside the UK was made by Lord Griffiths in *Liangsiriprasert v Government of the United States*:

> As a broad general statement it is true to say that English criminal law is local in its effect and that the common law does not concern itself with crimes committed abroad. The reason for this is obvious; the criminal law is developed to protect English society and not that of other nations which must be left to make and enforce such laws as they see fit to protect their own societies. To put the matter bluntly it is no direct concern of English society if a crime is committed in another country. It was for this reason that the law of extradition was introduced between civilised nations so that fugitive offenders might be returned for trial in the country against whose laws they had offended.[46]

The protection of the interests of those who owe obedience to English law, the maintenance of law and order within the realm and the protection of English society are the stated purposes of the law from these cases. Clearly these remain central today. The relevant and interesting questions arising are whether and how these purposes inform the application of criminal law across borders and whether they can assist in its comprehension. As will be seen in Chapters 3 and 5, those purposes undoubtedly do affect the application of the criminal law across borders, aid in understanding why the law is so applied and shed light upon the limits of that application.

Human rights law – nature and function

Human rights law is of course very different from criminal law. It is akin to it, however, in that it is almost exclusively applies in a vertical manner – between the state and the citizen. It entails the bestowal of entitlements by the state upon private individuals which may be enforced against the state in certain circumstances. Unlike the criminal law, however, under human rights law the state is the subject of the application or respondent – not the instigator of the appli-

45 [1957] AC 602 at 625. Michael Wood, Legal Advisor to the Foreign Office, in giving the Secretary of State advice leading up to the invasion of Iraq, discussed the Ministry of Defence's view of the crime of murder and the necessity for it to be within the Queen's peace, and concluded that the law is uncertain in the area as it is not laid down, at http://www.iraqinquiry.org.uk/media/43502/doc_2010_01_26_11_03_00_737.pdf, accessed 20 May 2011. For a discussion of the meaning and present relevance of the term 'Queen's peace', see Hirst, M., 'Murder Under the Queen's Peace' [2008] *Criminal Law Review* 541.

46 [1991] 1 AC 225 at 244.

cation. Whilst these basic facts are indubitably true, practice is not so simple. First, the state is comprised of numerous and distinct 'public authorities'. They are the entities which are explicitly subject to the application of UK human rights law. Section 6(1) of the Human Rights Act 1998 (HRA) provides that 'It is unlawful for a public authority to act in a way which is incompatible with a Convention right'. 'Public authorities' are defined by section 6(3) as including '(a) a court or tribunal, and (b) any person certain of whose functions are functions of a public nature, but does not include either House of Parliament or a person exercising functions in connection with proceedings in Parliament'. Public authorities in the context of the application of human rights law across borders have included the Secretary of State for the Home Office, the armed forces and members of the diplomatic service. All of these emanations of the state are clearly public in nature. The question arising, therefore, in the course of the application of human rights law across borders is not whether they must act compatibly with human rights in general but whether they must act compatibly in light of the geographical location of the past or future human rights violation. The first question, whether a body must act compatible per se, requires mention. This is because of the uncertainty and debate surrounding the issue of whether and if so how human rights obligations fall on private actors.

The HRA is silent on the application of human rights law in a horizontal sense. It is the fact that courts are public authorities and so must act compatibly with human rights which has, in part, led courts and numerous commentators to conclude that human rights obligations can indeed be placed upon private individuals and concerns. A further factor is the wide nature of the definition of public authority. In *YL v Birmingham City Council* Lord Mance cited with approval the passage by Lord Rodger in *Parochial Church Council of the Parish of Aston Cantlow, Wilmcote with Billesley, Warwickshire v Wallbank and another*:[47]

> Prima facie . . . when Parliament enacted the 1998 Act . . . the intention was to make provision in our domestic law to ensure that the bodies carrying out the functions of government in the United Kingdom observed the rights and freedoms set out in the Convention. Parliament chose to bring this about by enacting inter alia section 6(1), which makes it unlawful for 'a public authority' to act in a way that is incompatible with a Convention right. A purposive construction of that section accordingly indicates that the essential characteristic of a public authority is that it carries out a function of government which would engage the responsibility of the United Kingdom before the Strasbourg organs.[48]

In this case the House of Lords held that certain actions of a private care home acting under the direction of a local authority were not functions of a public

47 [2003] UKHL 37 at para 160.
48 [2004] 1 AC 546 at para 87.

nature under section 6(3)(b) of the HRA.[49] The courts, and academics, continue to grapple with the horizontal nature of human rights obligations in UK law. However, as noted above, in so far as the application of UK law across borders is concerned, the debate is of little relevance. To date, the jurisprudence and debate has not been concerned with what particular body or person is subject to the law as applied across borders but whether in fact that body is so subject in light of the particular circumstances.

It is considerably easier – as with the criminal law – to describe the nature of human rights law than its function or purpose. In an applied and practical vein the Labour Government's explanation and justification for enacting the HRA, *Bring Rights Home: The Human Rights Bill*, stated:

> We therefore believe that the time has come to enable people to enforce their Convention rights against the State in the British courts, rather than having to incur the delays and expense which are involved in taking a case to the European Human Rights Commission and Court in Strasbourg and which may altogether deter some people from pursuing their rights. Enabling courts in the United Kingdom to rule on the application of the Convention will also help to influence the development of case law on the Convention by the European Court of Human Rights on the basis of familiarity with our laws and customs and of sensitivity to practices and procedures in the United Kingdom.[50]

Lord Irving has written that the HRA would engender 'a constitutional change of major significance: protecting the individual citizen against the erosion of liberties, either deliberate or gradual. It will also help develop a process of justice based on the promotion of positive rights'.[51] The effects of the HRA, he noted, could be categorised under four heads: the domestication of freedom, the prioritisation of human rights, the imposition of substantive rights and principled decision making.[52]

Reflecting the function of the HRA as 'domesticating freedom' is the preamble to the Act itself. It provides that the HRA is 'An Act to give further effect to rights and freedoms guaranteed under the European Convention on

49 A decision that has engendered much criticism; see, e.g. Williams, A., '*YL v Birmingham City Council*: contracting out and functions of a public nature' [2008] *European Human Rights Law Review* 524.

50 Cmnd 3782, 1997, para 1.18.

51 Irving, D., 'The Development of Human Rights in Britain under an Incorporated Convention on Human Rights' [1998] *Public Law* 221 at p 221. On a more general level Lord Irvine cites as the reasons for the development of human rights in international law, in the form of provisions within the Charter of the United Nations, the removal of the threat of a return of conflict and genocide and 'as common justice [and] part of the process of guaranteeing peace', at p 222.

52 Ibid at pp 226–30.

Human Rights; to make provision with respect to holders of certain judicial offices who become judges of the European Court of Human Rights; and for connected purposes'. The preamble to the European Convention on Human Rights 1950 first refers to the Universal Declaration of Human Rights 1948 and then, *inter alia*, states: 'Reaffirming their profound belief in those Fundamental Freedoms which are the foundation of justice and peace in the world and are best maintained on the one hand by an effective political democracy and on the other by a common understanding and observance of the Human Rights upon which they depend'. Here, human rights are conceived as the 'foundation of justice and peace'.[53] As is clear, it is relatively easy in general terms to state the function and purpose of human rights law and the main human rights instruments and to descend into superficiality, circular reasoning and tautology. This is both understandable and unfortunate. It is understandable because the rationale for protecting persons from ill-treatment is largely intuitive – a narrative of why seems hardly necessary. As stated in the 1776 US Declaration of Independence: 'we hold these truths to be self-evident, that all men are created equal, that they are endowed by their Creator with certain unalienable rights, that among these are life, liberty and the pursuit of happiness'.[54] It is unfortunate because a detailed and clear picture of the function and purpose of human rights law can enable an understanding of the application of UK law across borders by aiding in the comprehension of what is the goal sought to be attained through the application of the law in such a way. This is particularly relevant when contrasting the application of human rights law to that of the criminal law, where the interests of the UK may be materially distinct. However, a general statement of the purpose and function of human rights law as being to hold the UK, in all its public manifestations, accountable for the violation of a number of entitlements of persons with which it is in a certain relationship takes us some way towards understanding. Indeed, as will be seen in Chapter 4, the explicit question at issue in courts is often not why the law applies but whether it does in the particular circumstances. Of course, it is a different question altogether whether this should be the case.

Issues and criticisms

A number of issues and criticisms underlie the application of UK non-private law across borders. They will emerge throughout this book, and be discussed

53 A Working Party from the 10 founding states of the Council of Europe concerned in the negotiations noted: 'The original purpose of the Council of Europe Convention on Human Rights was to enable public attention to be drawn to any revival of totalitarian methods of government and to provide a forum in which the appropriate action could be discussed and decided', as noted in Hoffman, L., 'The Universality of Human Rights' [2009] *Law Quarterly Review* 416, citing Simpson, A.W.B., *Human Rights and the End of Empire: Britain and the Genesis of the European Convention*, Oxford University Press, Oxford, 2001, at p 777.

54 As discussed in Hoffman, ibid.

specifically at points in Chapters 3, 4 and 5. It is useful, however, briefly to mention them here. The specific issues or concerns arising from the application of law across borders arise from, and return to, the point that it is generally undesirable for the UK, or any state, to act in such a manner. Effectiveness, cost, state sovereignty, conflict with extant national and international norms, perceived legal imperialism and chauvinism and human rights are amongst the reasons for this. Undoubtedly, the application of law across borders is often less effective than it could be – certainly in comparison with the law as applied within the UK. Issues of enforcement and evidence come to the fore here. Following on from debatable effectiveness is the question of cost. Expenditure incurred in a largely ineffective application of law across borders begs the question of whether those resources should be directed towards the application and enforcement of the law intra-territorially or indeed another purpose altogether. State sovereignty militates against the application of law across borders in that in the vast majority of cases the *situs* of the alleged crime or human rights violation will be within the territory of a foreign state. The exception to this is the high seas and areas *terra nullis*. The position of the rules protecting state sovereignty and territorial integrity in international law leads, in most cases, to the strongest entitlement to act being held by the state where the crime or violation took place. Indeed, the application of the law by a non-territorial state may well contravene the territorial state's sovereignty. In circumstances where it contravenes the sovereignty of a third state the application of law across borders may give rise to disquiet and claims of legal imperialism or chauvinism. Finally, the application of law across borders may give rise to claims of human rights violations itself – for example on the basis of Article 7 of the Convention relating to the non-retroactivity of criminal law. UK law and practice largely heed these factors. The UK generally retains a reliance on territory and the relationship between it and persons associated with it.[55] UK law is rarely applied across borders in an egregious manner – it is, however, generally applied on an ad hoc and reactive basis. This fact evidences

55 This has led to the minimisation of inter-state conflict. Lowe includes self-restraint as the second of four factors that can address the problems arising from law applied across borders; he states that they can be addressed through 'consultation procedures, unilateral restraint, harmonisation of laws, and agreed allocations of extraterritorial competence. Of these, the first two are of the greatest practical significance at present in the search for a solution. None of them, however, seems to offer a satisfactory basis for a general solution to the problem': Lowe, A.V., 'The Problems of Extraterritorial Jurisdiction: Economic Sovereignty and the Search for a Solution' [1985] 34 ICLQ 724 at p 728. This statement was made in the context of competition law being applied across borders. The generally limited approach that the UK takes to applying its law across borders is, of course, not beyond criticism. In regard to the criminal law, for example, the former Director of Public Prosecutions, Ken Macdonald, has argued for an amendment to the law so as to include as a ground for applying the crime of genocide mere presence in the UK, extending the law from its present residence requirement. See Macdonald, K., 'Britain: A Refuge for the Unspeakably Evil', *The Times*, 6 July 2009.

the further problem of a lack of coherence to the application of the law. A lack of central focus or principle applies to both the criminal law and human rights law. Whilst specific cases, novel circumstances and the differences between human rights law and the criminal law make the existence of a complete, coherent, principled approach in practice very difficult, clarity and principle are undoubtedly needed. It is suggested below that such a principled approach may in fact be beginning to emerge – based upon the concept of the proper law.

Themes

Description and analysis of the application of UK law across borders evinces two related themes. The first is that non-UK law and practice, including that coming from the two pre-eminent European bodies, public international law, and the law of third states has had, and is having, a material effect upon UK law in the area. Treaties, foreign cases and international guidelines, for example, have all played a role in conditioning the shape of the law. The second theme is that emerging from UK law and practice is a proper law approach to the application of its non-private law across borders. This generally entails reliance upon certain defined factors existing between the UK and crime, criminal or violation as justifying the application and, in some cases, consideration of the factors that exist in relation to third states. The two themes are related in that non-UK law and practice has, to an extent, contributed to the emerging proper law approach.

Non-UK influence on law across borders

The impact of European, international and foreign law upon UK law has been increasingly notable in affecting its application of law across borders. Of course, external influence in general is not new. The law in England and Wales, Scotland and Northern Ireland have all been influenced to a greater or lesser extent by developments outside these jurisdictions. In Scotland, for example, the influence of the 'Institutional Writers' was such that a notable civilian element within Scots law has come to exist.[56] In recent times the effect of the EU and the Council of Europe has been very significant – as will be discussed in Chapter 2 and seen throughout this book. For our present purposes, however, it is not this inward effect alone that it germane, but rather how the effect has led to and conditioned the application of UK law outside its territory – the outward effect of the non-UK influence. In addition to the influences of the EU and the Council of Europe are those of the United Nations and the Organisation of Economic Co-operation

56 See, e.g. Cairns, J.W., 'The Civil Law Tradition in Scottish Legal Thought', in Carey Miller, D. and Zimmermann, R. (eds), *The Civilian Tradition and Scots Law: Aberdeen Quincentenary Essays*, Duncker and Humblot, Berlin, 1997, at pp191–223; and Gordon, W. (ed.), *Roman Law, Scots Law and Legal History*, Edinburgh University Press, Edinburgh, 2007.

and Development (OECD), for example. The OECD Convention on Combating Bribery of Foreign Public Officials in International Business Transactions 1997 and the UN Convention Against Torture and other Inhuman and Degrading Treatment and Punishment 1984 are two prominent instances. There is also a not-inconsiderable reference in UK case law to decisions of the judiciaries of Commonwealth and other states. Cases from Canada, the United States and Israel, amongst others countries, have been mentioned in consideration of the application of UK law across borders. These include the Canadian case of *United States v Cotroni*[57] and the Israeli case of *Attorney-General v Eichmann*.[58] A notable example of an international instrument affecting the application of UK law across borders is the Attorney General and Lord Advocate's 'Guidance for Handling Criminal Cases with Concurrent Jurisdiction between the United Kingdom and the United States of America',[59] which will be discussed in Chapter 3. More generally and widely applicable are the numerous substantive criminal conventions and those relating to mutual criminal assistance and extradition to which the UK is party.

In addition to noting the fact that an increasing amount of extrinsic authority, be it guidelines, treaties, judicial decisions or otherwise, affects the application of UK law across borders, it is necessary to discuss the particular type of affect or influence. Non-UK law may, for example, merely act as an example or provide guidance. Here a UK court may examine a foreign judicial decision to ascertain what was held on a particular point. The UK court can, of course, choose to follow that example or not. Reference to the Canadian Supreme Court case of *United States v Cobb*[60] by the House of Lords in *McKinnon v Government of the United States*[61] is such an example. A second type of affect that non-UK law may have is a permissive one. Here the authority allows the UK to apply its law across borders if it decides to do so. An example can be found in criminally related conventions where state parties are permitted to apply a criminal sanction to an act where its national was a victim of that crime – so-called passive personality jurisdiction. An example of this is Article 6(2)(b) of the Convention for the Suppression of Unlawful Acts Against the Safety of Maritime Navigation 1988. It provides that state parties may establish jurisdiction over an offence defined by the Convention where 'during its commission a national of that state is seized, threatened, killed or injured'. A third type of affect or influence is where the foreign authority obliges the UK to act. Here one may cite as an example Article 1 of the Convention, which provides that 'The High Contracting Parties shall secure to everyone within their jurisdiction the rights and freedoms defined in Section I of this Convention'. The word 'shall' denotes

57 [1989] 1 SCR 1469.
58 (1962) 36 ILR 5.
59 The Guidance is available at http://www.publications.parliament.uk/pa/ld200607/ldlwa/70125ws1.pdf, accessed 20 May 2011.
60 [2001] 1 SCR 587.
61 [2008] UKHL 59.

that state parties must act on the obligation; it is not merely permissible. The question arising is the correct and definitive meaning of the term 'within their jurisdiction'. This is not in fact settled, as will be discussed in Chapter 4. A further example from a criminally related convention is Article 9 of the Convention on the Prohibition of the Use, Stockpiling and Transfer of Anti-Personnel Mines and on their Destruction 1997. This provides, *inter alia*, that 'Each State Party shall take all appropriate legal, administrative and other measures, including the imposition of penal sanctions, to prevent and suppress any activity prohibited to a State Party under this Convention'. There are, then, differing ways in which the variety of non-UK law can have an impact upon the extent and nature of the application of UK law across borders.

The proper law approach to jurisdiction

The second theme evinced in this book is that the application of UK law across borders is seeing the emergence of a proper law approach where the law is applied in an international or transnational sense. The term 'proper law approach' is here used to denote the process whereby the law is applied only in the presence of a material linkage or connection between the alleged criminal act or human rights violation and the UK. It can go further and entail awareness on the part of the UK of the existence of connections with third states as well as the weighing-up of those linkages with the connections that exist with the UK. The proper law approach to the application of law originated in areas of private law, and came to hold a firm place in private international law. In regard to English contract law the proper law doctrine was said to 'localise the contract by looking for the system of law with which the transaction was most closely connected'.[62] This book argues that the proper law approach has begun to emerge in the application of non-private law across borders.[63] This development contrasts with what has happened in private international law. The proper law approach is no longer applied in the law of contract in the UK, following the Contracts (Applicable Law) Act 1990, which implemented the EEC Convention on the Law Applicable to Contractual Obligations 1980 ('the Rome Convention'). Therefore, whilst the proper law approach is having lesser relevance in the sphere of private law, it is seeing a greater impact in non-private law. An important caveat, however, must be made when transposing the approach from the private to non-private sphere. This is that in the area of private law the application of a proper law approach may lead to a state applying the law of a third state in its courts – something the approach accepted as possible and, in certain instances, reasonable. However, states do not of course apply the non-private law of other states. The

62 Fawcett, J. and Carruthers, J., *Cheshire, North and Fawcett: Private International Law* (n 15 above), at p 666.

63 It has also found a place in the area of competition law. Amongst the voluminous literature, see Roth, P.M., 'Reasonable Extraterritoriality: Correcting the "Balance of Interests"' [1992] ICLQ 245.

distinction made in private international law between 'jurisdiction' and 'applicable law' is not made in non-private law. In the private international law sense these terms denote the legitimate ability of a forum to hear a dispute (jurisdiction) and the issue of which set of rules are to govern (applicable law). This distinction is not made and has no direct relevance in the non-private area. In regard to the criminal law and human rights law the two issues of the legitimate (and indeed optimal) forum to hear a case and the set of rules that are to be applied are fused. In the non-private sphere the approach solely concerns the application of a state's law which, if it is to be effective, necessarily entails the institutions and machinery – its courts, prosecutorial authorities and, if applicable, prison service – that operate to impose it.

The proper law approach can be seen to assume a greater relevance in the non-private sphere than the private sphere when one appreciates that a state's overall judicial and executive competence and the applicability of its law are conjoined. It in effect entails a process whereby two choices are made – to apply or not apply a particular body of law and to engage a particular state's legal system. The relevance of the proper law approach can be seen from three different perspectives: states, the individual and the rule of law. From the perspective of states its operation legitimises the application of law. States may point to the linkages between themselves and the alleged crime or human rights violation as substantiating the legitimacy and legality of their behaviour. Where there may be competing claims to apply the law or protest by the subject of application the approach can be wielded as a defence. From the perspective of individuals the proper law approach is relevant in providing a basis for ascertaining possible liability or protection. Individuals should as far as possible know what laws and legal systems apply to them for the purpose of the applicability of criminal sanction as well as human rights protection. From the perspective of the rule of law the approach forms part of a system of allocation of competencies of states where crime and human rights violations occur internationally or transnationally. In almost every such case there will be differing relationships and linkages between the crime, the accused and human rights violation and two or more states. Both states and the individuals concerned will have expectations as to what law and legal system will govern. The rule of law militates in favour of a transparent, predictable and defensible system of allocation of competencies and the proper law approach goes some way in addressing this need.

2 The context

UK law and practice do not take place in isolation. The context in which they occur is increasingly relevant generally and especially where the law is applied across borders. Public international law, including treaties emanating from the Council of Europe, EU law, the rules within approximately 200 third states and the norms and guidelines promulgated by international organisations, can and do have an effect. These laws and guidelines operate contemporaneously. Where UK law is applied across borders it is inevitable that at least one of these forms of law and the state or organisation from which it originates will be engaged or affected. Indeed, in most cases two, three or more states or organisations may have an interest in the application of UK law across borders. From a UK perspective more relevant is the influence or affect these extrinsic rules have upon its law and practice as opposed to the possible effect the application of its law has upon third states. As noted in Chapter 1, the affect of non-UK law and practice is one of themes in this book. From both these perspectives – that of third states and international organisations and the UK itself – it is necessary to describe and analyse the context in which UK law is applied across borders. It will be seen that the legal and institutional landscape is crowded and complex, and that it demands and requires restraint and co-operation.

1 'Application' has been discussed in Chapter 1. The two further material words in the subject of examination, 'the application of UK law across borders', 'law' and 'across', do not need specific discussion here. 'Law', as will be seen throughout this book, comprises legislation enacted by the UK Parliament and the Scottish Parliament, the common law and on occasion statutory instruments. The meaning of 'across' is largely self-evident. It denotes the transcending of a line, the territorial edge of the UK. Applied 'across' borders means that the law is related to something that is, at least in part, outside the UK or has taken, or would take, place there. It should be noted here that following this understanding included as law which is applied 'across' the UK border are certain human rights cases arising in the area of extradition and expulsion – something that certain analyses of extra-territorial human rights exclude; see further Chapter 4.

The UK border

In order to fully comprehend the context of the application of UK law across borders it is necessary to describe the UK and its border.[1] At first glance both seem to be axiomatic. The UK is comprised of England, Wales, Scotland and Northern Ireland, and being an island nation the subject of the UK border generally does not arise – save the border between Northern Ireland and the Republic of Ireland.[2] This view, however, is not correct. A search for greater and authoritative precision quickly brings to light a degree of complexity and indeed uncertainty. A starting point in defining the UK is the Interpretation Act 1978.[3] Section 5 and Schedule 1 provide that the UK is comprised of Great Britain and Northern Ireland.[4] It does not define 'Great Britain'. Article 1 of the Treaty of Union between Scotland and England 1706, however, states 'That the Two Kingdoms of England and Scotland shall upon the first day of May which shall be in the year seven hundred and seven and for ever after be united into one Kingdom by the name of Great Britain'.[5] The Treaty of Union is also said to have incorporated Wales into Great Britain.[6] The legal position of Ireland and Northern Ireland with and within the UK is a complicated subject.[7] Generally, however, the United Kingdom of Great Britain and Ireland was first formed by the Union of Ireland Act 1800. Over a century later the Government of Ireland Act 1920 established two Parliaments, in Belfast and Dublin. The Irish Free State (Agreement) Act 1922 saw the UK Parliament recognise the Irish Free States, and created the United Kingdom of Great Britain and Northern Ireland. The legal position of Northern Ireland presently is governed

2 See, generally, Brazier, R., 'The Constitution of the United Kingdom' (1999) 58 *Cambridge Law Journal* 96.

3 It should be noted that the definitions within the 1978 Act exist explicitly for the purposes of statutory interpretation. Section 2(2) of the Parliamentary Titles Act 1927 provides that references to the United Kingdom in public documents shall 'unless the context otherwise requires, mean Great Britain and Northern Ireland'.

4 The Channel Islands and the Isle of Man are not part of the UK; however they are part of the British Islands together with the UK. Schedule 1 to the Interpretation and Legislative Reform (Scotland) Act 2010 similarly provides that the 'UK' means Great Britain and Northern Ireland.

5 Acts were passed in each of the Scottish and English Parliaments implementing the Treaty in January 1707 (Scottish Act: APS XI 406) and March 1707 (English Act: 6 Anne c 11) respectively.

6 Bradley, A.W. and Ewing, K.D., *Constitutional Law*, 15th edn, Pearson Education Limited, Harlow, 2011, at p 34. In 1536 an Act of the English Parliament united Wales with England. English common law was applied as from 1543. They share a common legal system. For example ss 7–9 of the Constitutional Reform Act 2005 provide in regard to the President of the courts of both England and Wales. See, generally, Andrews, J. (ed.), *Welsh Studies in Public Law*, University of Wales Press, Cardiff, 1970.

7 See, e.g. Hadfield, B., *The Constitution of Northern Ireland*, SLS Legal Publications, Belfast, 1989; and McCrudden, C., 'Northern Ireland and the British Constitution', in Jowell, J. and Oliver, D. (eds), *The Changing Constitution*, 6th edn, Oxford University Press, Oxford, 2007, Ch 10.

by section 1(1) of the Northern Ireland Act 1998, which states: 'It is hereby declared that Northern Ireland in its entirety remains part of the United Kingdom and shall not cease to be so without the consent of a majority of the people of Northern Ireland voting in a poll held for the purposes of this section in accordance with Schedule 1'.[8]

An understanding that the UK comprises England, Wales, Scotland and Northern Ireland takes us some way. It begs the question, however, of what exactly is each of these constituent parts? The approach taken by the Interpretation Act 1978 is to define England and Wales by reference to the local government areas existing in each.[9] England is defined by the 1978 Act as 'subject to any alteration of boundaries under Part IV of the Local Government Act 1972, the area consisting of the counties established by section 1 of that Act, Greater London and the Isles of Scilly'. Section 1(2) of the Local Government Act 1972 provides that the metropolitan and non-metropolitan counties named in Parts 1 and 2 of Schedule 1 are the constituent parts of England for the purpose of local government. Similarly, Wales is defined as 'the combined area of the counties which were created by section 20 of the Local Government Act 1972 as originally enacted, but subject to any alteration made under section 73 of that Act (consequential alteration of boundary following alteration of watercourse)'. The local government areas existing in Scotland are those found in Schedule 1 to the Local Government etc. (Scotland) Act 1994.[10] The local government districts that comprise Northern Ireland are those listed in section 1(2) of the Local Government (Boundaries) Act (Northern Ireland) Act 2008.[11]

Perhaps of greater importance for our purposes is not what comprise England, Wales, Scotland and Northern Ireland, but the related question of what are the external borders of each. Prior to discussing this it should be noted that this book is not immediately concerned with the application of law within and between the three separate UK legal systems. As such, the border between Scotland and England is not directly relevant.[12] Its significance for our purposes is limited to the fact that it divides the two areas, and that both separate legal systems can and do apply their law across the external UK border.[13] The border

8 The 1998 Act repealed the previously applicable statute, the Government of Ireland Act 1920.

9 Another possible approach to understanding what exactly are England, Wales, Scotland and Northern Ireland is through reference to parliamentary constituencies. On a UK-wide basis the Parliamentary Constituencies Act 1986 governs the process by which the UK is divided into constituencies. Note, however, the effect of the Parliamentary Voting System and Constituencies Act 2011.

10 Under s 1(2).

11 As enacted by the Northern Ireland Assembly.

12 The border between England and Wales even less so in that they share a legal system.

13 There is no explicit legislative statement of the Scottish–English border. It can be found in the northern boundaries of Northumbria and Cumbria as set by the Ordnance Survey as required by the UK Local Government Act 1972, Sched 1, Pt 3. See further Hirst, H., *Jurisdiction and the Ambit of the Criminal Law*, Oxford University Press, Oxford, 2003, Ch 1, esp. pp 63–6.

between Northern Ireland and the Republic of Ireland is, of course, a line demarcating the edge of UK territory. It was provided for by section 1(2) of the Government of Ireland Act 1920, which states: 'For the purposes of this Act, Northern Ireland shall consist of the parliamentary counties of Antrim, Armagh, Down, Fermanagh, Londonderry and Tyrone, and the parliamentary boroughs of Belfast and Londonderry'. The Act has been repealed by the Northern Ireland Act 1998. The border as set originally in the 1920 Act, however, remains. Generally, then, the UK has both internal and external borders – internal within the UK and external facing the sea and the Republic of Ireland.[14]

It is the UK's external border with the high seas that is of the most relevance for our purpose. This is because it demarcates what is within and outside the UK in almost all cases. Most importantly from our perspective the criminal law and human rights law generally and normally apply inside the UK's external border only, not outside it.[15] In regard to the precise sea border, historically the criminal law applied to the land within the realm and extended to 'the foreshore or sea beach where the land meets the open sea'.[16] However, the applicability of the law has been extended to the territorial sea – those waters seaward of UK internal waters by section 2 of the Territorial Sea Act 1878. Section 1 of the Territorial Sea Act 1987 extended the breadth of the territorial sea to 12 nautical miles from the coast. Therefore, it is correct to state that the UK's seaward border is generally 12 nautical miles from its coast, at the outer edge of the UK's territorial sea.[17] The rule of public international law which stipulates that states may establish a territorial sea of up to 12 miles from its baselines – in essence the outer edge of its internal waters and landmass – is Article 3 of the Convention on the Law of the Sea 1982. In regard to the extension of the criminal law to the territorial sea, section 2 of the 1878 Act provides, *inter alia*, that 'An offence committed by a person, whether he is or is not a subject of Her Majesty, on the open sea within the territorial waters of Her Majesty's dominions, is an offence within the jurisdiction of the Admiral, although it may have been committed on board or by means of a foreign ship'. Section 7 of the Act excludes summary offences from this extension of the law. The 1878 Act did not distinguish between waters off England and Wales and the other parts of Great Britain. However, the Scotland Act 1998 and the Northern Ireland Act

14 The notion of a sea border is perhaps counterintuitive in that crossing it may not entail entry into a third state. However, it is apt in that it shares the characteristic of delimiting the application of law in most cases.

15 The position in regard to human rights law is more complex, however, as the limitation on its spatial application is not explicitly territorial, but rather 'jurisdictional'. Article 1 of the European Convention on Human Rights and Fundamental Freedoms 1950 ('the Convention') provides that state parties secure rights to persons 'within their jurisdiction'. This point is analysed below and in some depth in Chapter 4.

16 Hirst (n 13 above), at p 62.

17 There are exceptions where the neighbouring country or juridical entity is less than 24 nautical miles from the UK's baselines, such as France and the Isle of Man.

1998 specifically refer to the waters apart of each. Section 126(1) of the Scotland Act 1998 states that '"Scotland" includes so much of the internal waters and territorial sea of the United Kingdom as are adjacent to Scotland'[18], and section 98 of the Northern Ireland Act 1998 provides, *inter alia*, that '"Northern Ireland" includes so much of the internal waters and territorial sea of the United Kingdom as are adjacent to Northern Ireland'. These provide that Scotland and Northern Ireland include the territorial waters off their respective coasts, and so facilitate the application of Scots and Northern Irish law within them.[19]

A final point about the UK border must be made prior to moving on to a discussion of the relevant public international law. This is that the territory within the border surrounding the UK at the edge of the territorial sea and with the Republic of Ireland is not the totality of the area that can be deemed part of the UK. There are a number of areas that are rightfully considered quasi-territorial. Whilst these areas are not, or not always, part of the UK-proper, they are also not wholly extraterritorial areas over which a third state can lawfully apply its law or areas *terra nullius*. These areas include consular and diplomatic premises abroad and offshore platforms.[20] UK-registered ships and aircraft are also properly considered as quasi-territorial.[21] There is also the *sui generis* position of the Channel Tunnel.[22] Even the relatively settled position of the territorial sea has been modified to a certain extent by the creation of 'Marine Areas' off Scotland and the rest of the UK.[23] A number of these areas will be mentioned

18 Schedule 1 to the Interpretation and Legislative Reform (Scotland) Act 2010 defines Scotland with reference to s 126 of the Scotland Act 1998.

19 A notable provision in regard to the territory of Scotland and its territorial sea is s 1 of the Island of Rockall Act 1972, as amended. It states, *inter alia*, that 'As from the date of the passing of this Act, the Island of Rockall . . . shall be incorporated into that part of the United Kingdom known as Scotland and shall form part of the Western Isles, and the law of Scotland shall apply accordingly'.

20 Human rights were at issue in regard to consular premises in Australia in *R v Secretary of State for the Foreign and Commonwealth Office ex p B and others* [2004] EWCA 1344, [2005] QB 643. Article 3 of the Criminal Jurisdiction (Offshore Activities) Order 1987, SI 1987/2198 extends the application of the criminal law to oil and gas installations within areas designated under s 1(7) of the Continental Shelf Act 1964.

21 Section 281 of the Merchant Shipping Act 1995 provides for the extension of the criminal law to 'United Kingdom ships'. Section 92 of the Civil Aviation Act 1982 provides similarly in regard to 'British controlled aircraft'. Both UK ships and British-controlled aircraft can be considered quasi-territorial in that they are regulated by UK law wherever they go. See further Chapter 3.

22 The Channel Tunnel Act 1987 relates to the applicability of English criminal law within the Channel Tunnel. The Channel Tunnel (International Arrangements) Order 1993, SI 1993/1813, art 3 provides that where the locus of a crime is unclear, either England or France can apply its law.

23 Section 1(1) of the Marine (Scotland) Act 2010 defines the Scottish marine area as 'the area of sea within the seaward limits of the territorial sea of the United Kingdom adjacent to Scotland and includes the bed and subsoil of the sea within that area'. The UK marine area, defined by s 42(1) of the Marine and Coastal Access Act 2009, consists of the territorial sea adjacent to the UK, the sea within the limits of the exclusive economic zone and the area

in Chapters 3 and 4. Here it is merely important to note that whilst the UK border is significant in that it demarcates between the territorial and extra-territorial application of law, it is not possible clearly and simply to draw that line.

Public international law and practice

Public international law provides the underlying context of the application of UK law across borders. It does so because it governs the behaviour of states. Public international law recognises states as the predominant legal persons within it and also provides that they are legal equals – by virtue of their statehood.[24] This constitutional principle, begetting an international society predicated upon the equality and independence of states, has been codified and strengthened in the post-Second World War period. It runs through the most fundamental of international instruments – the Charter of the United Nations. Article 2 contains a list of principles expressing and expanding upon the basic premise, amongst which are:

1. The Organisation is based upon the principle of the sovereign equality of all its Members.
   [. . .]
4. All Members shall refrain in their international relations from the threat or use of force against the territorial integrity or political independence of any state, or in any other manner inconsistent with the Purposes of the United Nations.
   [. . .]
7. Nothing contained in the present Charter shall authorise the United Nations to intervene in matters which are essentially within the domestic jurisdiction of any state.

These principles have been restated and clarified in subsequent instruments, a significant instance of which is General Assembly Resolution 2625 (XXV),[25] adopted without a vote on 24 October 1970. The Resolution, entitled 'General Assembly Declaration on Principles of International Law Concerning Friendly Relations and Co-operation Among States in Accordance With the Charter of

of sea within the limits of the UK sector of the continental shelf including the seabed and subsoil of the sea within those areas.

24 There are 192 state parties to the United Nations, a useful indicator of the number of states generally. The membership is listed at http://www.un.org/en/members/, accessed 21 May 2011. The membership of the Council of Europe and European Union is mentioned below. A further relevant institution is the Commonwealth, with 54 Member States with largely similar legal backgrounds coming together, see http://www.thecommonwealth.org/Internal/142227/members/, accessed 21 May 2011.

25 Series I, Vol XIII, 1970–71, p 337.

the United Nations', contains the principle that 'States shall refrain in their international relations from the threat or use of force against the territorial integrity or political independence of any State, or in any other manner inconsistent with the purposes of the United Nations'. Additionally, it refers to 'the duty not to intervene in matters within the domestic jurisdiction of any State in accordance with the Charter' and the 'principle of the sovereign equality of States'. This last principle means that:

(a) states are juridically equal;
(b) each State enjoys the rights inherent in full sovereignty;
(c) each State has the duty to respect the personality of other States;
(d) the territorial integrity and political independence of the State are inviolable;
(e) each State has the right freely to choose and develop its political, social, economic and cultural systems;
(f) each State has the duty to comply fully and in good faith with its international obligations and to live in peace with other States.

In addition to conventional international law and so-called soft law supporting these international constitutional principles, there is authority in support of them in custom, at least in regard to the prohibition contained in Article 2(4) of the Charter. In the case of *Military and Paramilitary Activities in and Against Nicaragua (Nicaragua v U.S.), Merits*, the ICJ stated: 'The principle of the non-use of force . . . may . . . be regarded as a principle of customary international law'.[26]

Not only do the rules protecting state sovereignty and territorial integrity exist in convention and custom, but there is support for the view that at least some of them have the character of *jus cogens*. The *Nicaragua Case* cites the International Law Commission, Nicaragua and the United States as all subscribing to that position in regard to the prohibition of the use of force.[27] A number of academics agree, with Brownlie, for example, citing the prohibition of the use of force as among the least controversial examples of *jus cogens*.[28] Beyond the prohibition on the use of force, other principles found in General Assembly Resolution 2625 (XXV) are also said to exist in customary international law, including the principle of the 'non-intervention in matters within the domestic jurisdiction of States'.[29] These rules form the basic constitutional structure of global society. Whilst it is perhaps pedestrian to note the nature and status of these basic constitutive public international norms, it is necessary to do so because the application of law across borders, in whatever

26 [1986] ICJ Rep 14, (1986) 76 ILR 1, at para 188 (hereinafter the *Nicaragua Case*).
27 Ibid at para 190.
28 Brownlie, I., *Principles of Public International Law*, 4th edn, Oxford, Clarendon Press, at p 513.
29 The *Nicaragua Case* at paras 191 and 192.

form (judicial, executive or legislative) and area (criminal or human rights), engages these rules, and may well be in conflict with them.[30]

Public international law is of central importance in an analysis of the application of UK law across borders. Clearly, an egregious application, for example through the exercise of executive authority in a third state without consent or authorisation, is a violation of international law.[31] More commonly, as will be discussed below, international law provides the parameters for the application of law in the form of the rules governing jurisdiction. Further, however, the value in detailing the central tenets of public international law in large part lies in the fact that such exposition brings to the fore the pervasive importance in international law of state sovereignty. Being created by existing states, public international law inevitably acts to defend them. It exists for largely conservative reasons – to protect the status quo and to delimit competencies. The former is accomplished by international law protecting state sovereignty through the prohibition on the use of force against states and intervention within their domestic jurisdiction.[32] However, states are not hermetically sealed – trade, travel and multifarious other forms of interaction by individuals and states themselves take place between and across countries. Reconciliation of the ramifications of international interaction and the protection of state sovereignty falls to the law on state jurisdiction. Jurisdiction is both a 'manifestation of State sovereignty'[33] and a central tool employed in its protection.

Jurisdiction in public international law

The rules of state jurisdiction in public international law permit states to apply their law across borders in certain circumstances.[34] Mann has stated: 'When public international lawyers pose the problem of jurisdiction, they have in mind the State's right under international law to regulate conduct in matters not exclusively of domestic concern'.[35] *Oppenheim's International Law* provides that state jurisdiction 'concerns essentially the extent of each state's right to regulate

30 The subject of the non-interference within the domestic jurisdiction of states remains very relevant today: see Jamnejad, M. and Wood, W., 'The Principle of Non-Intervention' [2009] *Leiden Journal of International Law* 345.

31 This will be discussed below in regard to the application of human rights law in Iraq.

32 Not all types of intervention are unlawful. Jennings and Watts write that 'interference [must be] forcible or dictatorial interference by a state in the affairs of another state, calculated to impose certain conduct or consequences on that other state': Jennings, R.Y. and Watts, A.D., *Oppenheim's International Law*, 9th edn, Longham, London, 1992, at p 428. It is suggested below that the application of law across borders may in certain circumstances amount to unlawful intervention.

33 Bowett, D.W., 'Jurisdiction: Changing Patterns of Authority over Activities and Resources' (1982) 53 BYIL 1.

34 See, generally, Ryngaert, C., *Jurisdiction in International Law*, Oxford University Press, Oxford, 2008.

35 Mann, F.A., 'The Doctrine of Jurisdiction in International Law' (1964- I) RdC 1.

conduct or the consequences of events'.[36] With reference solely to crime, Article 1(b) of the Harvard Draft Convention on Jurisdiction with Respect to Crime 1935 provides that 'A State's "jurisdiction" is its competence under international law to prosecute and punish for crime'.[37] Common to these definitions is the notion that international law permits the application of law across borders by states if certain conditions are met. It is important to state this basic point clearly because one of the leading authorities in the area – the opinion of the Permanent Court of International Justice in the *Case of the SS Lotus*,[38] appears to weigh against it. In the *Lotus* case France challenged Turkey's instigation of criminal proceedings against the captain of a French ship. This followed a collision with a Turkish vessel in the Mediterranean but outside Turkish waters. The relevant passage of the case states:

> Now the first and foremost restriction imposed by international law upon a State is that – failing the existence of a permissive rule to the contrary – it may not exercise its power in any form in the territory of another State. In this sense jurisdiction is certainly territorial . . . It does not, however, follow that international law prohibits a State from exercising jurisdiction in its own territory, in respect of any case which relates to acts which have taken place abroad, and which in it cannot rely on some permissive rule of international law. Such a view would only be tenable if international law contained a general prohibition to States to extend the application of their laws and the jurisdiction of their courts to persons, property and acts outside their territory. . . . But this is certainly not the case under international law as it stands at present. Far from laying down a general prohibition to the effect that States may not extend the application of their laws and their jurisdiction . . . it leaves them in this respect a wide measure of discretion which is only limited in certain cases by prohibitive rules; as regards other cases, every State remains free to adopt the principles which it regards as best and most suitable.[39]

This passage can be interpreted to mean that states are free to apply their law unless expressly forbidden by international law in the particular circumstances. This is clearly not the case in international law today.

Nowadays it is beyond doubt that international law generally prohibits the application of law across borders, allowing it in defined situations only. Authority

36 Jennings and Watts (n 32 above), at p 456.

37 (1935) 29 AJIL (Supp) 439 (hereinafter 'Harvard Draft Convention'). The law relating to state jurisdiction, and the principles, bases or categories thereof, discussed below, have developed with reference to the criminal law. Human rights law has generally been overlooked in analyses of the subject. This simply follows from the novelty of it being applied across borders, and the fact that the criminal law and human rights law are considered discrete subjects. For a collection of human rights analyses, see Coomans, F. and Kamminga, M.T. (eds), *Extraterritorial Application of Human Rights Treaties*, Intersentia, Oxford, 2004.

38 *Case of the SS Lotus, (France v Turkey)* (1927) PCIJ Rep, Series A, No 10.

39 Ibid at pp 18–19.

for this is found in the long-standing practice of states, supported by academic opinion. Therefore, the passage cited above from the *Lotus* case is either not what it appears, or is bad law.[40] The pre-eminent authority in support of this view of international law must be, of course, state practice. It is, perhaps surprisingly, not difficult to find. The crime of piracy in public international law provides the paradigmatic example. In a rule unusual in its strength and near universal acceptance, international law provides that all states are entitled to apply their law to alleged pirates. It has been stated in this regard that 'whereas *according to international law the criminal jurisdiction of municipal law is ordinarily restricted* to crimes committed on its *terra firma* or territorial waters or on its own ships, and to crime by its own nationals wherever committed, it is also recognized as extending to piracy'.[41] A conventional authority providing similarly is Article 13 of the Treaty on International Penal Law 1889, which provides that 'Crimes considered as piracy by public international law fall within the jurisdiction of the State under whose power the criminals come'.[42] If international law generally allowed the application of municipal law abroad such specific permissible provision would not be necessary. In other words there would be no need for explicitly facilitative rules if states were free to apply their law in all cases. The strength of this illustration is heightened because piracy necessarily occurs outside the territory of all states.[43] If international law freely allowed states to apply their law across borders it would undoubtedly do so on the high seas. Finally on this point, Jennings deduces from collective state practice that:

> States do not give themselves unlimited discretion in the matter [of applying their laws]. Their municipal laws – even those of States which make extensive claims to extraterritorial jurisdiction – contain principles of jurisdiction. . . . It seems reasonable to infer from the existence of these principles of extraterritorial jurisdiction, firmly entrenched as they are in the practice of States, that some justifying principle is thought to be necessary to found extraterritorial jurisdiction; that it is not a matter for sovereign discretion.[44]

40 In regard to the passage being bad law, Mann notes that it seems 'to propagate the idea of the delimitation of jurisdiction by the state itself rather than international law or, in the words of Sir Hersch Lauterpacht, they proclaim the principle of presumptive freedom of State action, and may therefore, have to be read as countenancing a most unfortunate and retrograde theory. It can be confidently asserted that they have been condemned by the majority of the immense number of writers who have discussed them, and today they probably cannot claim to be good law': Mann, (n 35 above), at p 35, footnotes omitted.

41 *In re Piracy Jure Gentium* [1934] AC 58 at 589, per Viscount Sankey LC (emphasis added).

42 (1935) 29 AJIL (Supp) 638, a translation from 18 Martens, *Nouveau Recueil Général de Traités* (2nd sér), at p 432.

43 The definition of international piracy is today found in the Law of the Sea Convention 1982 (1982) 21 ILM 1261, Art 101.

44 Jennings, R.Y., 'Extraterritorial Jurisdiction and U.S. Antitrust Laws' (1957) 33 BYIL 146 at p 150.

Concluding, and lending support to the argument that a proper law is emerging, Jennings further notes: 'It would be intolerable if States were permitted without any justifying legitimate interest to attempt to control the doings of foreigners in their own countries'.[45] The 'justifying legitimate interest' evidenced by a material connection between the UK, crime or human rights violation forms the basis of the proper law approach, as discussed in Chapter 5.

The bases, principles or categories of jurisdiction[46]

International law undoubtedly permits and regulates the application of law across borders. It permits it in certain circumstances and forbids it in their absence. The question arising, then, is what are the circumstances in which the application of law across borders is permissible? The answer depends, first, on what form of law is being applied – executive, legislative or judicial. The circumstances in which executive application is permissible are very limited. The general rules stated above prohibiting the use of force and intervention within the 'domestic jurisdiction' of states forbid executive action within the territory of a third state without that state's consent or UN Security Council authorisation. Therefore, the conditions requisite for the application of UK human rights law across borders on a wholly extraterritorial basis are rare.[47] These are the presence of a UK public authority abroad exercising the requisite degree of control over a person. The circumstances in which a state may apply its law legislatively or judicially are generally considerably wider. They are discerned with reference to the categories of jurisdiction, which relate to territory, nationality of the accused and victim(s) and the affectation of certain core interests of states both individually and collectively. Each forms a category of jurisdiction: the territorial,[48] active personality,[49] passive personality,[50]

45 Ibid at p 151.

46 The literature refers to 'bases', 'principles' and 'categories' interchangeably. 'Categories' is to be preferred in that it denotes inert groupings of similar links that have been accepted as able to substantiate a requisite connection between a state and a person, crime or human rights violation.

47 The application of human rights law across borders takes one of two forms: wholly extraterritorial, where the UK's actions and the violation are outside its territory; and extradition and expulsion cases, where the UK acts within its territory in regard to possible violations outside it. These are described in detail in Chapter 4.

48 It is outside the scope of this book to delve into the precise nature and limits of the categories. For such an examination, see Arnell, P., 'Criminal Jurisdiction in International Law' [2000] *Juridical Review* 179. See also Blakesley, C.L., 'A Conceptual Framework for Extradition and Jurisdiction Over Extraterritorial Crime' [1984] *Utah Law Review* 1. For analysis of the territorial category in particular, see Berge, W., 'Criminal Jurisdiction and the Territorial Principle' (1931–2) 30 *Michigan Law Review* 238 and Fitzgerald, P., 'The Territorial Principle in Penal Law: An Attempted Justification' (1970) 1 *Georgia Journal of International and Comparative Law* 29.

49 See Arnell, P., 'The Case for Nationality Based Jurisdiction' (2001) 50 ICLQ 955 and Watson, G.R., 'Offenders Abroad: The Case for Nationality Based Criminal Jurisdiction' (1992) 17 *Yale Journal of International Law* 41.

protective[51] and universal.[52] Whilst the categories have been developed with the criminal law in mind, they have been applied to other areas of law such as competition law.[53] Human rights law to date has been applied across borders exclusively with reference to territory, albeit including on what is known as a subjective territorial basis and on a quasi-territorial basis.[54] The subjective territorial basis is implicitly utilised in extradition and expulsion cases and the quasi-territorial basis is applied in wholly extraterritorial cases arising in diplomatic premises and areas where the UK exercises effective control.

The categories of jurisdiction are, in effect, repositories of examples of genuine and accepted linkages or connections between the state and the person, crime or violation.[55] In the presence of such a link a state may lawfully apply its law. Brownlie has noted that international law is developing in the light of 'a principle of substantial and genuine connection between the subject-matter of jurisdiction, and the territorial base and reasonable interests of the jurisdiction sought to be exercised'.[56] *Oppenheim's International Law* states that there is a tendency:

> to regard these various categories [of jurisdiction] as parts of a single broad principle according to which the right to exercise jurisdiction depends on there being between the subject matter and the state exercising jurisdiction a sufficiently close connection to justify that state in regulating the matter and perhaps also to override any competing rights of other states.[57]

50 See Watson, G.R., 'The Passive Personality Principle' (1993) 28 *Texas International Law Journal* 1.

51 See Meyer, E.T., 'Drug Smuggling and the Protective Principle: A Journey into Uncharted Waters' (1979) 39 *Louisiana Law Review* 1189 and Cameron, I., *The Protective Principle of International Criminal Jurisdiction*, Aldershot, Dartmouth Publishing Co., 1993.

52 Randall, K.C., 'Universal Jurisdiction Under International Law' (1988) 66 *Texas Law Review* 785; Graefrath, B., 'Universal Criminal Jurisdiction and an International Criminal Court' (1990–1) 1 EJIL 67; and O'Keefe, R., 'Universal Jurisdiction: Clarifying the Basic Concept' (2004) 2 *Journal of International Criminal Justice* 735.

53 Roth discusses whether the application of competition law is reasonably justified with reference to the protective principle or objective territorial principle, in Roth, P.M., 'Reasonable Extraterritoriality: Correcting the "Balance of Interests"' [1992] ICLQ 245 at p 284. Objective territoriality denotes where the act or offence concludes within a state, and subjective territoriality where it commences within a state.

54 In *R (Smith) (FC) v Secretary of State for Defence and another* [2010] UKSC 29 an argument was made that UK human rights law applied on something akin to a nationality basis to UK armed forces personnel abroad. The case and the UK's approach to jurisdiction are discussed in Chapters 3 and 4.

55 Akehurst makes the point of the evidential nature of the categories of jurisdiction, albeit in a somewhat different context, stating that the categories of jurisdiction are 'specific heads of jurisdiction which are proved to be legal', in Akehurst, M., 'Jurisdiction in International Law' (1972–3) 43 BYIL 145 at p 167.

56 Brownlie (n 28 above), at p 298.

57 Jennings and Watts (n 32 above), at pp 457–8.

The categories are linked by the fact that they are all examples of sufficiently close and genuine links. The link is the common denominator amongst the disjunctive and seemingly *ad hoc* categories of jurisdiction. This point is clearly related to the proper law approach to the application of law.

The conventional context

Related to public international law and the law of state jurisdiction are numerous conventions which provide further context to the application of UK law across borders. This is because treaties form a central source of international law and at times explicitly relate to state jurisdiction. The treaties that are relevant for our purposes apply to both the criminal law and human rights specifically, as well as international law more generally. There are three types of treaty, with each acting in a different way. The firsts limits and restricts the application of law abroad. The leading example of which, mentioned above, is the Charter of the United Nations. The second type does the opposite and permits and indeed may require state parties to apply their law outside their territory.[58] A third type relates to or creates competency-based rules applying to especial areas or situations. We will focus here on the last two – the first having been mentioned. The majority of the treaties that permit or require the application of law relate to the criminal law, with human rights law affected less so. Not one of these, however, addresses the application of municipal law across borders – be it criminal or human rights law – in general terms. Ideally, there would be such treaty or treaties, allocating competencies and governing dispute settlement where more than one state had an interest in a crime or human rights violation. It is perhaps understandable, however, that such conventions do not exist – states are naturally reluctant to limit their lawful ability to apply their law, certainly in the area of criminal law. One merely has to note that the crimes of treason and the counterfeiting of currency are intended to affect central state interests directly and that they can readily occur outside a state's territory to comprehend why there is a reluctance on the part of states to address the subject and constrain their competence. That noted, there was an attempt to regulate the application of criminal law across borders in 1935. This took the form of the Harvard Draft Convention with Respect to Crime 1935 – which did not move beyond draft form.[59] There has never been an attempt specifically to regulate the application of municipal human rights law across borders by way of convention. The bulk of the conventional treatment in the area, then, comprises treaties which permit or require the application of the law to specific crimes. Also relevant, however, are several general human rights treaties that

58 Related to these conventions are those which govern extradition and mutual legal assistance.

59 (1935) 29 AJIL (Supp) 439. This is not to suggest that it has little or no value. Indeed, the erudition evident within the Harvard Draft Convention has resulted in it being one of the leading authorities in the area of criminal jurisdiction.

contain provision on their application, and a number of conventions that create especial areas or regimes governing the application of municipal law outside the territory of state parties.[60]

The majority of the conventions that exist in the area of the criminal law permit or require the application of municipal law to acts or persons. The UK is party to a significant number of these conventions, including treaties relating to piracy, torture, crimes against maritime installations, hijacking of aircraft, drug-trafficking, money-laundering and corruption. Two examples will suffice in illustrating the type of obligations within these treaties relating to the application of the law, and the UK response. The first is the Convention on the Prohibition of the Use, Stockpiling and Transfer of Anti-Personnel Mines and on their Destruction 1997 ('the Ottawa Convention') and the Landmines Act 1998. Article 9 of the Ottawa Convention provides: 'Each State Party shall take all appropriate legal, administrative and other measures, including the imposition of penal sanctions, to prevent and suppress any activity prohibited to a State Party under this Convention undertaken by persons or on territory under its jurisdiction or control'. This is a comparatively broad and general competence-related provision. It relies on the concepts of 'jurisdiction' and 'control'. The UK's response to this obligation is section 3 of the Landmines Act 1998. It provides that the prohibitions found in section 2(1) and (2) of the Act, relating, *inter alia*, to the usage of anti-personnel mines, apply outside the UK:

> (1) Section 2(1) applies to conduct in the United Kingdom or elsewhere.
>
> (2) Section 2(2) applies to assistance, encouragement and inducements in the United Kingdom or elsewhere, and it so applies irrespective of whether the conduct assisted, encouraged or induced takes place, or (if it takes place) will take place, in the United Kingdom or elsewhere.
>
> (3) Subsections (1) and (2) of section 2, so far as they apply respectively to –
> (a) conduct outside the United Kingdom, and
> (b) assistance, encouragement and inducements outside the United Kingdom, impose prohibitions only on United Kingdom nationals, Scottish partnerships and bodies incorporated under the law of a part of the United Kingdom.

As will be seen in Chapter 3, this approach is generally applied by the UK when implementing this type of conventional obligation. It applies the criminal law on a territorial basis, first, and then extends it to nationals or residents and in certain cases to bodies corporate. A second example, and an exception to this

60 It should be noted that this considerable body of conventional law evidences the second underlying theme within this book – the increasing importance and effect of non-UK law and practice in the area.

general pattern, is in regard to torture in UK law. Article 5 of the Convention against Torture and Other Cruel, Inhuman or Degrading Treatment or Punishment 1984 ('the Torture Convention') provides:

1. Each State Party shall take such measures as may be necessary to establish its jurisdiction over the offences referred to in article 4 in the following cases:
   (a) When the offences are committed in any territory under its jurisdiction or on board a ship or aircraft registered in that State;
   (b) When the alleged offender is a national of that State;
   (c) When the victim is a national of that State if that State considers it appropriate.

The UK has enacted section 134(1) and (2) of the Criminal Justice Act 1988 to meet this obligation, which provide:

(1) A public official or person acting in an official capacity, whatever his nationality, commits the offence of torture if in the United Kingdom or elsewhere he intentionally inflicts severe pain or suffering on another in the performance or purported performance of his official duties.
(2) A person not falling within subsection (1) above commits the offence of torture, whatever his nationality, if –
   (a) in the United Kingdom or elsewhere he intentionally inflicts severe pain or suffering on another at the instigation or with the consent or acquiescence –
      (i) of a public official; or
      (ii) of a person acting in an official capacity; and
(b) the official or other person is performing or purporting to perform his official duties when he instigates the commission of the offence or consents to or acquiesces in it.

Unusually, the UK has gone beyond the requirements of the Torture Convention. It has provided that the crime of torture may apply without reference to territory, nationality or any other link to the UK and instead may apply merely on the basis of the nature of the crime itself.

There are a considerably smaller number of human rights-related treaties affecting the application of UK law across borders than those in the criminal sphere. Those that do exist generally fail to address the subject explicitly or effectively. It is necessary, first, to mention the European Convention on Human Rights and Fundamental Freedoms 1950. Article 1 provides that 'The High Contracting Parties shall secure to everyone within their jurisdiction the rights and freedoms defined in Section 1 of the Convention'. Clearly, this provision does not explicitly permit or require the application of the Convention across the borders of state parties. There is, however, considerable jurisprudence which has interpreted it to apply in this way in certain circumstances. The Convention is undoubtedly the most important convention affecting UK human rights law. There are other treaties, however, that also have some relevance. The International Covenant on Civil and Political Rights 1966 (ICCPR) is one such treaty. The Covenant has 165 parties, including the UK. The Human Rights Committee of the United Nations has consistently held that the ICCPR can apply outside state parties.[61] However, because the UK has not signed or ratified the Optional Protocol to the ICCPR allowing individual communications to the Human Rights Committee, this is of limited practical impact – not to mention the very close relationship between UK law and the Convention. An altogether different type of convention that has influenced the application of UK human rights law across borders is that governing extradition. Indeed, the law of extradition (together with deportation) has given rise to one of the two ways in which human rights law is applied across borders –the consideration of arguments made by a person subject to extradition or expulsion that their human rights will be violated as a result. The most high profile example of such a treaty is the Extradition Treaty between the Government of the United Kingdom and the Government of the United States 2003.[62] Notably, the Treaty itself does not mention human rights; rather, it is the Extradition Act 2003 which provides that in considering an extradition a judge must consider human rights. In regard to 'Category 2' states, including the United States, section 87 provides:

(1) If the judge is required to proceed under this section (by virtue of section 84, 85 or 86) he must decide whether the person's extradition would be compatible with the Convention rights within the meaning of the Human Rights Act 1998 (c. 42).
(2) If the judge decides the question in subsection (1) in the negative he must order the person's discharge.
(3) If the judge decides that question in the affirmative he must send the case to the Secretary of State for his decision whether the person is to be extradited.

The process of extradition has given rise to the leading European Court of Human Rights (ECtHR) case in the area, *Soering v United Kingdom*.[63] Here the Court held that arguments on the basis of human rights concerns in the requesting state inevitably involve an 'assessment of conditions in the requesting

61 See McGoldrick, D., 'The Extraterritorial Application of the International Covenant on Civil and Political Rights', in Coomans and Kamminga, *Extraterritorial Application of Human Rights Treaties* (n 37 above), at p 41.

62 2003, No 1, Cmnd 5821, cited at http://www.official-documents.gov.uk/document/cm71/7146/7146.asp, accessed 29 May 2011.

63 (1989) 11 ECHR (Series A).

country'.[64] In other words, extradition necessarily entails the application of human rights law across borders where arguments are made relating to the conditions in third states in that the situation in that country is measured against the Convention and UK human rights law.

The third type of treaty affecting the application of UK law across borders relates to or creates competency-based rules applying to especial areas or situations. These include treaties governing diplomatic and consular premises, specific areas of the seas, Antarctica and the International Criminal Court. The Vienna Convention on Consular Relations 1963 was of some relevance in *R v Secretary of State for the Foreign and Commonwealth Office ex p B and others*[65] where the possible applicability of the Human Rights Act 1998 to the UK Consulate in Melbourne was at issue. The United Nations Law of the Sea Convention 1982, mentioned above in regard to the UK border, provides for the application of UK law to areas of the seas and ships.[66] A further especial regime has been created to cover the Antarctic. The Antarctic Treaty 1961 forms the central part the Antarctic Treaty System which, *inter alia*, provides for a delimitation of competencies over the area. Article 8 of the Antarctic Treaty provides that observers 'shall be subject only to the jurisdiction of the Contracting Party of which they are nationals in respect of all acts or omissions occurring while they are in Antarctica for the purpose of exercising their functions'.[67] The International Criminal Court is governed by the Rome Statute for the International Criminal Court 1998.[68] The UK is a party to the Statute and accordingly has enacted the International Criminal Court Act 2001 and the International Criminal Court (Scotland) Act 2001. These Acts implement the principle of 'complementarity' into UK law, whereby both the UK and the International Criminal Court share the competence to try crimes under the Rome Statute.[69] The specific rules within the UK relating to crimes under the Rome Statute will be examined in Chapter 3; here, it is merely relevant to note that there are such rules and that there are especial regimes and areas – not just in relation to the International Criminal Court but more generally – that form part of the context of the application of UK law across borders.

64 Ibid at para 91. See also *Chahal v United Kingdom*, (1997) 23 EHRR 413. Article 3(2) of the Convention against Torture and Other Cruel, Inhuman or Degrading Treatment or Punishment 1984, 1465 UNTS 85, specifically mandates the consideration of circumstances in a foreign state where there are allegations that torture may result from an extradition or expulsion.

65 [2004] EWCA Civ 1344.

66 See, generally, Churchill, R.R. and Lowe, A.V., *The Law of the Sea*, Manchester University Press, Manchester, 1999.

67 See Joyner, C.J. and Chopra, S.K., *The Antarctic Legal Regime*, Martinus Nijhoff, Dordrecht, 1988.

68 The Court's website is found at http://www.icc-cpi.int/, accessed 21 May 2011.

69 See, in regard to Scotland, Arnell, P., 'The International Criminal Court in Scotland: Part One' (2001) *290 Scottish Legal Action Group Legal Journal* 216, and Arnell, P., 'The International Criminal Court in Scotland: Part Two' (2002) 291 *Scottish Legal Action Group Legal Journal* 7.

The Council of Europe

A description of the context in which the UK applies its law across borders must include reference to the Council of Europe and the European Union. UK law and practice in the area is materially influenced by these organisations. Both the Council of Europe and the EU engage in a wide range of activity, and have been doing so for over a half a century. It is impossible here to do other than outline the most pertinent features affecting the application of UK law across borders. The aim of the Council of Europe is found in Article 1(a) of its Statute,[70] which provides:

> The aim of the Council of Europe is to achieve a greater unity between its members for the purpose of safeguarding and realising the ideals and principles which are their common heritage and facilitating their economic and social progress.

Article 3 states:

> Every member of the Council of Europe must accept the principles of the rule of law and of the enjoyment by all persons within its jurisdiction of human rights and fundamental freedoms, and collaborate sincerely and effectively in the realisation of the aim of the Council as specified in Chapter I.

At the Third Summit of the Heads of State and Government of the Council of Europe in 2005 a declaration re-stating the objectives of the organisation was promulgated. This, in part, states:

> The Council of Europe shall pursue its core objective of preserving and promoting human rights, democracy and the rule of law. All its activities must contribute to this fundamental objective. We commit ourselves to developing those principles, with a view to ensuring their effective implementation by all member states.[71]

In carrying out its aims and objectives the Council of Europe has been responsible for the conclusion of over 200 conventions, covering a wide range of subject matter. For our purposes, however, the European Convention on Human Rights and Fundamental Freedoms 1950 is pre-eminent. The Convention is important not only because it contains substantive human rights but also because it created the European Court of Human Rights, which gives authoritative interpretations of the rights within the Convention – including on the important question of their geographic applicability. In addition to the Convention, however, it should

70 There are 47 Member States of the Council of Europe.

71 Cited at http://www.coe.int/t/dcr/summit/20050517_decl_varsovie_en.asp, accessed 21 May 2011.

be noted that there are a number of other Council of Europe treaties that relate to the application of UK law across borders. These include treaties that mandate the criminalisation of an activity within the UK and which may be applied outside it, such as the Criminal Law Convention on Corruption 1999,[72] the Convention on Laundering, Search, Seizure, and Confiscation from the Proceeds of Crime 1990[73] and the Convention on the Protection of the Environment through Criminal Law 1998. A relevant different type of Council of Europe convention relates to mutual assistance and extradition – including the European Convention on Mutual Assistance in Criminal Matters 1959, the European Convention on Extradition 1957 and the Additional Protocol to the European Convention on Extradition 1975.[74]

The European Union

Like the Council of Europe, the EU's activities have directly affected the application of UK law across borders. The competences of the EU are stipulated in the Treaty on the Functioning of the European Union (TFEU).[75] Article 3(1) provides for the exclusive competence of the EU in a number of areas. It states:

> The Union shall have exclusive competence in the following areas: (a) customs union; (b) the establishing of the competition rules necessary for the functioning of the internal market; (c) monetary policy for the Member States whose currency is the euro; (d) the conservation of marine biological resources under the common fisheries policy; (e) common commercial policy.

The areas where competence is shared between the EU and its 27 Member States are provided for in Article 4(3):

> Shared competence between the Union and the Member States applies in the following principal areas: (a) internal market; (b) social policy, for the aspects defined in this Treaty; (c) economic, social and territorial cohesion; (d) agriculture and fisheries, excluding the conservation of marine biological resources; (e) environment; (f) consumer protection; (g) transport; (h) trans-European networks; (i) energy; (j) area of freedom, security and justice; (k) common safety concerns in public health matters, for the aspects defined in this Treaty.

72 See also the Additional Protocol to the Criminal Law Convention on Corruption 2003.
73 Expanding upon this Convention is the Convention on Laundering, Search, Seizure and Confiscation from the Proceeds of Crime and on the Financing of Terrorism 2005.
74 See also the Second Additional Protocol on Extradition 1978.
75 2010/C 83/01, cited at http://eur-lex.europa.eu/LexUriServ/LexUriServ.do?uri=OJ:C:2010:083:FULL:EN:PDF, accessed 29 May 2011.

Article 6 provides for EU competence in supporting, etc. the acts of the Member States:

> The Union shall have competence to carry out actions to support, coordinate or supplement the actions of the Member States. The areas of such action shall, at European level, be: (a) protection and improvement of human health; (b) industry; (c) culture; (d) tourism; (e) education, vocational training, youth and sport; (f) civil protection; (g) administrative cooperation.

Clearly, the range of competences is wide, and the amount of regulation spawned by the EU is accordingly vast. For our purposes, however, only a relatively narrow aspect of EU law is relevant. This relates to extradition, and the European arrest warrant scheme. As will be seen in Chapters 3 and 4, the law of extradition has had a significant impact upon the application of UK law across borders – both criminally and in regard to human rights.[76] This is not to suggest that EU law does not have influence in other ways. Indeed, EU competition law has given rise to a considerable amount of commentary on the application of EU law across borders.[77]

The UK overseas

A concomitant feature of the application of UK law across borders is, in most cases, the presence and activity of UK nationals, residents, the civil service, armed forces and others acting outside it. This is self-evident. The objects of the application of the law in criminal cases are often nationals and residents, and, as discussed in Chapter 1, the subjects of the application of human rights law are emanations of the UK itself. Of course, the law can be applied to persons, natural or legal, with no affinity with the UK; however, this is exceptional. As a result, it is useful to note the extent of nationals, companies and various manifestations of the state situated or operating abroad. The number of UK residents travelling abroad is considerable. In the 12-month period to January 2011, UK residents made approximately 54.9 million visits abroad.[78] The vast majority of these were to Europe. In terms of the military, as of 1 April 2010 37,690 service and Ministry of Defence civilian personnel were stationed outside the

76 The UK has secured an 'opt-out' from the application of the Charter of Fundamental Rights of the EU, by the Protocol on the Application of the Charter of Fundamental Rights on the European Union to Poland and to the United Kingdom. It has also opted out from areas of EU competence relating to justice and home affairs, by Protocol 21 on the Position of the United Kingdom and Ireland in Respect of the Area of Freedom, Security and Justice.

77 Competition law per se is excluded from the subject matter of the book. It has had an influence, however, on the development of a proper law approach and as such will be referred to in Chapter 5. Articles 101 and 102 of the TFEU provide the treaty basis for EU competition law.

78 Office of National Statistics, http://www.statistics.gov.uk/hub/travel-transport/index.html, accessed 21 May 2011.

UK.[79] This figure does not include those persons deployed on operations and temporary assignments. Politically, the UK has a significant presence outwith its territory. This largely involves the diplomatic service under the auspices of the Foreign and Commonwealth Office. In 2010 the Foreign and Commonwealth Office stated that of its 14,400 employees in over 170 countries, one-third were UK nationals.[80] These employees work in embassies or consular premises around the world. Finally, of note in regard to the presence of persons and institutions related to the UK abroad are its overseas territories. The international legal obligations that the UK agrees to apply to its 14 overseas territories vary. The Memorandum on Application issued by the Foreign and Commonwealth Office (FCO) provides that the FCO will make a statement on the application of treaties to which it becomes party upon ratification.[81] The presence of emanations of the UK itself and its nationals and residents abroad clearly affects the application of UK law across borders. Indeed, in light of the scale of that presence it is perhaps surprising that the phenomenon is not more common than it is.

79 Defence Analytical Services and Advice, UK Regular Forces Stationed Location, 1 April 2010, cited at http://www.dasa.mod.uk/, accessed 21 May 2011.

80 See http://www.fco.gov.uk/, accessed 21 May 2011.

81 Cited at http://www.fco.gov.uk/en/publications-and-documents/treaties/uk-overseas-territories/memorandum-application, accessed 21 May 2011. The question of the extension of human rights law to an overseas territory was discussed in *R (Quark Fishing Ltd) v Foreign Secretary* [2005] UKHL 57.

3 UK criminal law across borders

The issues

The criminal law has been applied across borders for longer than any other field of law, and has experienced the greatest change. Both the history and evolution of practice illustrate a number of issues or problems associated with the application of criminal law across borders. A number of these issues are discussed further in Chapter 5; however, it is necessary to introduce them here. The issues surrounding the application of UK criminal are contingent upon the perspective taken. There are four different perspectives: that of the UK, accused persons, third states and international law. From the UK's point of view – or any state for that matter – the issue is simply that criminals and crime fail to respect borders. Lord Griffiths, in a well-known passage, has stated:

> Unfortunately in this century crime has ceased to be largely local in origin and effect. Crime is now established on an international scale and the common law must face this new reality. Their Lordships can find nothing in precedent, comity or good sense that should inhibit the common law from regarding as justiciable in England inchoate crimes committed abroad which are intended to result in the commission of criminal offences in England.[1]

A strict intra-territorial approach will at times be ineffectual in meeting the desire to tackle criminality – especially with the limitations of extradition law and practice and inter-state co-operation. Nowadays, it is not exceptional for an act thought to require the application of UK criminal law to be committed either fully or partially outside UK territory. In comparison with instances of intra-territorial crimes these acts are rare. However, their significance is not diminished by their rarity. Indeed, that the criminal law has been extended to such acts denotes their importance. Simply, then, the central issue from the UK's point of view is that criminality, especially serious criminality, fails to respect borders.

1 *Somchai Liangsiriprasert v Government of the United States of America and another* [1991] 1 AC 225 at 251.

A further issue, from the UK's perspective, which is addressed or rather accommodated through the application of its criminal law across borders, is the actual and perceived inefficiencies within the criminal justice systems of third states and the rendition and co-operation agreements applied to accused persons. Were the criminal justice systems of third states considered efficient, effective and sufficiently akin to that of the UK the application of UK law in a number of circumstances would not be necessary. The underlying point here is that the failure to prosecute and punish persons outside the UK can give rise to the perceived need to do so within it. An example is in regard to so-called sex-tourism crimes. If the criminal justice systems and substantive law in the states where the crimes are committed were such as to be able effectively to prosecute and punish UK residents engaged in these acts the need for the UK to do so would greatly decrease. Admittedly the symbolic nature of, and moral impetus behind, criminalising such odious behaviour would remain, but the need to punish offenders in the UK would be largely vitiated. Leading up to the enactment of the Sexual Offences Act 2003, Lord Falconer of Thoroton in the House of Lords stated:

> The Government are committed to tackling the sexual exploitation of children wherever it occurs in the world. This includes where UK citizens go abroad with the intention of abusing children. We have already put in place a number of measures to deal with this problem, but the Sexual Offences Bill, currently before Parliament, provides us with an opportunity to ensure that we are doing everything we can to deal with those who commit sexual offences overseas.[2]

Clearly, if the exploitation of children by UK nationals and residents was addressed in the place in which it is committed the purpose behind the application of its law – prosecution and punishment – would be met overseas.

From the perspective of an accused the application of UK criminal law across borders gives rise to two distinct issues: violation of human rights and multiple criminal liability. Possible human rights violations can take two forms: a breach of Article 7 of the European Convention on Human Rights and in particular the principle of *nullum crimen, nulla poena sine lege*, and a breach of Article 5. A breach of the principle *nullum crimen, nulla poena sine lege* can occur where the law is applied to a person outwith the UK in a place where his or her behaviour is not criminal. Whilst UK law would exist and apply in the particular circumstances, an argument could be made that the principle is violated because the act is lawful according to the *lex loci delicti*. Article 7 provides that 'No one

2 *Hansard*, HL, Written Answers, 6 March 2003, col WA 123. A further aspect of the desire to prevent the abuse of children overseas is that registered sex offenders must give notice of their intention to travel overseas for a period greater than three days; in Scotland this is governed by the Sexual Offences Act 2003 (Travel Notification Requirements) (Scotland) Regulations 2004, SI 2004/205 made under s 86(2) of the Sexual Offences Act 2003.

shall be held guilty of any criminal offence on account of any act or omission which did not constitute a criminal offence under national or international law at the time when it was committed'. The question arising is whether criminality under any national law is sufficient, or rather that criminality under the law where the accused committed the act is required. The Grand Chamber of the European Court of Human Rights (ECtHR) has stated:

> Article 7 § 1 of the Convention goes beyond prohibition of the retrospective application of criminal law to the detriment of the accused. It also sets forth, more generally, the principle that only the law can define a crime and prescribe a penalty (nullum crimen, nulla poena sine lege).[3]

Whilst this statement provides authority for the principle of *nullum crimen, nulla poena sine lege* coming within Article 7, it does not address the question whether a particular national law must prescribe the act. Whilst there have been arguments relying on *nullum crimen, nulla poena sine lege* in cases where crimes purported to exist in customary international law were being applied, there have not, as far as the author is aware, been similar arguments where national law was applied across borders.[4]

This issue of a possible breach of the principle of *nullum crimen, nulla poena sine lege*, whilst real, is prevented from arising in most cases where UK criminal law is applied across borders, for two reasons. First, the UK applies its law only in regard to acts widely accepted as meriting criminalisation – such as murder or child sex crimes. More particularly, the extension of the law is often conditioned with the requirement that the behaviour is also criminal in the country in which it is committed. An example is found in section 72(2) of the Sexual Offences Act 2003. It provides:

> (2) If (a) a United Kingdom resident does an act in a country outside the United Kingdom, (b) the act constitutes an offence under the law in force in that country, and (c) the act, if done in England and Wales or Northern Ireland, would constitute a sexual offence to which this section applies, the United Kingdom resident is guilty in that part of the United Kingdom of that sexual offence.

Notably, the requirement that the offence must constitute one under the law where it is committed extends only to UK residents, not nationals. A national,

3 Application No 10249/03 *Scoppola v Italy (No 2)*, September 2009 at para 93.

4 For a discussion of the application of the principle in Spanish law following its prosecution of an Argentinean former general, see Pinzauti, G., 'An Instance of Reasonable Universality: The Scilingo Case' [2005] 3 *Journal of International Criminal Justice* 1092. The ECtHR has held in *Jorgic v Germany* (2008) 47 EHRR 6 that a prosecution in Germany of the crime of genocide allegedly committed in the former Yugoslavia did not entail a violation of Art 7 of the Convention.

therefore, can be found guilty for a crime under the Sexual Offences Act 2003 for an act that is not criminal in the country in which it is committed. This is because the act is criminal in the law of England and Wales, and the law of the place of its commission is not material. A national is bound, the view holds, to act in conformity with these particular prohibitions wherever he or she may be, and ignorance of the law is no excuse. If this view is correct then the application of the particular provision within the Sexual Offences Act 2003 to nationals without regard to the *lex loci delicti* (and to residents with reference to it and not at all to non-nationals and non-residents) is legitimate and does not entail a violation of *nullum crimen, nulla poena sine lege*. On the other hand, it is well known that the UK takes a largely territorial approach to the criminal law. Its extension is not generally presumed. It is perhaps not unreasonable, in light of the territorial emphasis of the criminal law, to suggest that an argument on the basis of *nullum crimen, nulla poena sine lege* has some merit.

A further human rights-related issue that may arise for accused persons where UK criminal law is applied across borders is a possible violation of Article 5 of the Convention, which protects the right to liberty and security of the person. This is, in a sense, opposite to the majority of human rights cases applying law across borders – where arguments are made that a violation may occur in a third state following an extradition or expulsion. This type of case occurs where irregularities are argued to have occurred in the course of an accused's rendition to the UK. Two leading authorities in this area are *R v Horseferry Magistrates' Court ex p Bennett*[5] and *HM Advocate v Vervuren*,[6] in England and Scotland respectively. Both cases are examples of arguments made, although not necessarily sustained, that irregularities in the rendition of an accused can engender a human rights violation or otherwise be an abuse of process within the UK. These cases are exceptional. UK authorities are not generally engaged in extra-legal apprehension of accused persons overseas. However, the point must be noted that a possible consequence of the application of UK criminal law across borders is irregularity in rendition, which may entail a violation of Article 5 of the Convention.

The second issue from the perspective of an accused that may arise from the application of criminal law across borders is multiple criminal liability. Indeed, this is likely to be the case with the law of the *lex loci delicti* and UK law applying. In such a case the substantive criminal law of two states would apply to the single person or act. Further, there may be cases where more than two bodies of criminal law apply – the categories of criminal jurisdiction discussed in Chapter 2 permit states to apply their law in a number of circumstances, including where one of their nationals is the victim of a crime. It should be noted

5 [1993] 3 All ER 138. See Warbrick, C., 'Judicial Jurisdiction and Abuse of Process' (2000) 49 ICLQ 489.

6 [2002] SLT 555. See Arnell, P., 'Male captus bene detentus in Scotland' [2004] *Juridical Review* 251.

that the existence of multiple liability in itself is not necessarily to the detriment of an accused. Indeed, it may well act in his or her favour if the state with the least punitive criminal justice system acts to apply its law. In several recent cases, mentioned below, arguments were made in an attempt to ensure that this happened – in the form of a prosecution in England as opposed to the United States. On the other hand, a factor that weighs against multiple criminal liability relates to the point just made, that a degree of 'prosecutorial forum shopping' may result in a state with a more punitive criminal justice system prosecuting the alleged offender. Exacerbating this problem for an accused is the absence of an established system governing cases of multiple liability. The custodial state has priority by virtue of that custody; it can either try an accused or extradite or deport him or her to any third state it wishes – subject to any obligations under a relevant treaty. This may lead to a decision being made for reasons inimical to the interest of the accused and instead on the basis of greatest possible punishment or highest likelihood of conviction. Ideally there would be an established system governing multiple criminal liability which refers to factors such as territory and nationality of the accused and victim and provides which state has priority.

Issues or problems for third states can arise following the application of UK criminal law across borders. Perhaps the paramount issue is that the application of law can be perceived as an interference with a third state's sovereignty and territorial integrity. This would certainly be the case where the act criminalised by the UK is lawful in the third state. For the reasons noted above, this is rare. Not mentioned above, however, is the principle of double criminality in extradition law, which would prevent such issues from arising where an accused is sought through this process. The principle provides that for a person to be subjected to extradition his or her alleged crime must be criminal in both the requesting and requested state. Even where the behaviour is criminal where committed, however, the territorial state may take umbrage at a third state putatively regulating the act, particularly where the territorial state is less able to enforce its law than the UK because of deficiencies in its legal system or the fact that the accused has assets in that state. In both cases, however, where the act is lawful or criminal in the place of commission, the application of UK law to it will entail an interference with the competence of the territorial state. Whilst an explicit hierarchy of the links between a crime and a state does not exist in international or domestic law, it is clear that the link of territory is pre-eminent. As was discussed in Chapter 2, some of the most authoritative and widespread rules of public international law act to protect the sovereignty and territorial integrity of states.

The issues arising from the application of criminal law across borders from the perspective of international law mirror, to a certain extent, those of third states and accused persons. The rules protecting state sovereignty and territorial integrity are of international derivation. A violation of state sovereignty entails a breach of international law, engaging the responsibility of the state so acting. An extension of criminal law, therefore, can entail a violation of international law in certain circumstances. Such a violation, however, is rare. This follows from the prosecution of crime generally being in the interests of all states, with the consequence that international law is generous in allocating competencies. A second issue from the perspective of international law engendered by the application of law across borders is that it can encourage the side-stepping of extant mechanisms designed to facilitate international co-operation. This arises particularly through the use of enforcement or executive jurisdiction across borders. It takes us back to point made above regarding irregular renditions. Clearly, abduction from the territory of a third state is a violation of the rules protecting sovereignty as well as evidencing contempt for any extant lawful and regular mechanisms for the transference of persons from one state to another. Again as above, the point to be made here is that the application of UK criminal law across borders may in certain cases contravene rules of international law where it is tantamount to interference with the domestic competence of a third state.

History

The history of UK criminal law applied across borders has witnessed a considerably greater evolution and development than that of human rights law.[7] This is simply because it has existed for longer. A further reason is that it is based in both common law and statute. Generally, the criminal law has evolved from a position where the territorial nature of the law was almost absolute, to one where it is possible today to construct an argument that territory as a basis of the criminal law is inappropriate and anachronistic. There is abundant authority in support of the territorial nature of the criminal law in England and Wales and Scotland.[8] In regard to Scotland, Lord Young, in *HM Advocate v Hall*, stated:

> The general rule is that criminal law is strictly territorial – so that a man is subject only to the criminal law of the country where he is, and that his conduct there, whether by acting, speaking, or writing, shall be judged of as criminal or not by that law and no other.[9]

The corollary of Scottish criminal law applying predominately within Scotland is that is does not apply abroad. Hume stated:

7 See generally in regard to the criminal law, Hirst, M., *Jurisdiction and the Ambit of the Criminal Law*, Oxford University Press, Oxford, 2003, esp Ch 2, 'Historical, International and Other Influences', pp 28–59 (hereinafter Hirst, *Jurisdiction and Ambit*).

8 For a discussion of the civilian approach to jurisdiction, see Blakesley, C.L. and Lagodny, O., 'Finding Harmony Amidst Disagreement Over Extradition, Jurisdiction, the Role of Human Rights, and Issues of Extraterritorialty Under International Criminal Law' (1991) 24 *Vanderbilt Journal of Transnational Law* 1.

9 (1881) 4 Couper 438.

> A person domiciliated here, whether a Scotsman or a foreigner, for any crime he may have committed abroad, is not liable to be tried before our courts. They are not instituted to administer justice over the whole world, but in our country, or a particular district of it only; and, therefore, if the crime charged has been committed beyond those limits, they are neither called upon nor entitled to step forward for its correction.[10]

In English law, Viscount Simonds stated in *Cox v Army Council* that 'apart from those exceptional cases in which specific provision is made in regard to acts committed abroad, the whole body of the criminal law of England deals only with acts committed in England'.[11] Clearly, the general rule is that 'offences committed by British subjects out of England are not punishable by the criminal law of this country'.[12] The territoriality of the criminal law is reflected in the presumption that offences apply within the territory of the UK only. In *Air India v Wiggins* Lord Diplock stated:

> My Lords, in construing Acts of Parliament there is a well-established presumption that, in the absence of clear and specific words to the contrary, an 'offence-creating section' of an Act of Parliament . . . was not intended to make conduct taking place outside the territorial jurisdiction of the Crown an offence triable in an English criminal court.[13]

Notably, and understandably, this rule applies with greater force to non-nationals. As Lord Diplock stated:

> The presumption against a parliamentary intention to make acts done by foreigners abroad offences triable by English criminal courts is even stronger. As Lord Russell of Killowen C.J. said in *R v Jameson*[[14]] 'One other general canon of construction is this – that if any construction otherwise be possible, an Act will not be construed as applying to foreigners in respect to acts done by them outside the dominions of the sovereign power enacting'.[15]

Following on from the point that the criminal law was traditionally territorial is the question, why was this the case? The obvious answer is that the lesser mobility of persons in the previous centuries, generally and in particular due to the island status of Great Britain, led to there being little need to conceive

10 Hume, D., *Commentaries on the Law of Scotland Respecting Crimes, 1844*, Law Society of Scotland, Edinburgh, 1986, vol 2 at para 52.
11 [1963] AC 48 at 67.
12 *R v Page* [1953] 2 All ER 1355 at 1356, per Lord Goddard CJ.
13 [1980] 1 WLR 815 at 819.
14 [1896] 1 QB 425 at 430.
15 Ibid.

of the law in any other way. This is undoubtedly part of the answer; however there are further factors. Hirst has noted that the pre-eminence of territory arose from the role of venue and that the common law 'generally required that any indictable offence – treason, felony, or misdemeanour – should be tried in the county in which the relevant acts were alleged to have occurred, by a jury drawn from the residents of that county'.[16] He continues: 'the fundamental point was that a jury drawn from the *vicenage* was more qualified than any other body to ascertain the facts at issue' and the 'venue doctrine almost accidentally contributed to the principle of territoriality, under which events abroad were regarded as beyond the criminal law's concern'.[17] O'Brien agrees, noting that:

> The United Kingdom has, from the 19th century, been a strong supporter of the territorial system: (a) because in criminal law matters it is for the people of the relevant territory to determine the rules they wish to live under; (b) it is practical in that English criminal procedure places considerable reliance on the testing of oral testimony by cross-examination. That is best achieved in the relevant territory.[18]

These factors explain the general reluctance to extend English criminal law across borders. Also relevant, however, was the belief that there was insufficient interest in doing so. Again, as Hirst notes, the reason the law was not extended can be seen to lie in the fact that 'until relatively recent times, there was little (if any) perceived need for widespread change . . . Crime . . . was generally considered to be entirely a local or territorial concern'.[19] The UK's historical attachment to the primacy of territory in the application of the criminal law remains. It has, however, come under considerable pressure, and numerous exceptions to it now exist. Behind these pressures is the internationalisation of criminality, an evolution in the accepted purposes of the criminal law and perceived deficiencies in extradition, third state criminal justice and international law more generally. The diminution of territory in the criminal law has led to the position today where exceptions have almost become the rule.[20] These exceptions are described and analysed below.

The current law

UK law contains an increasing number of instances where the law is applied on the basis of the relationship between it and an accused. Considerably less common are instances where the law has been extended with reference to the

16 Hirst, *Jurisdiction and Ambit* (n 7 above), at p 29.

17 Ibid at pp 30–33.

18 O'Brien, J., *International Law*, Cavendish Publishing, London, 2001, at p 237.

19 Hirst, *Jurisdiction and Ambit* (n 7 above), at p 56.

20 Hirst notes that in stating the general rule a problem arises in distinguishing the rule itself and the principal exceptions or qualifications to it: ibid at p 4.

victim of a crime and to the crime alone. However, UK criminal law is usually applied across borders with reference to territory. The attachment to territory has paradoxically remained whilst the law has been extended – in a sense, 'territory' itself has been stretched. Whilst the criminal law is generally applied across borders with reference to territory, the nature of that application is far from simple for two reasons: because it has developed in an ad hoc way and because it has been extended to cover situations which are not objectively and literally 'territorial'.

Criminal law applied territorially

Over the years judges and legislators (and academics) within the UK have grappled with the difficulties engendered by the increasingly international nature of criminality. The hitherto importance of territory has clearly diminished. In relatively recent times the law has come to accept – in part through an evolution of the view of territory and in part as a result of the obligations within international agreements – that territory has become only one of the factors that can and should justify the application of the criminal law.[21] Different methodologies are used in presenting descriptions and explanations of UK criminal law applied across borders yet retaining a notional link to territory. Generally, analyses of domestic UK law have focused on the specific and technical approaches discerned from decided cases. Leading authorities and writers here include Glanville Williams,[22] Julian Lew[23] and Michael Hirst.[24] In addition are reports and articles on particular aspects of the application of the criminal law abroad, such as fraud and inchoate offences.[25] There is also an influential English Law Commission Report, *The Territorial and Extraterritorial Extent of the Criminal Law*,[26] as well as non-UK official reports.[27] Discussions of the application of law across borders from an international legal perspective, in

21 As noted in Chapter 2 a distinction must be drawn between the competence of a court to try an alleged crime and the application of the law to any particular act. These two distinctions – the 'jurisdiction' of a court and the 'ambit' of the law in Hirst's phraseology, ibid – are distinct but related concepts.

22 Williams, G., 'Venue and Ambit of the Criminal Law' (1965) 81 *Law Quarterly Review* 276.

23 Lew, J., 'The Extraterritorial Jurisdiction of English Courts' (1978) 27 ICLQ 168.

24 Hirst, *Jurisdiction and Ambit* (n 7 above). Amongst his other writings are Hirst, M., 'The Criminal Law Abroad' [1982] CLR 496 and Hirst, M., 'Jurisdiction over Cross Frontier Offences' (1981) 97 LQR 80.

25 See, e.g. Law Commission, *Conspiracy and Attempts*, Report No 318, December 2009, esp Pt 7, cited at http://www.justice.gov.uk/lawcommission/publications/733.htm, accessed 22 May 2011; and Holroyd, J. and Chuah, J., 'Trying Frauds with a Foreign Element' (1994) 58 *Journal of Criminal Law* 388.

26 Law Commission No 91, 1978.

27 These include the Law Reform Commission of Canada, *Extraterritorial Jurisdiction*, Working Paper No 37, 1984 and the European Committee on Crime Problems, *Extraterritorial Jurisdiction*, 1990.

contrast, normally address territorial competence and its two sub-species – objective and subjective territoriality.[28] The analytical approach taken below will, in large part, mirror that taken by international lawyers. This is not because the UK has adopted a view explicitly in accordance with international law and its terminology (although it is argued in Chapter 5 that the influence of international law and practice is manifest), but simply because it is not unreasonable to categorise 'territorial' law applied across borders with reference to where a crime began and where it ended or had its effect.[29]

There are four different types of territorial link between a crime and the UK. First, the law can demand a complete connection, with the requirement that the totality of the offence occur within the UK. Second, the law can demand that the territorial connection be partial in the form of the last act, effect(s) or gist of the offence occurring within the UK. Third, it can require a partial connection in the form of the initial acts comprising the offence occurring within the UK. Fourth, and finally, the law can eschew the requirement of any particular act (last or initial act or otherwise) occurring within the territory of the UK and instead require a connection of a requisite degree whatever its nature. The first form of territorial connection, a complete one, exists largely as a consequence of the nature of certain criminal offences. For example, a number of offences under the Road Traffic Regulation Act 1984 are only capable of occurring within the UK. Section 89(1) provides: 'A person who drives a motor vehicle on a road at a speed exceeding a limit imposed by or under any enactment to which this section applies shall be guilty of an offence'. 'Road' is defined by section 142 as 'in England and Wales . . . any length of highway or of any other road to which the public has access, and includes bridges over which a road passes'. Notably, other traffic-related offences are not so restricted. In *Lawson v Fox*[30] the House of Lords held that for the purposes of computing the number of hours driven in the consideration of the limits set by section 96 of the Transport Act 1968, the time spent driving abroad was to be included. Admittedly, the driving abroad was not unlawful per se; rather it was the driving within England without sufficient rest – a portion of which time was spent driving outside the country. This aside, there are generally relatively few crimes that are limited in scope by their nature to the territory of the UK.

The UK's criminal justice systems have traditionally and generally adopted the second approach identified above, somewhat akin to the objective territorial approach in international law – which has been named 'the terminatory theory'. It is suggested that it is not unreasonable to equate the objective territorial

28 Riesemann, W.M. (ed.), *Jurisdiction in International Law*, Ashgate 1999; Akehurst, M., 'Jurisdiction in International Law' (1972–3) 46 BYIL 145; Arnell, P., 'Criminal Jurisdiction in International Law' [2000] *Juridical Review* 179; and the classic Harvard Research Group, Draft Convention on Jurisdiction with Respect to Crime (1935) 29 AJIL (Supp) 480.

29 As will be seen below, this is not as simple as it may seem with, *inter alia*, inchoate and participatory crimes causing not inconsiderable difficulty.

30 [1974] AC 803.

approach with the terminatory theory, especially in light of its present definition. It is suggested that the objective territorial approach can be construed broadly to mean that the law is applied to cross-border situations where the main or last act, essence, gist or effect of the offence has taken place within the territory of a state.[31] In other words, the objective approach includes the terminatory theory, and more. The terminatory approach is concerned with the legal question of where and when the offence was 'completed' and the objective approach traditionally was thought to relate to where an offence has its effects or consequences. These are not, of course, necessarily the same. Here, the distinction between 'conduct crimes' and 'result crimes' comes to the fore. The conduct/result categorisation is said to have originated[32] in the first edition of the *Criminal Law of Scotland* by Sir Gerald Gordon.[33] Conduct crimes are those in which relevant behaviour itself comprises the offence – regardless of any result or consequences of that conduct. Result crimes are those where the result or consequence is an integral part of the offence. In regard to both conduct and result crimes, the courts can be seen to take a similar approach, considering 'an offence to be committed where it is completed'.[34] This is not to suggest that the classification of crimes as either conduct crimes or result crimes is not significant; it can be. What can generally be stated is that conduct crimes raise fewer problems in the application of law across borders. For example, conduct crimes by definition do not raise issues of causation (which can be exacerbated by borders) and, from a *situs* perspective, the locus of a conduct crime is normally straightforward in that the alleged offender's whereabouts are normally an obvious question of fact. However, as just noted in *Lawson v Fox*,[35] conduct crimes can themselves lead to some uncertainty when applied across borders. Indeed, the law has developed the concept of the continuing act, through which a conduct crime may be committed in a territory where the offender is not present. The leading authority on this point is the well-known case *DPP v Stonehouse*.[36]

It is in regard to result crimes that the terminatory or objective approach has come to the fore. This is because courts have become seized of these cases more often, deciding whether the law applies in a specific case. An early legislative example dates from 1548, with it being provided that:

31 Hirst notes that the subjective and objective approach 'does not represent, and has never represented, the approach adopted under English law. To make sense of English cases . . . one must think instead in terms of what Glanville Williams christened the 'terminatory' or 'metaphysical' theory of jurisdiction': Hirst, *Jurisdiction and Ambit* (n 7 above), at p 115, citing Williams, G., 'Venue and Ambit of the Criminal Law' (1965) 81 *Law Quarterly Review* 276.

32 Hirst, *Jurisdiction and Ambit* (n 7 above), at p 118.

33 W Green, Edinburgh, 1967. When using the terms, Lord Roskill, in *R v Berry* [1985] AC 246 at 252, stated that he 'adopted the nomenclature borrowed from Scots criminal law by my noble and learned friend, Lord Diplock, in *R v Treacy* [1971] AC 537 at 560'.

34 Hirst, *Jurisdiction and Ambit* (n 7 above), at p 119.

35 [1974] AC 803.

36 [1978] AC 55.

> where any person or persons hereafter shall be feloniously stricken or poisoned in one county, and die of the same stroke or poisoning in another county, that then an indictment thereof founden by jurors of the county where the death shall happen . . . shall be as good and effectual in the law, as if the stroke or poisoning had been committed and done in the same county where the party shall die[37]

This section governed venue within England and not the commission of a crime across an international border. The latter was provided for three centuries later, by (1828) 9 George IV (c 31). Judicially, an example of a Scottish authority taking a terminatory or objective approach is *Laird v HM Advocate* where Lord Wheatly stated:

> it seems to me that where a crime is of such a nature that it has to originate with the forming of a fraudulent plan, and that thereafter various steps have to be taken to bring that fraudulent plan to fruition, if some of these subsequent steps take place in one jurisdiction and some in another, then if the totality of the events in one country play a material part in the operation and fulfilment of the fraudulent scheme as a whole there should be jurisdiction in that country.[38]

In another Scottish case, *HMA v Witherington*,[39] it was held that the courts had properly taken cognisance of crimes of falsehood, fraud and wilful imposition even though the accused was outwith Scotland during the relevant period. The Lord Justice-General stated:

> The objection is rested on these considerations, that the panel is an Englishman; that the only fraud or criminal act alleged against him was committed in England: that he was never in Scotland, and is not subject to the criminal law or to the jurisdiction of the criminal Courts of Scotland; that criminal jurisdiction does not extend *extra territorium*, and that the true foundation of ordinary criminal jurisdiction is the *locus delicti*.[40]

He continued: 'The argument is certainly plausible, and there is, at first sight, something startling and paradoxical in the proposition that a man may commit a crime in a place in which he was never personally present. This proposition is nevertheless technically or constructively, but actually, true'.[41]

In England and Wales authority for a terminatory or objective approach is found in *R v Harden*[42] where, in regard to the crime of obtaining property by

37 (1548) 2 and 3 Edw VI (c 24).
38 [1985] JC 37.
39 (1880–1) 8 SC (JC) 41.
40 Ibid at p 46.
41 Ibid.

deception, it was stated 'that the gist of the offence of obtaining by false pretences lies in the act of obtaining, and that if this act is done within the jurisdiction it matters not that the false pretence was made abroad'.[43] A more recent authority is *R v Manning*[44] where the court stated, in a discussion of the authorities surrounding the law applicable to offences with a cross-border element:

> We further consider that those and other cases demonstrate that the last act or terminatory theory remains the binding common law of England and Wales. We have carefully considered whether that position can be regarded as set aside by the decision of this court in *Reg. v Smith (Wallace Duncan) (No. 1)* [1996 2 Cr App R 1], but we have to conclude that that decision cannot stand against the authorities to which we have just referred.[45]

R v Manning and *R v Smith (Wallace Duncan) (No 1)*[46] will be referred to below because the law has taken a step away from the terminatory theory, in large part due to *R v Smith (Wallace Duncan) (No 4)*.[47]

Perhaps the most interesting aspect of the terminatory or objective approach arises where inchoate crimes in one sense or another occur across borders. As will be seen below, there is considerable and complex legislation governing circumstances where an accused acts within the UK with an intention to attempt or incite, etc. a criminal act abroad. In the opposite situation, where persons have, whilst abroad, conspired or attempted to commit a crime within the UK, there has instead been an evolution of the common law. It is obvious that a particular problem for the terminatory or objective approach arises here because there is no conclusion in the form of a completed crime or effect within the UK. The leading authority is decision of the Privy Council in *Somchai Liangsiriprasert v Government of the United States*.[48] It is worth re-stating the relevant passage of Lord Griffiths:

> Unfortunately in this century crime has ceased to be largely local in origin and effect. Crime is now established on an international scale and the common law must face this new reality. Their Lordships can find nothing in precedent, comity or good sense that should inhibit the common law from regarding as justiciable in England inchoate crimes committed abroad which are intended to result in the commission of criminal offences in

42 [1963] 1 QB 8, referring to *R v Ellis* [1899] 1 QB 230.
43 Ibid at p 19.
44 [1999] QB 980.
45 Ibid at p 989. As will be discussed below, the law applying in this case has been superseded by the rules in the Criminal Justice Act 1993.
46 [1996] 2 Cr App R 1.
47 [2004] EWCA Crim 631.
48 [1991] 1 AC 225.

> England. Accordingly a conspiracy entered into in Thailand with the intention of committing the criminal offence of trafficking in drugs in Hong Kong is justiciable in Hong Kong even if no overt act pursuant to the conspiracy has yet occurred in Hong Kong.[49]

This case has been applied by the Court of Appeal in *R v Sansom*[50] and followed in Scotland in *HM Advocate v Al-Megrahi (Abdelbaset Ali) (No 1)*.[51]

The opposite of the terminatory or objective approach is the initiatory or subjective approach – the third approach identified above. This provides that the law applies where a crime *commences* within a territory. In spite of the historical weight behind the terminatory view, long-standing support of the initiatory theory can also be found in UK law. A leading example is section 10 of the Offences Against the Person Act 1861, which states:

> Where any person . . . being criminally stricken, poisoned, or otherwise hurt in any place in England or Ireland, shall die of such stroke, poisoning, or hurt upon the sea, or at any place out of England or Ireland, every offence committed in respect of any such case, whether the same shall amount to the offence of murder or manslaughter . . . may be dealt with, inquired of, tried, determined, and punished . . . in England and Ireland.[52]

An inchoate offence is found in section 4 of the Act. It relates to conspiracy to murder, stating that 'whosoever shall solicit, encourage, persuade, or endeavour to persuade, or shall propose to any person, to murder any other person, whether he be a subject of Her Majesty or not, and whether he be within the Queen's dominions or not, shall be guilty of a misdemeanor, and being convicted thereof shall be liable to imprisonment for life'. This section was applied against Abu Hamza, and his appeal against conviction was heard in 2006 in *R v Abu Hamza*.[53] It was held that the section did, in fact, apply to the circumstances of his case.[54]

A comparatively recent statutory enactment along similar lines to sections 4 and 10 of the Offences Against the Person Act 1861 is the Criminal Justice Act 1993, which substantially altered the rules surrounding a number of crimes – broadly under the rubric fraud and blackmail, As such, it merits scrutiny. The Act changed the law as applied in *R v Manning*[55] mentioned above. There it was held that section 20(2) of the Theft Act 1969 did not apply as Manning had practised deception in England but procured cheques to be executed in Athens

49 Ibid at p 252.
50 [1991] 2 QB 130.
51 [2000] JC 555.
52 Note that this provision also provides for the converse situation.
53 [2006] EWCA Civ 2918.
54 The case is discussed further below.
55 [1999] QB 980.

– the last act was not committed in England. The Criminal Justice Act 1993 altered the rules under which the courts can hold that an offence has been committed in England and Wales. As noted above the terminatory or objective approach was the dominant approach in English law. Indeed it was so 'well established . . . that legislation was needed to change it'.[56] The terminatory theory was supplanted by new rules in Part 1 of the 1993 Act for a considerable number of offences. The Act created two groups of offences, Group A and Group B. Group A offences include those under the Theft Act 1968, the Fraud Act 2006, the Forgery and Counterfeiting Act 1981 and the Identity Cards Act 2006. Group B offences consist of conspiracies, incitements and attempts to commit Group A offences and conspiracy to defraud. Note, however, that the law in regard to conspiracies generally has been replaced by the Criminal Justice (Terrorism and Conspiracy) Act 1998, sections 5–7, discussed below. Section 2 of the 1993 Act extends Group A offences to circumstances where they are committed across borders. It does so through the concept of 'relevant event', which is generally defined in section 2(1) as 'any act or omission or other event (including any result of one or more acts or omissions) proof of which is required for conviction of the offence'.[57] Section 2(3) then provides that 'A person may be guilty of a Group A offence if any of the events which are relevant events in relation to the offence occurred in England and Wales'. Therefore, if any relevant event (described by Sullivan and Warbrick as denoting 'a constituent part of the offence'[58]) takes place in England or Wales a crime can be held to have been committed. In regard to Group B offences, section 5 of the 1993 Act generally amends the law so as to apply to situations where attempts and incitements relating to Category A offences and conspiracies to defraud commence or otherwise begin in England and Wales and are intended to be completed abroad.[59] This reversed the law as it was applied in *R v Cox*[60] and *Attorney General's Reference (No 1 of 1982)*.[61] Notably, section 6 of the 1993 Act limits the application of section 5 offences to the effect that the acts attempted, incited or conspired must be unlawful in the place where their final commission of was intended.

The rules governing conspiracies to commit offences outside the UK were amended by the Criminal Justice (Terrorism and Conspiracy) Act 1998. The Act was passed in the wake of the terrorist bombing in Omagh, and extended the rules in regard to conspiracy generally, not merely in relation to terrorist

56 Sullivan, G.R. and Warbick, C., 'Territorial Jurisdiction: Criminal Justice Act 1993' [1994] ICLQ 460 at p 462.

57 Section 2(1A) provides specifically for the offence of fraud under the Fraud Act 2006.

58 Sullivan and Warbick, 'Territorial Jurisdiction: Criminal Justice Act 1993' (n 56 above), at p 462.

59 Criminal Justice Act 1993, s 5(2) inserted a new s 1A into the Criminal Attempts Act 1981.

60 [1968] 1 WLR 88.

61 [1982] 2 All ER 721.

conspiracies. Section 5 of the 1998 Act[62] inserted section 1A into the Criminal Law Act 1977, which makes it an offence under English law, under certain conditions, to conspire in England to commit an offence abroad (as well as in other parts of the UK – by the Coroners and Justice Act 2009).[63] Generally, the Act criminalises agreements to commit offences outside the UK where there is a link between the agreement and the UK.[64] This is subject to the requirement that the offence to which the conspiracy relates is recognised as such in the territory in which it is intended it will be committed, as well as the UK. In regard to England and Wales this condition is found in section 1A(3) of the 1977 Act. An example of the extended offence being applied is found in *R v Patel (Sophia)*.[65] Here, Patel and others were convicted or pleaded guilty under section 1A of the 1977 Act to conspiring to take immigrants unlawfully into the United States. As explained in the judgment:

> The plain purpose of that amendment was to give the English courts extra-territorial jurisdiction in relation to conspiracies which are formed or carried out, at least in part, in England and Wales and where the object is the commission of a foreign offence. That purpose is achieved by the method of extending the application of the existing domestic law of conspiracy, as it is familiarly set out in s.1(1) of the 1977 Act, to such conspiracies, providing that four conditions are met. In other words, the amendment does not create a distinct offence of conspiracy. It applies the ordinary English statute law as per s.1(1) where the specified conditions are met.[66]

A largely similar offence applies in Scotland, with section 7 of the Criminal Justice (Terrorism and Conspiracy) Act 1998 introducing a new section 11A into the Criminal Procedure (Scotland) Act 1995. Section 11A provides:

> (1) This section applies to any act done by a person in Scotland which would amount to conspiracy to commit an offence but for the fact that the criminal purpose is intended to occur in a country or territory outside the United Kingdom.

62 The relevant provisions in this Act superseded and repealed somewhat similar provisions to those in s 5(1) of the Criminal Justice Act 1993 before they had entered into force.

63 See, generally, Campbell, C., 'Two Steps Backwards: the Criminal Justice (Terrorism and Conspiracy) Act 1998' [1999] *Criminal Law Review* 941 and Hirst, *Jurisdiction and Ambit* (n 7 above), at pp 142–8; and in regard to sentencing under the section, see Thomas, D.T., 'Sentencing: conspiracy to commit offence abroad – Criminal Law Act 1977, section 1A – maximum sentence' [2009] *Criminal Law Review* 466.

64 Campbell, ibid, at p 955.

65 [2009] EWCA Crim 67.

66 Ibid at para 6.

> (2) Where a person does an act to which this section applies, the criminal purpose shall be treated as the offence mentioned in subsection (1) above and he shall, accordingly, be guilty of conspiracy to commit the offence.

These sections, it should be emphasised, apply to conspiracies within the UK to commit crimes abroad that would not otherwise be criminal under any other enactment. Where there is an existing extraterritorial provision, that provision is applicable. To borrow an example from Hirst, a conspiracy to murder in Brazil entered into in England by a Nigerian national is triable under section 1A of the Criminal Law Act 1977, whilst a conspiracy to murder in Brazil entered into in England by a Spanish national is triable under section 1 of the 1998 Act.[67] The distinction hinges upon the fact that under the Suppression of Terrorism Act 1978 the latter act is criminal on an extraterritorial basis in the circumstances and the former is not.[68]

A further legislative extension of the law on an initiatory or subjective basis is the Sexual Offences (Conspiracy and Incitement) Act 1996, section 1 of which criminalises conspiracy and incitement to commit sexual acts against children outside the UK. This has been repealed in regard to England and Wales by the Criminal Justice (Terrorism and Conspiracy) Act 1998; however, it still applies in Scotland and Northern Ireland. In regard to Scotland, section 6 inserts a new section 16A into the Criminal Law (Consolidation) (Scotland) Act 1996, which provides:

> (1) This section applies to any act done by a person in Scotland which would amount to the offence of conspiracy or incitement to commit a listed sexual offence but for the fact that the criminal purpose or, as the case may be, what he had in view is intended to occur in a country or territory outside the United Kingdom . . .

It should be noted that the Sexual Offences Act 2003, in England and Wales and Northern Ireland, and the Criminal Law (Consolidation) (Scotland) Act 1996, in Scotland, have subsequently criminalised a number of substantive crimes of a sexual nature committed abroad on the basis of nationality and residence decreasing, to an extent, the importance of these provisions – which will be discussed below. The final provision to be mentioned that applies the law on an initiatory or subjective basis is section 59 of the Terrorism Act 2000. It provides that 'A person commits an offence if (a) he incited another person to commit an act of terrorism wholly or partly outside the United Kingdom and (b) the act would, if committed in England and Wales, constitute one of the

67 Hirst, *Jurisdiction and Ambit* (n 7 above), at p 146, fn 123.

68 The distinction is because Spain is a designated country under the Suppression of Terrorism Act 1978 (being a party to the European Convention for the Suppression of Terrorism 1977), under the Suppression of Terrorism (1978) Designation of Countries) Order 1981, SI 1981/1389, art 2.

offences listed in subsection (2)'. Those offences include murder and an offence under section 1(2) of the Criminal Damage Act 1971. The incited act must have been an act of terrorism, as defined by section 1 of the 2000 Act.

The fourth form of territorial requirement demanded by UK criminal law is a general one. It has been called 'inclusionary' in that it eschews the non-application of law on the basis of what may be termed 'technicalities'.[69] It requires a connection of a requisite degree, regardless of whether the criminal act ends or commences in the UK or whether the gist or main act of the offence can be said to have taken place there. This approach is increasingly adopted by the courts. As will be discussed in Chapter 5, this development supports the argument that the law is witnessing the emergence of a proper law approach to its application in that it is not focused upon technical requirements such as the final act, but is instead taking an overall, holistic view as to whether there is a sufficient link between the crime and criminal and the UK. This general and inclusionary approach can be seen to originate in the *obiter* comments in the opinion of Lord Diplock in *Treacy v DPP*.[70] Lord Diplock held that where there was no geographical limitation to a statutory offence the existence and extent of any limitation is found by applying a presumption as to Parliament's intention extraneous to the definition of the offence. That presumption is found, he held, in the rules of international comity, which merely provide that states should not punish persons for their conduct within the territory of another state where that conduct has had no harmful consequences within it. It was held in *Treacy* that the offence of blackmail was completed when a letter containing the demand for money was posted on the Isle of Wight; receipt of the letter in Germany was not required. The last constituent element of the offence, the posting of the letter, took place in England. Therefore, the offence was completed within England. *Treacy*, then, is an authority in support of the terminatory theory.

Significantly for the purposes of the inclusionary approach, Lord Diplock in *Treacy* discussed the assumptions which underlie the notion that a choice must be made between the terminatory and initiatory theories. Of the first assumption, he stated 'that the definition of the crime under consideration includes a requirement that the physical acts of the accused should be followed by specific consequences – otherwise, the initiatory and terminatory characteristics of the crime coincide'; and, of the second, 'that the existence of jurisdiction in the courts of one state to try the accused for a particular crime, however the crime may be defined, necessarily excludes the jurisdiction for the courts of any other state to try the accused for his physical acts which either alone or in conjunction

69 Said by Hirst, in Hirst, M., 'Assisted Suicide After *Purdy*: The Unresolved Issue' [2009] *Criminal Law Review* 870 at p 874 (hereinafter Hirst, *Purdy*); first being advanced by Lord Diplock in *Treacy v DPP* [1971] AC 537 at 561.

70 [1971] AC 537. Hirst states that Lord Diplock's attempt to identify wider policy considerations was laudable in principle but unsatisfactory in practice: Hirst, *Jurisdiction and Ambit* (n 7 above), at p 8.

with their consequences constitute the crime defined'.[71] Lord Diplock then challenged this second assumption, stating:

> There is no rule of comity to prevent Parliament from prohibiting under pain of punishment persons who are present in the United Kingdom, and so owe local obedience to our law, from doing physical acts in England, notwithstanding that the consequences of those acts take effect outside the United Kingdom. Indeed, where the prohibited acts are of a kind calculated to cause harm to private individuals it would savour of chauvinism rather than comity to treat them as excusable merely on the ground that the victim was not in the United Kingdom itself but in some other state. Nor, as the converse of this, can I see any reason in comity to prevent Parliament from rendering liable to punishment, if they subsequently come to England, persons who have done outside the United Kingdom physical acts which have had harmful consequences upon victims in England. The state is under a correlative duty to those who owe obedience to its laws to protect their interests and one of the purposes of criminal law is to afford such protection by deterring by threat of punishment conduct by other persons which is calculated to harm those interests.[72]

The judicial treatment of the inclusionary approach discussed by Lord Diplock in *Treacy* has been mixed.[73] It has been applied in cases including *R v Bevan*,[74] *R v Abu Hamza*[75] and *R v Smith (Wallace Duncan) (No 1)*.[76] The approach has been criticised in cases including *R v Manning*,[77] noted above. The divergent lines of authority were directly considered in *R v Smith (Wallace Duncan) (No 4)*,[78] subsequent to which has been *R (Purdy) v DPP (Society for the Protection of Unborn Children Intervening)*.[79] In light of all these authorities, it can be discerned that the law has moved towards the adoption of an approach broadly in line with that postulated by Lord Diplock in *Treacy*. It is useful to discuss several of these authorities in that they highlight the developing approach taken to the requirement of a territorial connection.

R v Smith (Wallace Duncan) (No 1) was an appeal against conviction, *inter alia*, of obtaining property by deception under section 15(1) of the Theft Act 1968.[80]

71 Ibid at p 561.
72 Ibid at pp 561–2.
73 Hirst notes that 'Prior to the ruling in Purdy [mentioned below] . . . the weight of judicial authority remained heavily against [the inclusionary approach]': Hirst, *Purdy*, at p 874.
74 (1987) 84 Cr App R 143.
75 [2006] EWCA Crim 2918.
76 [1996] 2 Cr App R 1.
77 [1999] QB 980.
78 [2004] EWCA Crim 631.
79 [2009] UKHL 45.
80 Note that in such a case today the jurisdictional arguments would not arise following the entry into force of the relevant provisions of the Criminal Justice Act 1993, mentioned above.

Smith had been founder, chairman and managing director of a merchant bank that had gone into liquidation. It was alleged that through various bogus agreements, the profits and size of the bank had been inflated. The gist of Smith's argument in regard to the non-applicability of the crime of obtaining property by deception was that although the deception had taken place in London, the obtaining had occurred in New York – hence, the offences were committed in the United States. In discussing the issues Rose LJ noted the two approaches to the application of the law, which he identified as 'gist of the offence' and 'comity'.[81] He sided firmly with the latter, stating:

> In our judgment it would be astonishing if the English courts did not have jurisdiction in such a case and certainly there would be nothing inimical to international comity in the English courts assuming jurisdiction. Questions of jurisdiction, though involving substantive law, contain a strong procedural element. There have in recent years been significant advances in electronic communications both within and across national boundaries. These have brought added sophistication to the ways in which offences involving frauds are committed . . . If the issue of jurisdiction in cases of obtaining is to depend solely upon where the obtaining took place it is likely that the courts, and especially juries, will be confronted with complex and, at times, obscure factual issues which have no bearing on the merits of the case. This Court must recognise the need to adapt its approach to the question of jurisdiction in the light of such changes.[82]

Rose LJ went on to refer to the well-known conspiracy cases of *Liangsiriprasert v Government of the United States of America*[83] and *R v Sansom*,[84] stating that in relation to the applicability of the law the court could see no distinction between conspiracy and obtaining by deception. This ground of appeal was dismissed.

Over eight years subsequent to *R v Smith (Wallace Duncan) (No 1)* the Court of Appeal again considered the issue of the application of the Theft Act 1968 to the circumstances of the case in *R v Smith (Wallace Duncan) (No 4)*.[85] The case was referred to the Court of Appeal by the Criminal Cases Review Commission in part because of the effect of *R v Preddy*,[86] where the House of Lords reconsidered the nature of the crime of obtaining property by deception under section 15(1) of the Theft Act 1968. As a result of this case the Crown in *R v Smith (Wallace Duncan) (No 4)* conceded that the convictions for obtaining property

81 [1996] 2 Cr App R 1 at 18.
82 Ibid at pp 19–20.
83 [1991] 1 AC 225.
84 [1991] 2 QB 130.
85 [2004] EWCA Crim 631. For a useful description of the evolution of the law, see Hodgson, T.W., 'From Famine to Feast: the Prosecution of Multi-jurisdictional Financial Crime in the Electronic Age' [2008] *Journal of Financial Crime* 320.
86 [1996] AC 815.

by deception could not be sustained. However, it argued that the court should substitute convictions of offences under section 1 of the Theft Act 1968 of obtaining services by deception. What was required by the court in *R v Smith (Wallace Duncan) (No 4)* therefore was determination of whether courts in England and Wales were able to apply the offence to be substituted. In discussing the position, Woolf CJ addressed head-on the conflicting lines of authority represented by *R v Smith (Wallace Duncan) (No 1)* and *R v Manning*. Notably, Woolf CJ began his discussion with the statement that:

> The issue [of conflicting authorities on jurisdiction] is an important one. The importance goes beyond the issue of jurisdiction that is directly involved on this appeal. It involves determining the extent to which it is appropriate for this court to develop the common law as to jurisdiction in order to meet the changing requirements of society.[87]

The judgment then summarised the position as it understood it from *R v Smith (Wallace Duncan) (No 1)*. This was, first, that *R v Harden*[88] was correct but should no longer be regarded as setting out as exclusive the terminatory theory. It held further that where there are no reasons of comity which require a different approach and that when substantial activities (particularly in relation to complex fraud) constituting the crime take place in England, the crime should be held to be justiciable here. The court also held that it is necessary to have different rules in regard to the application of the law for different crimes. Finally, and importantly, it was held that questions relating to the application of the law, since they have a strong procedural element, are less immutable than issues of pure substantive law.[89] Woolf CJ noted that Buxton LJ in *R v Manning* may not have appreciated that Rose LJ was advancing an alternative and additional approach to the terminatory or last rule approach – one that holds that the law applies if either the last act took place in England or a substantial part of the crime was committed here and there were no reasons of comity why it should not be tried here. The court concluded that the correct approach was to follow the decision of Rose LJ in *R v Smith (Wallace Duncan) (No 1)*. Amongst the reasons for this were that a more flexible approach to the binding effect of decisions relating to the applicability of the law was appropriate, the law as stated in *R v Manning* was not in accord with the inclusionary approach developed or advocated by Lord Diplock, Lord Wilberforce and Lord Griffiths,[90] and that it was consistent with the changes in the law that had taken place in regard to conspiracy and attempts. Finally, it was stated by Woolf CJ that 'It would undermine the inherent nature of the common law if courts were prevented as

87 [2004] EWCA Crim 631 at para 48.
88 [1963] 1 QB 8.
89 [2004] EWCA Crim 631 at para 56.
90 In *DPP v Treacy*, *R v Doot* [1973] AC 807 and *Somchai Liangsiriprasert v Government of the United States of America* respectively.

a matter of principle from developing the law to meet the needs of contemporary society in the present situation'.[91]

Reinforcing the emergence of the more general or inclusionary approach to the requisite connection to territory is *R (Purdy) v CPP (Society for the Protection of Unborn Children Intervening)*.[92] In this case the House of Lords, to some extent at least, considered the scope of section 2(1) of the Suicide Act 1961. Whilst the essence of the case considered the appellant's human rights and the application of Article 8 and Article 8(1) of the European Convention on Human Rights to the failure of the DPP to publish details of the policy applied to decisions over the instigation of prosecutions under the section, the application of section 2(1) was considered by Lord Hope and Lord Phillips.[93] What is material here for our present purposes are Lord Hope's comments on the law as stated in *Smith (Wallace Duncan) (No 4)*.[94] He noted that that case 'settled the law on the point'.[95] However, Hirst, whose views as to the continuing applicability of the terminiatory approach were rebuffed by Lord Hope, argued that it is still good law, but stated that 'Following the support given to it in *Purdy*, however, the case for an inclusionary approach to cross-frontier crime is now that much stronger, and since this follows *Smith (No.4)* one senses that the tide of judicial opinion may now be running in its favour'.[96] Indeed, subsequent to *Purdy* the test for the application of the law as stated in *Smith (Wallace Duncan) (No 4)* was applied in *R v Sheppard (Simon Guy)*.[97]

In addition to the four forms of territorial requirement that UK law demands exist in certain circumstances for the law to apply is a fifth, *sui generis* form. It is unique in that it relates to quasi-territorial areas, such as on board ships and aircraft. It is appropriate to mention this type of extension of the law because it entails the application of UK law across borders – albeit to quasi-territorial

91 [2004] EWCA Crim 631 at p 1438.

92 [2009] UKHL 45.

93 The Coroners and Justice Act 2009, s 59 amends the Suicide Act 1961. The effect of the amendment is to make the jurisdictional argument redundant because what is now criminalised is the doing of an act capable of encouraging or assisting suicide – which would be complete within England in the circumstances such as those present in the *Purdy* case.

94 Lord Hope and Lord Phillips disagreed as to the applicability of s 2(1) where a suicide took place, or was intended to take place, outside England and Wales.

95 *Purdy*, at para 23.

96 Hirst, *Purdy*, at p 874.

97 [2010] EWCA Civ 65. The Law Commission in 2007 stated: 'A recent academic article has described *Smith (Wallace Duncan) (No 4)* as "controversial" and based on "policy rather than principle" [Ormerod, D. and Rees, T., 'Jurisdiction: jurisdiction of English courts – obtaining by Deception' (2004) *Criminal Law Review* 951]. However, it appears that until the House of Lords considers the issue, the current law is that jurisdiction can be determined by reference to either the terminatory theory or the comity theory. This is subject to the proviso that the latter theory can only be relied upon where the alleged offence has a substantial connection with this jurisdiction', in Law Commission, *Participating in Crime*, May 2007, http://www.lawcom.gov.uk/assisting_crime.htm, accessed 22 May 2011.

areas. Whilst it is correct to aver that ships, aircraft, etc. are capable of being equated with UK territory, they are not, of course, legally equivalent. Instead, they are especial areas over which the criminal law has been extended to apply – in some cases on a complete basis. These areas are, generally, the space on (and sometimes nearby) UK-registered ships, aircraft and fixed platforms. The extension of the law to these areas is complex and varied. As Hirst notes:

> Distinctions may need to be drawn for jurisdictional purposes between aircraft, ships and fixed platforms; between British and foreign ships or aircraft; between different categories of ship; between British citizens and others; between a ship's crew and passengers; and between jurisdiction that is statutory and that which is derived from the ancient jurisdiction of the Admiral.[98]

Modern extensions of the law to ships, aircraft and fixed platforms have in certain cases been mandated by international agreement, and in others the extension is recognised by such an agreement. Several examples will illustrate the affect of international law in the area. The Vienna Convention Against Illicit Traffic in Narcotic Drugs and Pyschotropic Substances 1988 led to the enactment of section 18 of the Criminal Justice (International Cooperation) Act 1990 applying drug-trafficking offences to British ships, and the Tokyo Convention on Offences and Certain Other Acts Committed on Board Aircraft 1963 led to the Tokyo Convention Act 1967 – since repealed.[99] Article 92 of the United Nations Convention on the Law of the Sea 1982, on the other hand, recognises the right of states to apply their criminal law to ships which fly its flag.

The extension of the law to ships is through statute and the common law. At common law Admiralty jurisdiction extends to all indictable offences committed 'on any kind of British ship or boat'.[100] Bovill CJ in *R v Anderson* stated, in regard to the question of whether the criminal law of England applied to an offence committed on a British ship when on a river in France:

> the Common Law of England . . . is in my judgment sufficient to decide this case. Here the offence is committed on board a British vessel by one of her crew. If this offence had been committed upon the high seas, there could have been no doubt upon the question either on principle or

98 Hirst, *Jurisdiction and Ambit* (n 7 above), at p 282; see, generally, Chapter 6.

99 In regard to aircraft generally the Civil Aviation Act 1982 extends the criminal law to British-controlled aircraft and in some cases to foreign-registered aircraft. Section 92 as amended provides, *inter alia*: '(1) Any act of omission taking place on board a British-controlled aircraft . . . which, if taking place in, or in a part of, the United Kingdom, would constitute an offence under the law in force in, or in that part or, the United Kingdom shall constitute that offence'.

100 Hirst, *Jurisdiction and Ambit* (n 7 above), at p 285.

> authority, and the offence then would have been committed clearly within the jurisdiction of the Admiralty, and therefore the Central Criminal Court would have stood in the same position as if the offence had been committed within its jurisdiction on land.[101]

Admiralty jurisdiction in England and Wales is now exercised by the Crown Court under section 46(2) of the Supreme Court Act 1981. Supplementing Admiralty jurisdiction are the provisions in the Merchant Shipping Act 1995. These apply a considerable number of offences within that Act to ships. Section 281 states:

> Where any person is charged with having committed any offence under this Act then (a) if he is a British citizen and is charged with having committed it (i) on board any United Kingdom ship on the high seas, (ii) in any foreign port or harbour, or (iii) on board any foreign ship to which he does not belong; or (b) if he is not a British citizen and is charged with having committed it on board any United Kingdom ship on the high seas; and he is found within the jurisdiction of any court in any part of the United Kingdom which would have had jurisdiction in relation to the offence if it had been committed on board a United Kingdom ship within the limits of its ordinary jurisdiction to try the offence that court shall have jurisdiction to try the offence as if it had been so committed.

In regard to fixed platforms, the Criminal Jurisdiction (Offshore Activities) Order 1987[102] extends the criminal law *in toto*. Article 3 provides that:

> Any act or omission which (a) takes place on, under or above an installation in waters to which this Order applies or any waters within five hundred metres of any such installation; and (b) would, if taking place in any part of the United Kingdom, constitute an offence under the law in force in that part, shall be treated for the purposes of that law as taking place in that part.

It must be noted that the extensions of the law to the quasi-territorial areas mentioned by no means comprise an exhaustive iteration of the law in the area.[103] They are put forward as examples to make the point that the law deems certain areas outside UK territory in a literal sense as territorial for the purposes of its application.

101 (1865–72) CCR 161 at 166–7.

102 SI 1987/2198.

103 A further example is that of diplomatic premises, a type of quasi-territorial area that has been at issue in regard to the application of UK human rights law across borders, discussed in Chapter 4.

Relationship-based criminal law

The second most important connection required by UK criminal law forming a basis for its application and extension across borders is the relationship the accused has with the state. This has been called various things, including nationality-based jurisdiction and active personality-based jurisdiction.[104] The latter, denoting a wider range of relationships between an alleged offender and the state than just nationality, is more precise. Unfortunately, there are a relatively large number of such relationships and descriptions and definitions thereof. As Hirst notes, the law refers to different designations including 'any subject of Her Majesty', 'a British subject', 'a British officer or subject', 'a citizen of the United Kingdom and colonies', 'a British citizen', 'a United Kingdom national, a United Kingdom resident or a person subject to United Kingdom service jurisdiction', 'resident in the United Kingdom', 'resident in the United Kingdom, the Isle of Man or any of the Channel Islands' and 'a United Kingdom person'.[105] Clearly, the use of these varied terms is not ideal. Several date from some time ago, for example 'any subject of Her Majesty' dates from the Offences Against the Person Act 1861. In recent times, however, legislation has increasingly referred to 'UK nationals'. For example, section 4(3) of the Cluster Munitions (Prohibition) Act 2010 applies the offences created by the Act outside the UK where committed by UK nationals, Scottish partnerships, and bodies incorporated under the law of any part of the UK. Section 4(6) provides that for the purposes of the section, UK nationals means 'an individual who is (a) a British citizen, a British overseas territories citizen, a British National (Overseas) or a British Overseas citizen, (b) a person who under the British Nationality Act 1981 is a British subject, or (c) a British protected person within the meaning of that Act'. This definition is commonly employed in recent statutes, a further example being section 72 of the Sexual Offences Act 2003, as inserted by the Criminal Justice and Immigration Act 2008. Notably, the Bribery Act 2010, section 12(1) applies the offences under sections 1, 2 and 6 (bribing another person, being bribed and bribery of a foreign public official) to circumstances where any act or omission forming part of the offence takes place within the UK. Section 12(1) is supplemented by section 12(2)–(4) which employ a 'close connection' requirement. This has the effect of applying these crimes on a relationship basis in the absence of a territorial connection. By section 12(4) a person has a close connection with the UK if and only if at the time of the act or omission he or she was a British citizen, a British overseas

104 The former was used by the present author in Arnell, P., 'The Case for Nationality Based Jurisdiction' (2001) 50 ICLQ 955, and the latter in the International Bar Association's Legal Practice Division, *Report of the Task Force on Extraterritorial Jurisdiction*, 2009, cited at http://tinyurl.com/taskforce-etj-pdf, accessed 29 May 2011.

105 Hirst, *Jurisdiction and Ambit* (n 7 above), at p 204. For a discussion of 'residence' in relation to the International Criminal Court Act 2001, see McGoldrick, D., Williams, S., Cryer, R. and Mora, P.D., 'The Coroners and Justice Act 2009 and international criminal law: backing into the future?' (2010) 59 ICLQ 803.

territories citizen, a British National (Overseas), a British Overseas citizen, a person who under the British Nationality Act 1981 was a British subject, an individual ordinarily resident in the United Kingdom, a body incorporated under the law of any part of the United Kingdom and a Scottish partnership.

The Bribery Act 2010 is one of a number of statutes employing 'residence' in addition to 'nationality' as a basis for the extension of the law. Further examples include the War Crimes Act 1991 (British citizen or resident in the United Kingdom, the Isle of Man or any of the Channel Islands), the Sex Offenders Act 1997 (British citizen and resident) and the Sexual Offences Act 2003 (UK national and resident). The latter interestingly applies a number of sexual offences to acts committed abroad by UK nationals, UK residents and those who, after the offence has been committed, become a UK national or resident. Section 72 of the Sexual Offences Act 2003 provides:

> (1) If (a) a United Kingdom national does an act in a country outside the United Kingdom, and (b) the act, if done in England and Wales or Northern Ireland, would constitute a sexual offence to which this section applies, the United Kingdom national is guilty in that part of the United Kingdom of that sexual offence.
>
> (2) If (a) a United Kingdom resident does an act in a country outside the United Kingdom, (b) the act constituted an offence under the law in force in that country, and (c) the act, if done in England and Wales or Northern Ireland, would constitute a sexual offence to which this section applies, the United Kingdom resident is guilty in that part of the United Kingdom of that sexual offence.
>
> (3) If (a) a person does an act in a country outside the United Kingdom at a time when the person was not a United Kingdom national or a United Kingdom resident, (b) the act constituted an offence under the law in force in that country, (c) the act, if done in England and Wales or Northern Ireland, would have constituted a sexual offence to which this section applies, and (d) the person meets the residence or nationality condition at the relevant time, proceedings may be brought against the person in that part of the United Kingdom for that sexual offence as if the person had done the act there. . . .

The residence or nationality condition in section 72(3)(d) is met if the person is a resident or national at the time the proceedings are brought. The definition of 'United Kingdom resident' is found in section 72(9), which states that a 'United Kingdom resident means an individual who is resident in the United Kingdom'. This circular definition is of very limited assistance in coming to an understanding of who in fact is a resident.

A much more detailed and complex definition of 'resident' has been inserted into the International Criminal Court (Scotland) Act 2001 and the International

Criminal Court Act 2001.[106] The definition is similar in both statutes, and is worth citing in full. Section 8A of the International Criminal Court (Scotland) Act 2001 provides that a UK resident means a person who is resident in the UK and continues:

(2) To the extent that it would not otherwise be the case, the following individuals are to be treated for the purposes of this Part as being resident in the United Kingdom –
  (a) an individual who has indefinite leave to remain in the United Kingdom,
  (b) any other individual who has made an application for such leave (whether or not it has been determined) and who is in the United Kingdom,
  (c) an individual who has leave to enter or remain in the United Kingdom for the purposes of work or study and who is in the United Kingdom,
  (d) an individual who has made an asylum claim, or a human rights claim, which has been granted,
  (e) any other individual who has made an asylum claim or a human rights claim (whether or not the claim has been determined) and who is in the United Kingdom,
  (f) an individual named in an application for indefinite leave to remain, an asylum claim or a human rights claim as a dependant of the individual making the application or claim if –
    (i) the application or claim has been granted, or
    (ii) the named individual is in the United Kingdom (whether or not the application or claim has been determined),
  (g) an individual who would be liable to removal or deportation from the United Kingdom but cannot be removed or deported because of section 6 of the Human Rights Act 1998 (c.42) or for practical reasons,
  (h) an individual –
    (i) against whom a decision to make a deportation order under section 5(1) of the Immigration Act 1971 (c.77) by virtue of section 3(5)(a) of that Act (deportation conducive to the public good) has been made,
    (ii) who has appealed against the decision to make the order (whether or not the appeal has been determined), and
    (iii) who is in the United Kingdom,
  (i) an individual who is an illegal entrant within the meaning of section 33(1) of the Immigration Act 1971 or who is liable to removal under section 10 of the Immigration and Asylum Act 1999 (c.33),
  (j) an individual who is detained in lawful custody in the United Kingdom.

106 Section 32 of the Criminal Justice and Licensing (Scotland) 2010 Act inserted a new s 8A into the International Criminal Court (Scotland) Act 2001 and s 70(4) of the Coroners and Justice Act 2009 inserted a new s 67A into the International Criminal Court Act 2001.

Section 8A(3) provides for persons not covered in (a)–(j). It states that in deciding whether any other person is resident in the UK regard is to be had to all other considerations including the length of time a person has been or intends to be in the country, the purpose of that presence, any familial connections and any interest in residential property in the UK. Clearly, this is a novel and detailed iteration of residence. It remains to be seen whether it will be extended to the numerous other statutes relying on residence as a basis for the application of UK criminal law across borders.

Joining UK nationals and residents as amenable to the application of certain crimes committed across borders are corporations and other legal persons, Crown servants and members of the armed forces.[107] The Bribery Act 2010 is an interesting example where the law is extended to apply to legal persons (as well as natural persons). Section 7 of the Act criminalises the failure of commercial organisations to prevent bribery. A 'commercial organisation' is defined as:

(a) a body which is incorporated under the law of any part of the United Kingdom and which carries on a business (whether there or elsewhere),
(b) any other body corporate (wherever incorporated) which carries on a business, or part of a business, in any part of the United Kingdom,
(c) a partnership which is formed under the law of any part of the United Kingdom and which carries on a business (whether there or elsewhere) or
(d) any other partnership (wherever formed) which carries on a business, or part of a business, in any part of the United Kingdom.

Crown servants and members of the armed forces, also subject to the law on the basis of their relationship with the UK, are unique in that the criminal law *in toto* applies to them when they commit crimes in the course of their employment, unlike the ad hoc application of the law in the case of nationals and residents generally.[108] The Criminal Justice Act 1948, section 21 and the Criminal Jurisdiction Act 1802, section 1 generally govern the application of the criminal law to Crown servants. As described by Hirst:

> the 1948 provision applies only to indictable offences committed by Crown servants in foreign countries and in the course of their employment, whereas the 1802 provision applies to offences committed by such persons anywhere in the world, so long as they were at the time employed in (or the holder of) an office or position somewhere outside Great Britain, and as long as the office in question was committed in the exercise etc. of that office etc.[109]

107 The offences under the Merchant Shipping Act 1995 are extended by s 282 to land outwith the UK when committed by British seamen.

108 See, e.g. Hirst, *Jurisdiction and Ambit* (n 7 above), at pp 209–16.

109 Ibid at p 210.

The application of the law to members of the armed forces is governed by the Armed Forces Act 2006. Whilst a detailed examination of this is beyond the scope of this work, the essence of the regime of service law is that the regular criminal law is applied to acts of members of the armed forces whilst abroad – in addition to a variety of specific offences and a separate system of prosecution.[110]

Three types of crime are applied across borders on the basis of the relationship between the alleged offender and the UK. These are long-established crimes of indigenous origin, modern crimes, also of indigenous origin and crimes which exist as a result of international agreement or obligation. Treason is the paradigmatic example of the first type. It is criminalised by the Treason Act 1351.[111] Also within this group are the crimes under the Offences Against the People Act 1861 (bigamy,[112] murder and manslaughter) that extend across borders on the basis of the relationship between the accused and the UK. Section 9 of the 1861 Act provides:

> Where any murder or manslaughter shall be committed on land out of the United Kingdom, whether within the Queen's dominions or without, and whether the person killed were a subject of Her Majesty or not, every offence committed by any subject of Her Majesty in respect of any such case, whether the same shall amount to the offence of murder or manslaughter . . . may be dealt with, inquired of, tried, determined, and punished . . . in England or Ireland . . . [P]rovided, that nothing herein contained shall prevent any person from being tried in any place out of England or Ireland for murder or manslaughter committed out of England or Ireland, in the same manner as such person might have been tried before the passing of this Act.[113]

Similarly applicable offences of considerable pedigree are found in the Slave Trade Act 1824 read with the Slave Trade Act 1873, the Foreign Enlistment Act 1870,[114] the Unlawful Oaths Acts 1797–1812 and the Explosive Substances Act 1883.[115]

110 See, generally, the *Manual of Service Law*, Vol 1, cited at http://www.mod.uk/NR/rdonlyres/4E67FD01-64B5-476D-8AD5-C12D977C1AE1/0/vol1and2mslver1.pdf, accessed 23 May 2011.

111 For treason being applied extraterritorially (and infamously), see *Joyce v DPP* [1946] AC 347.

112 See *The Trial of Earl Russell* [1901] AC 446.

113 This has been applied to Mohan Singh Kular, who was convicted for the murder of his wife in Punjab: see *The Times*, 4 November 1997. See further below.

114 For an example of the extraterritorial application of the Act, see *R v Jameson* [1896] 2 QB 431.

115 Section 2 of the Explosive Substances Act 1883, as amended, states: 'A person who in the United Kingdom or (being a citizen of the United Kingdom and Colonies) in the Republic of Ireland unlawfully and maliciously causes by any explosive substance an explosion of a nature likely to endanger life or cause serious injury to property . . . shall be guilty of an offence'. This extension of the law is notable in that whilst it applies outside

The number and range of crimes applied across borders on the basis of the relationship between the accused and the UK has grown considerably in recent times. These crimes form the second type identified above – modern crimes of indigenous origin. The increasing 'range' denotes the widening of the subject matter of such offences. It can be seen that the law has developed from predominately concerning acts of a political nature which affect the interests of the UK as a state (as seen above, there are exceptions to this) to including acts that affect, at least directly, private interests. Sex-related crimes fall within this expanded range. An example is the Sexual Offences (Scotland) Act 2009, which extends the application of a number of 'listed offences' on the basis of nationality and residence. As noted, the Sexual Offences Act 2003 provides similarly for England and Wales and Northern Ireland. Listed offences are found in Schedule 4, Part 2 to the 2003 Act. The 2009 Act covers both the incitement to commit offences outside the UK and extraterritorial offences themselves – so combining prescription on an initiatory or subjective basis with that of a relationship basis. The 2009 Act itself contains crimes that apply across borders, for example rape (if committed against a person under 18), and extends the application of offences found in third statutes, for example under section 52 of the Civic Government (Scotland) Act 1982 relating to the taking and distribution of indecent images of children.[116] Further relatively recent extensions of the law include those in the Immigration Act 1971, the Representation of the People Act 1983,[117] and the Official Secrets Act 1989.[118] These act to protect public interests. There exist a number of other examples of crimes of indigenous origin where the law has been extended on the basis of the relationship between the accused and the UK.[119]

The third type of relationship-based criminal law is distinguished from the other two by the fact that it is derived from conventional obligation. As noted above, the UK is party to a considerable number of treaties relating to the criminal law. Often these conventions oblige, or permit, state-parties to criminalise certain behaviour and to extend the scope of those crimes beyond their borders. Examples are the crimes relating to landmines, found in the Landmines Act 1998. These include, in section 2(1) and (2), the prohibition on the use of

the UK, it is limited to the Republic of Ireland. The 1883 Act is referred to below in that its scope has been extended further in certain circumstances by the Terrorism Act 2000.

116 As will be seen below, most enforcement has been in regard to certain sexual offences.

117 Crimes under this Act are unusually extended in that they apply to Commonwealth and Irish subjects outside the UK – those groups of persons who would have a franchise if resident within the UK.

118 Section 15(1) of the Official Secrets Act 1989 states that 'Any act – (a) done by a British citizen or Crown servant; or (b) done by any person in any of the Channel Islands or the Isle of Man or any colony, shall, if it would be an offence by that person under any provision of this Act . . . [with limited exceptions] . . . when done in the United Kingdom, be an offence under that provision'.

119 See, further, Richardson, J., *Archbold: Criminal Pleading, Evidence and Practice*, Sweet and Maxwell, 2010, Chs 2 and 19–33; and Hirst, *Jurisdiction and Ambit* (n 7 above), at pp 219–83.

anti-personnel mines, the development or production of an anti-personnel mine, and the assistance, encouragement and inducement of such conduct. Section 3(1) of the 1998 Act provides that the crimes in section 2(1) and2(2) 'apply to conduct in the United Kingdom or elsewhere'. Section 3(2) provides that crimes prescribing the 'assistance, encouragement and inducements in the United Kingdom or elsewhere' apply regardless of the fact that the conduct takes place, or will take place, in the UK. These extensions of the law are limited by section 3(3), which provides that 'Subsection (1) and (2) of section 2, so far as they apply respectively to (a) conduct outside the United Kingdom, and (b) assistance, encouragement and inducements outside the United Kingdom, impose prohibitions only on United Kingdom nationals, Scottish partnerships and bodies incorporated under the law of a part of the United Kingdom'. The definition of 'United Kingdom national' is similar to that found in section 4(6) of the Cluster Munitions (Prohibition) Act 2010, noted above. The origin of the extension of the law in regard to landmines is Article 9 of the Convention on the Prohibition of the Use, Stockpiling, Production and Transfer of Anti-Personnel Mines and on Their Destruction 1997. It provides that 'Each State Party shall take all appropriate legal, administrative and other measures, including the imposition of penal sanctions, to prevent and suppress any activity prohibited to a State Party under this Convention undertaken by persons or on territory under its jurisdiction or control'.

Further examples of conventionally mandated extensions of the law on a relationship basis include those under the Nuclear Explosions (Prohibition and Inspections) Act 1998,[120] the International Criminal Court Act 2000[121] and the Suppression of Terrorism Act 1978. The latter is of particular interest in that section 4(1) extends the crimes of murder and manslaughter in English law to unlawful killings within the territory of the state parties to the European Convention on the Suppression of Terrorism 1977. This is, in effect, the application of a vicarious territorial approach to jurisdiction. A relationship-based extension of the law is effected by section 4(3) of the 1978 Act, which exceptionally extends the applicability of certain offences to the nationals of state parties – a vicarious, nationality-based extension of the law. Clearly, the approach taken by the European Convention on the Suppression of Terrorism 1977 is unusual. However, because it utilises the relationship between persons and the state as a basis upon which to extend the law it is rightfully included as one of the number of conventions that oblige or permit the UK to act in this way. The instances mentioned above are just a selection of these treaties; further treaties provide similarly.[122]

120 The Act was enacted to give effect to certain provisions of the Comprehensive Nuclear-Test-Ban Treaty 1996 and the Protocol thereto.

121 The Act enabled the UK to ratify the Rome Statute of the International Criminal Court 1998, cited at http://http://untreaty.un.org/cod/icc/index.html, accessed 23 May 2011. The International Criminal Court (Scotland) Act 2001 provided similarly for Scotland.

122 See, in regard to Scotland, Gordon, G. and Gane, C. (eds), *Renton and Brown: Criminal Procedure*, W Green, Edinburgh, 2010, at paras 1–22 to 1–40.

A second form of relationship-based crime – as opposed to type – extends the law not with reference to the alleged offender but rather to the victim. In international law this is termed as applying the law on a passive personality basis. It has not traditionally found favour within the UK. Indeed, it became part of UK law only in 2000, in the form of section 63C of the Terrorism Act 2000.[123] Section 63C, entitled 'Terrorist attacks abroad on UK nationals, residents and diplomatic staff etc: jurisdiction', provides:

> (1) If (a) a person does anything outside the United Kingdom as an act of terrorism or for the purposes of terrorism, (b) his action is done to, or in relation to, a United Kingdom national, a United Kingdom resident or a protected person, and (c) his action, if done in any part of the United Kingdom, would have constituted an offence listed in subsection (2), he shall be guilty in that part of the United Kingdom of the offence . . .

Section 63C(2) lists, *inter alia*, the offences of murder, rape, assault causing injury, kidnapping, abduction and false imprisonment. Material here is the meaning of 'an act of terrorism or for the purposes of terrorism'. By section 1 of the Terrorism Act 2000 'terrorism' means the use or threat of action *inter alia* comprising serious violence against a person or damage to property where the use or threat is designed to influence the government or an international governmental organisation or to intimidate the public or a section of the public, and the use or threat is made for the purpose of advancing a political, religious, racial or ideological cause. Section 63C was enacted to comply with Article 9(1) of the EU Framework Decision on Combating Terrorism, which states:

> Each Member State shall take the necessary measures to establish its jurisdiction over the offences referred to in Articles 1 to 4 where: . . . (e) the offence is committed against the institutions or people of the Member State in question or against an institution of the European Union or a body set up in accordance with the Treaty establishing the European Community or the Treaty on European Union and based in that Member State.[124]

The Explanatory Notes to the Crime (International Co-operation) Act 2003 state that Part 2 of that Act, which introduced to the Terrorism Act 2000 the sections extending the law, was to affect the implementation of the Framework Decision.[125] Notably, the Framework Decision also appears to allow the application of the law on the basis of the protection of state interests in that it refers

123 Hirst, M., 'Murder as an Offence Under English Law' (2004) 68 *Journal of Criminal Law* 315.

124 Cited at http://eur-lex.europa.eu/LexUriServ/LexUriServ.do?uri=OJ:L:2002:164:0003:0003:EN:PDF, accessed 23 May 2011.

125 Cited at http://www.opsi.gov.uk/acts/acts2003/en/ukpgaen_20030032_en_1, accessed 23 May 2011.

to an offence committed 'against the institutions . . . of the Member State in question'. The UK has generally eschewed this approach – termed protective jurisdiction in international law.[126] Instead, section 63D of the Terrorism Act 2000 limits the extension of the law to certain terrorist-related crimes directed at diplomatic premises and vehicles abroad.

Crime-centric criminal law

A limited number of crimes in UK law are subject to being applied purely on the basis of the crime itself – without the requirement for any other link between the UK and the person, crime or victim. These crimes are termed 'crime-centric' in that it is the nature of the crime itself that provides the connection. In the description of the law above, the focal point was the link or connection – territorial and relationship-based – between the UK and the crime, accused or victim. Crimes that are applied in the absence of any such link are, in the parlance of international law, applied on a universal basis.[127] The application of the law on a crime-centric or universal basis is clearly exceptional – internationally and especially in UK law. That noted, there is a not-inconsiderable group of such crimes in UK law. Examples include piracy, crimes against aircraft and ships, torture, hostage-taking and crimes against internationally protected persons and United Nations personnel. As will be seen, all of these crimes today have a basis in international law. Amongst these crimes piracy is particularly notable for its long-standing nature and common-law basis, in regard to which Viscount Sankey stated:

> With regard to crimes as defined by international law, that law has no means of trying or punishing them. The recognition of them as constituting crimes, and the trial and punishment of the criminals, are left to the municipal law of each country. But whereas according to international law the criminal jurisdiction of municipal law is ordinarily restricted to crimes committed on its *terra firma* or territorial waters or its own ships, and to crimes by its own nationals wherever committed, it is also recognised as

126 A case sometimes used as an example of the UK taking such an approach to the application of its law is *DPP v Joyce* [1946] AC 347. Shaw suggests that this 'seems to have been applied' in this case in Shaw, M., *International Law*, 6th edn, Cambridge University Press, Cambridge, 2008, at p 667; whilst Hirst, *Jurisdiction and Ambit* (n 7 above), at p 49 discounts this by highlighting the fact that Joyce was a British passport-holder and so the law could be applied on the basis of his relationship to the UK.

127 Universal jurisdiction has been considered to amount to 'the claim by a state to prosecute crimes in circumstances where none of the traditional links of territoriality, nationality, passive personality or the protective principle exists at the time of the commission of the alleged offence': *AU–EU Expert Report on the Principle of Universal Jurisdiction*, 16 April 2009, at p 7, cited at http://ec.europa.eu/development/icenter/repository/troika_ua_ue_rapport_competence_universelle_EN.pdf , accessed 23 May 2011.

> extending to piracy committed on the high seas by any national on any ship, because a person guilty of such piracy has placed himself beyond the protection of any State. He is no longer a national, but '*hostis humani generis*' and as such he is justicable by any State anywhere.[128]

Although piracy in UK law exists only at common law,[129] its definition is provided by international law. Section 26 of the Merchant Shipping and Maritime Security Act 1997 provides that the definition of piracy in the 'law of nations' is found in Article 101 of the Law of the Sea Convention 1982. It is replicated in Schedule 5 to the 1997 Act.[130]

UK law also applies to certain crimes against aircraft, ships and fixed platforms which have no connection with the UK territorially or otherwise. The relevant statutes are the Aviation Security Act 1982 and the Aviation and Maritime Security Act 1990. For example, section 9(1) of the Aviation and Maritime Security Act 1990 prescribes the hijacking of ships, providing:

> (1) A person who unlawfully, by the use of force or by threats of any kind, seizes a ship or exercises control of it, commits the offence of hijacking a ship, whatever his nationality and whether the ship is in the United Kingdom or elsewhere.

The purposes of the 1990 Act are found in its preamble, which provides that the Act is:

> An Act to give effect to the Protocol for the Suppression of Unlawful Acts of Violence at Airports Serving International Civil Aviation which supplements the Convention for the Suppression of Unlawful Acts against the Safety of Civil Aviation; to make further provision with respect to aviation security and civil aviation; to give effect to the Convention for the Suppression of Unlawful Acts against the Safety of Maritime Navigation and to the Protocol for the Suppression of Unlawful Acts against the Safety of Fixed Platforms Located on the Continental Shelf which supplements that Convention; to make other provision for the protection of ships and harbour areas against acts of violence; and for connected purposes.

The role of conventional international law in providing the impetus for the extension of the law on this crime-centric basis is clearly evident here.

128 *In re Piracy Jure Gentium* [1934] AC 586 at 589, per Viscount Sankey LC, quoting from Grotius, *De Jure Belli ac Pacis*, vol 2, cap 20, § 40.

129 See *Cameron v HMA* 1971 SLT 333.

130 Hirst calls piracy the 'doyenne' of extraterritorial offences under English law, stating that it arose through the criminal jurisdiction of the Admiral following a civil or Roman law procedure, thus forgoing the limitations caused by the issue of venue: Hirst, *Jurisdiction and Ambit* (n 7 above), at p 33.

Among further crimes that may be prosecuted within the UK in the absence of a territorial or relationship connection are torture, under section 134 of the Criminal Justice Act 1988,[131] and certain offences specified in the Internationally Protected Persons Act 1978,[132] the United Nations Personnel Act 1997, the Taking of Hostages Act 1982 and the Terrorism Act 2000. All of these offences are rooted in international conventions. These are the Convention Against Torture and Other Cruel Inhuman or Degrading Treatment or Punishment 1984, the Convention on the Prevention and Punishment of Crimes against Internationally Protected Persons 1973, the Convention on the Safety of United Nations and Associated Personnel 1994, the International Convention against the Taking of Hostages 1979, the Convention for the Suppression of Terrorist Bombings 1998 and the Convention for the Suppression of the Financing of Terrorism 1999. Section 62(1) of the Terrorism Act 2000 provides that: 'If (a) a person does anything outside the United Kingdom as an act of terrorism or for the purposes of terrorism, and (b) his action would have constituted the commission of one of the offences listed in subsection (2) if it had been done in the United Kingdom, he shall be guilty of the offence'. The offences listed in section 62(2) are those in sections 2, 3 and 5 of the Explosive Substances Act 1883, section 1 of the Biological Weapons Act 1974 and section 2 of the Chemical Weapons Act 1996. Finally, it should be noted that, perhaps surprisingly, war crimes, crimes against humanity and genocide do not apply on a crime-centric or universal basis in UK law. War crimes are criminalised by the War Crimes Act 1991, the Geneva Conventions Act 1957, the International Criminal Court Act 2001 and the International Criminal Court (Scotland) Act 2001. The crimes specified in these statutes are restricted in their application in one way or other. There is a geographic and temporal restriction within the War Crimes Act 1991, a contextual restriction within the Geneva Conventions Act 1957 (the crimes must take place in an international armed conflict or conflict against colonialism) and a relationship restriction within the International Criminal Court Act 2001 and International Criminal Court (Scotland) Act 2001.

131 The crime of torture was at issue in the proceedings relating to Augusto Pinochet. The UK's legal involvement with Pinochet began on 17 October 1998 with his arrest. It came to an end when he was flown back to Chile on 2 March 2000. The most pertinent judgments are the original decision of the Divisional Court on 28 October 1998, *The Times*, 3 November 1998, the original decision of the House of Lords of 25 November 1998, [1998] 3 WLR 1456, which was set aside as a result of the Committee not being properly constituted, [1999] 2 WLR 272, and the second substantive decision of the House of Lords on 24 March 1999, [1999] 2 All ER 97. Interestingly, the Convention Against Torture and Other Cruel, Inhuman or Degrading Treatment and Punishment 1984 does not require state parties to apply their law in such an expansive way. Article 5 requires the application of law on a territorial and nationality basis and is optional as to its application on a passive personality basis.

132 See *In Re Al-Fawwaz and others* [2001] UKHL 69, [2002] 1 All ER 545.

Enforcement

The enforcement of the law must be part of an examination of the general subject of the application of law across borders. As seen in Chapter 1, analyses often dissect the subject into executive, legislative and judicial elements. This section largely focuses on the executive and judicial application of the law. This topic is important because unenforced substantive law – whatever its purported scope – is of limited use in coming to an understanding of the problems and policies affecting the area of law. Whether their impetus is international convention or indigenous policy concerns, substantive prescriptions extended to persons and circumstances outside the UK do not in themselves directly and immediately affect individuals or third states.[133] It is their enforcement that does so. Further, insight into the nature of the concerns motivating the application of law across borders, as well as the important issue surrounding decisions to instigate criminal prosecution, is gained by looking at whether and how the substantive law is enforced. Addressed by the examination of the enforcement of criminal law across borders is the issue, as Hirst puts it, of whether substantive criminal prescriptions 'appear(s) to be "paper tigers": Draconian and far-reaching on paper, but unused (and perhaps almost unusable) in practice'.[134] Such examination entails two elements – the rules that have been enacted and concluded to facilitate that enforcement and cases where persons have been subjected to the law.

The law governing co-operation in criminal matters in found in statute and treaty. The Crime (International Co-operation) Act 2003 is the primary source of UK legislation governing international co-operation.[135] Another central source of legislation is the Extradition Act 2003. The Crime (International Co-operation) Act 2003 governs both outgoing assistance – in the form of governing service of process from the UK, etc. and incoming assistance – where the prosecuting authorities in the UK seek to serve process, obtain evidence, affect a freezing order, etc. outside the UK. Section 7(1) and (2) of the Crime (International Co-operation) Act 2003 provide:

> (1) If it appears to a judicial authority in the United Kingdom on an application made by a person mentioned in subsection (3)(a) that an offence has been committed or that there are reasonable grounds for suspecting that an offence has been committed, and (b) that proceedings in respect of the offence have been instituted or that the offence is being investigated, the judicial authority may request assistance under this section.

133 Of course, there can be an indirect effect on both – in the form of deterrence on individuals and a notional violation of the sovereignty of third states.

134 Hirst, *Jurisdiction and Ambit* (n 7 above), at p 7.

135 The Home Office produces guidelines regarding UK mutual assistance generally, entitled *Mutual Legal Assistance Guidelines for the United Kingdom 2010*, cited at http://www.homeoffice.gov.uk/publications/police/operational-policing/MLA-guidelines-8th-edition?view=Binary, accessed 23 May 2011.

> (2) The assistance that may be requested under this section is assistance in obtaining outside the United Kingdom any evidence specified in the request for use in the proceedings or investigation.

Closely related to this statute are a number of conventions in relation to assistance in criminal matters to which the UK is party. The most important multilateral treaty is the European Convention on Criminal Matters 1959, which entered into force for the UK in 1991. This has been supplemented by the Convention on Mutual Assistance in Criminal Matters between the Member States of the European Union 2000, established by the Council of the EU in accordance with Article 34 of the Treaty on European Union. Article 1(1) of the 1959 Convention states that 'The Contracting Parties undertake to afford each other, in accordance with the provisions of this Convention, the widest measure of mutual assistance in proceedings in respect of offences the punishment of which, at the time of the request for assistance, falls within the jurisdiction of the judicial authorities of the requesting Party'.

Covering a much wider geographical area than the European Convention in Criminal Matters 1959 – although the 1959 Convention can extend to states not party to the Council of Europe[136] – are the numerous bilateral, mutual, legal assistance treaties to which the UK is party. Whilst some of these are crime or subject-specific, such as the Agreement between the Government of the United Kingdom of Great Britain and Northern Ireland and the Government of the Argentine Republic concerning Mutual Judicial Assistance against Illicit Drug Trafficking 1991, others are general in scope. An example of the latter is the Treaty between the Government of the United Kingdom of Great Britain and Northern Ireland and the Government of the Kingdom of Thailand on Mutual Assistance in Criminal Matters 1997. Article 1 of the 1997 Treaty provides as follows:

> 1) The parties agree, in accordance with provisions of this Treaty, to provide mutual assistance in connection with investigations, prosecutions, and other proceedings relating to criminal matters.
> (2) Assistance shall include but not be limited to:
>   (a) taking the testimony and statement of persons;
>   (b) providing documents, records and evidence;
>   (c) serving documents;
>   (d) executing requests for searches and seizures;
>   (e) transferring persons in custody for testimonial purposes;
>   (f) locating persons;
>   (g) assisting in restraint and forfeiture proceedings.

136 The list of state parties as at 23 May 2011 is found at http://conventions.coe.int/Treaty/Commun/ChercheSig.asp?NT=030&CM=8&DF=26/05/2010&CL=ENG, accessed 23 May 2011. The only non-Council of Europe party is Israel.

(3) Assistance shall be provided without regard to whether the acts which are the subject of the investigation, prosecution, or proceedings in the Requesting Party are prohibited under the law of the Requested Party, or whether the courts of the Requested Party would have jurisdiction with respect to such acts in corresponding circumstances.

In addition to mutual legal assistance agreements, general and specific, are a number of conventions addressing a specific crime or policy concern which contain provision on co-operation, extradition and prosecution. Many of these have been mentioned above. An example is Article 4 of the Convention Against Torture and Other Cruel, Inhuman, Degrading Treatment and Punishment 1984. It places an obligation upon states having custody of an individual suspected of having committed torture to inform those states with an interest of this fact – an interested state being the territorial state and the state of the nationality of the accused. It further contains, in Article 7, the relatively common extradition or prosecution provision,[137] which obliges state parties either to prosecute a person within their territory suspected of the relevant offence or to extradite him or her to a state seeking to prosecute.

In the UK, the Extradition Act 2003 is the core piece of legislation governing the subject of extradition. The Act broadly operates in conjunction with a network of treaties. In the process of being applied, extradition law can raise the issue of the applicability of the criminal law (and human rights law) – hence, its particular relevance to the subject of this book. A person contesting an extradition may argue that the law does not apply to the acts that he or she allegedly committed. In such cases, a court will examine the applicability of the law to the facts in question. In cases where the UK is applying its criminal law across borders, therefore, extradition-related judicial authority often includes discussion of and judicial pronouncement on the extended scope of the law. This occurs not only where the UK is seeking to extradite a suspect who is abroad; it also occurs where a person is sought on account of the requirement – still applicable explicitly or de facto – of double criminality. More practically, in some cases extradition is vital where the accused is outside the UK. In other cases, however, it is not relevant because the accused has either returned to the UK of his or her own accord or he or she has committed an initiatory or subjective territorial offence and thus never left the country. The Extradition Act 2003 contains the framework to be followed when the UK seeks the extradition of a person from a foreign state – as well as the rules that apply when the UK authorities are extraditing an individual.[138] Different procedures must be

137 The International Law Commission has produced an analytical guide to the obligation to extradite or prosecute: Office of Legal Affairs, International Law Commission, 'Obligation to Extradite or Prosecute (aut dedere aut judicare)', January 2010, cited at http://untreaty.un.org/ilc/guide/7_6.htm, accessed 23 May 2011.

138 For a description of the main features of the Act, see Arnell, P., 'Scots Extradited' [2008] *Juridical Review* 241.

followed dependent, generally, on the relationship that the third state has with the UK. States that are party to the Council Framework Decision on the European Arrest Warrant 2002 (all 27 Member States of the EU) are classed Category 1 states, and all others are Category 2. Within Category 2 are states with which the UK has concluded an extradition treaty, as well as those with which it will co-operate on an ad hoc basis. The UK has concluded a bilateral extradition agreement with approximately 50 states.[139] This number excludes countries party to the multilateral European arrangements under the Framework Decision and the European Convention on Extradition 1957.

A final and relatively novel type of law or agreement governing or affecting the enforcement of law across borders relates explicitly and directly to prosecutorial co-operation. This takes the form of the Attorney General and Lord Advocate's 'Guidance for Handling Criminal Cases with Concurrent Jurisdiction between the United Kingdom and the United States of America and corresponding Domestic Guidance'.[140] The Guidance, as its name implies, is non-binding and is intended to promote prosecutorial co-operation between the UK and the United States and reduce the risk of criminal proceedings being brought in the two countries simultaneously.[141] Interestingly, it has been considered in several cases in England. In the *R (Syed Talha Ahsan) v Director of Public Prosecutions* it was held that the Guidance only applied where there were existing investigations in both countries that were taking place with a view to prosecute – it did not require the commencement of an investigation within the UK.[142]

Instances of enforcement

The enforcement of UK criminal law across borders in the form of criminal prosecution is relatively rare. This, together with only limited information on the subject, makes its description somewhat general and anecdotal. The infrequent enforcement stands in stark contrast to the considerable number of substantive common law and statutory crimes extended across borders and the thorough and widespread set of norms designed to facilitate their enforcement. There are several reasons for this relatively infrequent enforcement. It stems, first, from the basic fact that the vast majority of crime is wholly intra-territorial. Crime with a cross-border element has been, and is still, exceptional. A second factor, in regard to wholly extraterritorial crime, is that the underlying policy

139 A list of these states can be found on the Foreign and Commonwealth Office website at http://www.fco.gov.uk/en/publications-and-documents/treaties/lists-treaties/bilatextradition, accessed 23 May 2011.

140 The Guidance is available at http://www.publications.parliament.uk/pa/ld200607/ldlwa/70125ws1.pdf, accessed 23 May 2011.

141 See, generally, Brookson-Morris, K., 'Conflicts of Criminal Jurisdiction' (2007) 56 ICLQ 659.

142 [2008] EWHC 666 Admin at para 35. See also *Onwuzulike v USA* [2009] EWHC 1395 Admin. The Guidance is discussed in Chapter 5.

of prosecution services and the Government is that crime should, as far as possible, be prosecuted where committed. As a non-governmental organisation working towards increased prosecution of so-called sex tourists states: 'The overarching principle underpinning UK government policy that it is better to have the offender arrested and dealt with in the country where the offence takes place'.[143] A third factor, related to the second, is the numerous evidential and procedural difficulties arising in mounting a criminal prosecution in cases with an international element. This difficulty can affect decisions to prosecute because prosecutors must take into account the likelihood of conviction. More generally, there is the problem of ascertaining precise information on the frequency and nature of the law being enforced across borders. Statistics are available in regard to practice in extradition, but these tell an incomplete story. As mentioned, persons subjected to prosecution may never have left the UK, having acted from a base in the country, or may have returned voluntarily after committing an offence outside the country. These facts noted, it is possible to locate and analyse cases where the law has been enforced across borders. These can be categorised according to the link to the UK which is relied upon in founding the prosecution – territorial connection, the relationship of the accused to the UK and the nature of the crime itself. [144]

Territorial connection

The majority of cases in which the criminal law has been enforced across borders have had a territorial connection of some kind. In most, an act has occurred within the UK which has had, or was intended to have, some prescribed effect outside the UK. In *R v Abu Hamza*,[145] for example, Hamza was convicted in 2006, *inter alia*, of soliciting to murder under section 4 of the Offences Against the Person Act 1861. Section 4 as amended states that:

> whosoever shall solicit, encourage, persuade, or endeavour to persuade, or shall propose to any person, to murder any other person, whether he be a subject of Her Majesty or not, and whether he be in the Queen's dominions or not, shall be guilty of a misdemeanour and being convicted thereof shall be liable to . . . [imprisonment for life] . . .

The charges related to speeches made by Hamza whilst he was Iman at Finsbury Park Mosque. Hamza appealed on the ground, *inter alia*, that if he had indeed

143 Beddoe, C., *Return to Sender – British Child Sex Offenders Abroad: Why More Must Be Done*, End Child Prostitution, Child Pornography and the Trafficking of Children for Sexual Purposes (ECPAT), 2008, at p 7, cited at http://www.ecpat.org.uk/sites/default/files/return_to_sender_2008.pdf, accessed 23 May 2011 .

144 In no sense is this an exhaustive narrative of the instances where the law has been applied and enforced across borders. Rather, it is a description of a number of cases chosen on the basis of their utility as examples.

145 [2006] EWCA Crim 2918.

solicited to commit murder it was to do so outside the UK. As stated in the judgment:

> insofar as the appellant's speeches solicited those who heard them to commit murder, the solicitation was to do so in foreign countries. The appellant's speeches were directed to a wide audience. No evidence was given as to the nationality of any members of that audience. Mr Fitzgerald submits that no offence will be committed under section 4 of the 1861 Act in respect of soliciting murder outside this jurisdiction unless the person solicited is a British national.[146]

Illuminatingly, this point of argument, which had been termed the 'jurisdiction point', was said by Lord Phillips to be in fact a matter of statutory interpretation.[147] This reinforces the basic point, and the language used in this book, that the application of the law across borders or extraterritorially is distinct from whether a court has the competence, or jurisdiction, to hear a case. The court had to decide whether section 4 amounted to an exception to the general principle of the common law that an inchoate offence is not committed unless the conduct planned or incited would, if carried out, be indictable in England. This is because the act of murder by a person not a subject of Her Majesty abroad is not criminal and thus, if the general rule were applied, the solicitation of a foreign national to commit murder abroad would not be criminal under section 4. It was held that section 4 did indeed amount to an exception to the general rule for three reasons. First, it was held that the section was apparently enacted to address 'the activities of aliens in England in support of murders, or attempts to murder, committed by aliens outside the jurisdiction'.[148] Second, section 4 itself does not suggest that it should be limited to cases where the person incited abroad is a subject of Her Majesty. Third, the limitation of section 4 to such cases would produce an anomaly. The Court held:

> It is anomalous that a British subject who is apprehended within the jurisdiction can be prosecuted for committing a murder abroad, but an alien in the same position cannot. The only reason for this anomaly is international comity. It would be doubly anomalous, where no reason of comity exists, to distinguish between inciting a British subject within this jurisdiction to commit such a crime and inciting an alien to do so.[149]

Hamza's appeal against the ruling of the trial judge on this point was dismissed and, with his other grounds of appeal also failing, his convictions were upheld.

146 Ibid at para 7.
147 Ibid.
148 Ibid at para. 38; citing Hirst, *Jurisdiction and Ambit* (n 7 above), at p 139.
149 Ibid at para 41.

Subsequent to his appeal Hamza brought a case to the European Court of Human Rights on the basis of Article 6 of the European Convention of Human Rights, the right to a fair trial. It was declared inadmissible in January 2011.[150]

A second example of where criminal law has been applied and enforced across borders is *R v Parnell*.[151] This was an appeal against sentence. Parnell was convicted of attempting to incite a male under the age of 16 to commit buggery and to commit gross indecency. As the court noted, the charges and circumstances were unusual:

> Prosecution for attempted incitement is unusual in the experience of the members of this court and the facts are indeed somewhat unusual. The defendant was engaged by a touring opera and concert group to fly to Sri Lanka to take part as a pianist in performances that the group were going to give there. Shortly before his departure for Sri Lanka he sent an e-mail to a group internet site seeking a teenage boy for sexual activity.[152]

The acts that Parnell committed were not unlawful in Sri Lankan law. Parnell was arrested and prosecuted in the UK under the Sexual Offences (Conspiracy and Incitement) Act 1996 – which, as noted above, no longer applies in England and Wales.[153] The court held that the original sentences were not correct because the offences were not 'sexual offences' within the meaning of section 161 of the Powers of Criminal Courts (Sentencing) Act 2000 or section 1 of the Sex Offenders Act 1997. Describing the case, the court stated:

> The judge quite rightly observed that there is concern in Sri Lanka and elsewhere that men from wealthy countries try to exploit and corrupt underage youths from poorer countries. It is a concern shared by the United Kingdom Parliament and by this court. He said that the offences involved premeditation – which of course is correct – and what would have been a degree of grooming if the victim had been real. On the other hand, Mr Jones points out that there was in fact no victim in this case. The recipients of the e-mails, as it turned out, were the police. The matter went no further than an attempt to incite. The defendant when he went to Sri Lanka took no steps to arrange a meeting – he simply fulfilled his professional

150 [2011] ECHR 211. A further case involving Hamza is pending before the ECtHR where he is challenging his extradition to the United States: see Chapter 4 below.

151 [2004] EWCA Crim 2523.

152 Ibid at para 3.

153 The Crown Prosecution Service states that this was the first conviction under the 1996 Act: 'A concert pianist has become the first person to be convicted under Britain's new "sex tourism" laws following advice provided to police by CPS London. Brian Parnell, 66, was jailed for two years for attempting to incite an under-age boy in Sri Lanka to commit buggery', cited at http://www.cps.gov.uk/news/articles/sextourist020604/, accessed 23 May 2011.

> engagements and the matter went no further until he was interviewed by the authorities. Mr Jones also points out that the defendant was a man of previously entirely good character and the consequence of this conviction has been the loss of his livelihood as a musician.[154]

Parnell's sentences were reduced from concurrent two-year and one-year terms on counts 1 and 2 to concurrent six-month terms of imprisonment on each count.

Another example of UK criminal law being applied across borders is part of the well-known prosecution of those responsible for the Lockerbie bombing, *HM Advocate v Al-Megrahi (Abdelbaset Ali) (No 1)*.[155] The question for the Scottish court, in a preliminary diet, was whether a conspiracy charge was justiciable in Scotland in light of the fact that the accused engaged in the conspiracy outside the country. It was alleged that Al-Meghrahi and another conspired in Libya and elsewhere to place an explosive device on a civilian aircraft which subsequently exploded over Lockerbie.[156] Lord Sutherland held that there appeared to be no intention that the conspiracy result in a crime being committed in Scotland:

> I accept that the situations posed in the cases of Doot and Liangsiriprasert rely to some extent on the specific target being the country seeking jurisdiction, and it might be argued that a country not a specific target cannot have jurisdiction. If the conspiracy never reached fruition and if there was no overt act to carry on the conspiracy in the country concerned, I appreciate that that would be a formidable objection. Where however, a crime of the utmost gravity has been in fact committed in a particular country and it can be shown that that crime is the culmination of a long drawn out and complex conspiracy, it appears to me quite illogical to say that that country has no interest in putting the conspirators on trial for their part in what has happened, even though their activities were all carried out abroad . . . That view, in my opinion, is consistent with what has been said in the cases of Doot and Liangsiriprasert which, although they deal with the English law of conspiracy, appear to me to be entirely consistent with the law in Scotland.[157]

Al-Megrahi was convicted of murder, with the conspiracy charge being dropped by the Crown at the conclusion of its submissions. His appeal against conviction was refused.[158]

154 [2004] EWCA Crim 2523 at para 17.
155 [2000] JC 555.
156 See, further, Arnell, P., 'Her Majesty's Advocate v. Megrahi and Fhimah' [2000] *Juridical Review* 395.
157 [2000] JC 555 at paras 18–19.
158 *HM Advocate v Al-Megrahi (Abdelbaset Ali) (No 4)* 2002 JC 99. The case was subsequently referred to the High Court of Justiciary by the Scottish Criminal Cases Review

The crime of conspiracy in section 1A of the Criminal Law Act 1977, as amended by the Criminal Justice (Terrorism and Conspiracy) Act 1998, section 5, has been the subject of several judicial decisions.[159] In *R v Patel*,[160] Patel and others had pleaded guilty or were convicted of conspiracy. The convictions related to two conspiracies to affect unlawful immigration into the UK and the United States. The conviction pertaining to the United States relied upon the extended crime of conspiracy in section 1A. As the judgment notes: 'The plain purpose of that amendment was to give the English courts extra-territorial jurisdiction in relation to conspiracies which are formed or carried out, at least in part, in England and Wales and where the object is the commission of a foreign offence'.[161] One of the questions facing the court was whether the maximum permitted sentence for the conviction relating to the US immigration-related offence was to be solely governed by UK law, or that of the United States. Section 1A itself is silent as to sentence, with section 3 of the Criminal Law Act 1977 governing the question. It provides, in effect, that the maximum sentence for conspiracy is that applying to the substantive offence, and that is the equivalent English offence. The court held that this followed the correct interpretation of section 1A(6), which provided that 'In the application of this Part of this Act to an agreement in the case of which each of the above conditions is satisfied, a reference to an offence is to be read as a reference to what would be the offence in question but for the fact that it is not an offence triable in England and Wales'. The court held:

> That is as it should be. If that were not the construction, and it plainly is, an English defendant might be exposed by s.1A to a greater punishment than he would suffer by committing a wholly English conspiracy if it were the law of the foreign country that a higher maximum was provided. The present case happens to be one where the English maximum is the higher, but that cannot affect the construction of the section. Moreover, the sentence passed in England for a s.1A foreign conspiracy is a sentence which will be served in England. English rules as to its effect will apply. Particularly, English rules as to early release and licence will apply. A prison sentence of the same nominal length in a foreign country might be a very different animal and the English court will normally not be equipped to

Commission on the ground that a miscarriage of justice may have occurred, but on the intervention of Al-Megrahi this did not reach a conclusion: see *Al-Megrahi v HM Advocate* 2009 GWD 29-467. Al-Megrahi was released and permitted to return to Libya on compassionate grounds on 20 August 2009.

159 The leading extraterritorial conspiracy cases of *Somchai Liangsiriprasert v Government of the United States of America and another* [1991] 1 AC 225 and *R v Sansom* [1991] 2 QB 130 have been discussed above.

160 [2009] EWCA Crim 67; the case is mentioned above as an example of the law being extended on an initiatory or subjective basis.

161 Ibid at para 6.

> know in detail what its import is. Those practical considerations reinforce what is the plain construction of the section. The maximum in this case was therefore 14 years.[162]

A further conspiracy case relates to the traffic in drugs. *R v Clough*[163] was an appeal against sentence for conspiracy under section 1A of the Criminal Law Act 1977 and section 20 of the Misuse of Drugs Act 1971. Clough had pleaded guilty to conspiring to supply a class A drug, cocaine, outside the UK. He had been involved in an attempt to export 337 kilograms of the drug from Venezuela to Portugal. He had been sentenced to 18 years' imprisonment. On appeal the sentence was reduced to 17 years, four months.

Relationship-based connection

The second most common type of case where the criminal law is enforced across borders utilises a relationship-based connection. This is in line with the fact that the substantive criminal law is extended across borders on a relationship basis second only to that of territory. One of the leading cases is the only conviction under the War Crimes Act 1991, that of Anthony Sawoniuk. The case did not concern the question of the legal conditions required for the application of section 1 of the 1991 Act, which were not in dispute. The conditions were that the crime be murder, manslaughter or culpable homicide and committed in the theatre of the Second World War between 1 September 1935 and 5 June 1945. It was also necessary that the accused be a British citizen or UK resident from a specified time. Section 1(2) provides that 'No proceedings shall by virtue of this section be brought against any person unless he was on 8th March 1990, or has subsequently become, a British citizen or resident in the United Kingdom, the Isle of Man or any of the Channel Islands'. It was accepted that Sawoniuk was a resident at the required time. The case entailed an appeal against conviction on the basis that the evidence used against Sawoniuk was unreliable, largely because the proceedings were instituted 56 years after they allegedly occurred.[164] This argument was rejected in *R v Sawoniuk*.[165] The court held that:

> Given the unique circumstances of this case and the grave consequences of conviction to the appellant, we have considered with care whether there is any more general ground upon which these convictions should be regarded as unsafe. For reasons already given, we conclude that the jury was in a very advantageous position, having seen the site and heard the evidence, to form

162 Ibid at para 13.
163 [2009] EWCA Crim 1669.
164 See, further, Ormerod, D., 'A Prejudicial View?' (2000) *Criminal Law Review* 452.
165 [2000] 2 Cr App R 220.

> a reliable judgment on count 3. On count 1 we remind ourselves that the conviction rested very largely on the evidence of a witness who was, if his evidence was reliable, standing within feet of the appellant when this murder was committed. It was not a case of an identification made 56 years after the event, but one of contemporaneous recognition to which the witness deposed after that lapse of time. It is not easy to imagine any event which, if witnessed, would impress itself more indelibly on the mind of a 13 year old boy. The jury had to consider whether the witness was honest and reliable. They concluded that he was both. We can see no reason to question the soundness of that judgment. We accordingly dismiss this appeal.[166]

This case also highlights the significant procedural and evidential difficulties attendant to the prosecution of crimes committed across borders.

A second example of the law being enforced on a relationship basis is that of Mohan Singh Kular. He was charged and convicted under section 10 of the Offences Against the Persons Act 1861 following the murder in India of his second wife in 1987. His appeal against conviction was dismissed in *R v Kular (Mohan Singh)*.[167] It was argued on behalf of Kular that the evidence against him was insufficient and that therefore the trial judge should have ordered the proceedings to be stayed, and/or that in consequence the verdict of the jury was unsafe. The Court of Appeal examined the evidence and held that 'The reality of this case is that there was . . . an overwhelming body of evidence against this defendant'.[168]

Another interesting example of the law being enforced with reference to the relationship between the accused and the UK relates to a prosecution for trading in weapons. As in several of the cases above the issue in the case was not the application of the law across borders itself but the appropriate sentence. In *R v Knight*,[169] Knight appealed against sentence having pleaded guilty to a count under the Trade in Goods (Control Order) 2003.[170] This case was the first time

166 Ibid at p 246.

167 2000 WL 33148708.

168 Ibid at para 61. An unsuccessful Scottish prosecution is *HMA v McLeod* (1993), unreported, cited in Hirst, *Jurisdiction and Ambit* (n 7 above) at p 201.

169 [2008] EWCA Crim 478.

170 SI 2003/2765, which has since been revoked and replaced by the Export Control Order 2008, SI 2008/3231. An interesting human rights-related case arising in relation to the Export Control Order 2008 is *R (Zagorski) v Secretary of State for Business, Innovation and Skills* [2010] EWHC 3110 (Admin), where an argument attempting to stop the export of a drug thought to be used in carrying out the death penalty in the United States was rejected. It was agreed that the applicants, two prisoners on death row, were not within the UK's jurisdiction for the purposes of Art 1 of the European Convention on Human Rights. Instead, the applicants relied on the common law, the principle of legality and Art 4 of the Charter of Fundamental Rights of the European Union. It was held that the scope of the Charter was co-extensive with that of the Convention, at para 74.

an offence under the Order had come before the courts. Knight had been knowingly involved in the movement of controlled goods with intent to evade a prohibition relating to their movement between third countries under the Order. Knight had arranged the sale of machine guns from Iran to Kuwait, from his base within the UK. This case is therefore both territorial (under article 3(1) of the Order) and relationship based (under article 3(2)). The licensing scheme under the Order applied to the brokering activities of UK nationals, which included transactions effected outside the UK. Knight had had his application for a licence refused, but continued with the sale of 130 sub-machine guns. On pleading guilty he was sentenced to four years' imprisonment and issued with a confiscation order in the amount of £53,389. He appealed against the custodial element of the sentence. Article 9(4) of the Order provided in regard to sentence that a person guilty on indictment shall be liable to a term of imprisonment not exceeding ten years. The appeal against sentence was dismissed. Interestingly, the Court discussed the purpose of the Order, and its parent legislation, the Export Control Act 2002:

> The legislative purpose is plain enough. Responsible governments were becoming increasingly concerned about the worldwide proliferation of weapons, about supplies of arms, as well as other paramilitary goods, falling into the hands of wicked or irresponsible regimes or groups. Exports from the United Kingdom could be, and indeed were, the subject of controls within the United Kingdom. But to strengthen those controls a licensing regime was extended, amongst other things, to brokering activities of nationals which included transactions in restricted goods or in controlled goods such as arms, even where those transactions were to be effected outside the United Kingdom.[171]

In light of the relatively high-profile nature of the fight against the sexual exploitation of children abroad it would be reasonable to conclude that a considerable number of prosecutions have taken place. The number of prosecutions, however, is relatively low. Whilst it is difficult to ascertain precise statistics, the non-governmental organisation, ECPAT UK, stated in a 2008 report that 'Less than half a dozen cases have been prosecuted in the UK since 1997'. It compares this with certain other countries noting that there have been over 65 prosecutions in the United States and 28 in Australia.[172] One example of a UK prosecution is in regard to the rape of a 16-year-old de facto stepdaughter of the accused in *R v R (Peter)*.[173] This was an appeal against conviction for rape that had allegedly occurred in Barbados. The issue on appeal was straightforward – whether section 7 of the Sex Offenders Act 1997 applied on a retrospective

171 [2008] EWCA Crim 478 at para 3.
172 Beddoe, *Return to Sender – British Child Sex Offenders Abroad* (n 143 above), at p 7.
173 [2001] 1 WLR 1314.

basis, as the date of the alleged rape was prior to the entry into force of the section. It was argued on behalf of the appellant that section 7 'did not come into effect until 1 September 1997. Thus, the alleged rape in question, which took place between 16 April and 8 May 1997, rendered that offence non-justiciable in the UK. There is no provision in the Act to give the new power retrospective effect'.[174] The Crown acknowledged that the conviction was a nullity and quashed it.

In *R v Towner*,[175] a sentence of eight years' imprisonment was imposed on the accused after he pleaded guilty in June 2001 to 14 counts under the Sex Offenders Act 1997. Towner had engaged in the abuse of children in Cambodia; his activities were uncovered when his wife found photographic evidence on his computer.[176]

In January 2006 Alexander Kilpatrick became the first person to be jailed in the UK under the Sexual Offenders Act 2001. As part of his sentence Kilpatrick, who was imprisoned for the abuse of children in Africa, was banned from Africa, Thailand, Cambodia, Goa and Costa Rica.[177]

A final case to be noted is the conviction of Dean Hardy in April 2009. Hardy was sentenced to six years in prison after admitting, *inter alia*, four counts of taking indecent photographs of children and one count of possessing indecent photographs of children. He was charged under the Sexual Offences Act 2003. Again, the evidence leading to the conviction was found on Hardy's computer, when a hand appearing in one of the photographs was identified in court as belonging to the accused.[178]

Crime-centric connection

Even rarer than the law being enforced across borders on the basis of the relationship between the accused and the UK are cases where there is no connection at all in the normal sense of the word. Only one case enforced on a crime-centric basis can be identified, that of Farayadi Sawar Zardad. In 2005, after a second trial, Zardad was convicted in London of conspiracy to commit torture and take hostages in Afghanistan and sentenced to 20 years' imprisonment.[179] Zardad was charged with conspiracy to torture and conspiracy to take hostages contrary to section 1(1) of the Criminal Law Act 1977. Zardad was an Afghan national,

174 Ibid at p 1317.

175 Cited in Hirst, *Jurisdiction and Ambit* (n 7 above), at p 271.

176 See http://www.independent.co.uk/news/uk/crime/paedophile-first-to-be-jailed-under-sex-tourism-law-674632.html, accessed 23 May 2011.

177 See http://news.bbc.co.uk/1/hi/uk/4768562.stm, accessed 23 May 2011.

178 See http://www.telegraph.co.uk/news/uknews/law-and-order/5197508/Paedophile-caught-out-by-the-freckles-on-his-hands.html, accessed 23 May 2011.

179 See the Crown Prosecution Service's Press Release, 18 July 2005, at http://cps.gov.uk/news/press_releases/135_05/, accessed 23 May 2011.

and his victims were Afghani.[180] The Crown Prosecution Service stated: that it 'believes this is the first time in any country where offences of torture and hostage taking have been prosecuted in circumstances such as this. It is even more unusual for an English court to try matters when neither defendant nor witnesses are British subjects'.[181]

Double criminality and other cases

The final type of case under this head does not concern the enforcement of the UK law at all. Rather, it involves cases where UK courts consider the question of whether the law would have applied in the abstract. Most of these cases arise where courts consider the double criminality requirement in extradition. The question is whether the law would be applicable in the UK if it (the UK) was in the position of the state seeking extradition. The leading cases here include *R (Al-Fawwaz) v Governor of Brixton Prison*,[182] *R v Bow Street Metropolitan Stipendiary Magistrate and others ex p Pinochet Ugarte (No 3)*[183] and *Norris v Government of the United States of America*.[184] In *Al-Fawwaz*, it was stated: 'I would interpret "within jurisdiction" as including but being wider than "in the territory" of the foreign state. The question is thus whether the conduct complained of will be triable in the United States and if that conduct were transposed to England, would be triable in England'.[185] In that case, the crime was conspiracy to murder. Lord Hutton, in the House of Lords, stated:

> In the present case it is common ground that the United States of America has extraterritorial jurisdiction over the alleged offence and that the United Kingdom also has extraterritorial jurisdiction over the alleged offence. Therefore, in my opinion, no difficulty arises in respect of transposition. The offence is triable within the jurisdiction of the United States of America and, as transposed, is triable, as section 26 of the 1870 Act requires, 'within English jurisdiction'.[186]

In *Pinochet*, the House of Lords was faced with the question of the 'material date' in regard to the double criminality requirement and the existence of the crime of torture in UK law. In particular, it had to decide whether the material date was the date at which the extradition request was made or the date at which

180 See also House of Commons Briefing Papers, Universal Jurisdiction, 25 March 2010, cited at http://www.parliament.uk/briefingpapers/commons/lib/research/briefings/snia-05422.pdf, accessed 23 May 2011.

181 See n 179 above.

182 [2001] UKHL 69.

183 [2000] 1 AC 147.

184 [2008] UKHL 16.

185 [2001] UKHL 69 at para 31.

186 [2008] UKHL 16 at para 71.

the alleged torture took place. The court held that it was the latter, thus making inapplicable a number of the charges against Pinochet that preceded the entry into force of section 134 of the Criminal Justice 1998.

In *Norris*, the question facing the House of Lords was whether the US crime of price fixing had an equivalent in English law. The court held that it did not, and as the double criminality requirement was not met, Norris could not be extradited for that crime.[187]

187 The circumstances in *Norris* will be discussed again in Chapter 4 in relation to his challenge against extradition on the basis of his human rights.

4 UK human rights law across borders

The issues

A number of problems or issues surround the application of UK human rights law across borders.[1] As with the criminal law, these issues can be examined from four different perspectives: the UK, the victim of a human rights violation, third states and international law. From the UK's perspective the issues surrounding the application of human rights law across borders are materially distinct from those arising in the field of the criminal law. The difference arises from the basic fact that in the vast majority of cases the UK itself, in its many public manifestations, is the respondent. In the criminal sphere, of course, the UK is the prosecutor. On this general level, then, the application of the law (judicially) is an issue from the UK perspective because it is being argued that it has violated human rights. Clearly, this is simplistic. The UK has willingly subscribed to the European Convention on Human Rights and has enacted the Human Rights Act 1998 ('HRA'). It has enabled, and in a sense welcomed, litigation against it on the basis of human rights law. The UK Parliament has almost always abided by decisions of the European Court of Human Rights (ECtHR) and domestic courts when those decisions have gone against it. It is obliged to abide by the decisions of the ECtHR under Article 46 of the Convention. Therefore, an application of human rights law across borders judicially can be seen as a mechanism through which the UK polices itself and ensures that all emanations of the state – executive, legislative and judicial – act in conformity with human rights.

Countering the view that litigation is welcomed by the UK is the fact that it has defended itself vigorously in certain human rights cases where the law has been applied across borders. An example is *R (Smith) (FC) v Secretary of State for Defence and another*,[2] where the Government appealed a Court of Appeal ruling which held, in part, that the HRA applied to areas in Iraq outside

1 Some of the issues identified here form the basis of the criticisms of the law discussed in more depth in Chapter 5, as is the case with those mentioned in Chapter 3.

2 [2010] UKSC 29 (hereinafter *Smith*). See, further, Milanovic, M., 'Applicability of the ECHR to British soldiers in Iraq' (2011) 70(1) *Cambridge Law Journal* 4.

military bases and other areas where the army had control. The Supreme Court overturned the Court of Appeal on this point, holding in effect that the HRA ceased to apply when British troops serving abroad step off a British base. Whilst this case will be examined below, it is useful here to highlight the opposition to the extension of the law to areas outside military bases and the reaction to the judgment. Mr Eadie, for the Government, argued in *Smith* that 'When, however, [Smith] was not within territory controlled by the United Kingdom, he was not within article 1 jurisdiction. His position in those circumstances did not fall within any of the recognised exceptions to the general principle that article 1 jurisdiction was territorial'.[3] This is an unequivocal statement that the UK believes that the law did not extend as far as it was suggested. One reaction to the case was that of the Chief of the Defence Staff, Air Chief Marshall Sir Jock Stirrup, who stated:

> I am pleased that the Supreme Court has upheld the Government's appeal. This outcome is not about denying rights to our people, it is about ensuring that we have a clear and workable set of rules under which they can carry out their demanding and dangerous work. Within that context, commanders at all levels are committed to the safety of the men and women they lead. We will continue to do everything we can to keep our people from harm by providing the best possible equipment and training.[4]

From this it can be discerned that the issues surrounding the application of human rights law across borders from a UK perspective are complex. Whilst the UK has willingly acceded to the Convention, enacted the HRA and agreed to abide by decisions of the ECtHR, it also has argued for the limitation of the Convention and the HRA, territorially and more generally.

There are two possible problems surrounding the application of human rights law across borders from the perspective of the victim; both relate to uncertainty. The first arises from the fact that a *sine qua non* of the application of law is that the UK must have acted abroad or is proposing to affect the rendition of a person outside of its territory. As will be discussed below, these represent the two forms of the application of human rights law across borders, on a wholly extraterritorial basis and through extradition and expulsion. Clearly, acting abroad may be at odds with the rules protecting the global system of sovereign territorial states. This is certainly the case if the exercise of authority is within the boundaries of a third state and not agreed to by that state. This concerns an individual not because it may infringe international law but because that he or she may not have reasonably expected to be affected by UK actions in the first

3 [2010] UKSC 29 at para 32.

4 30 June 2010, cited at http://www.mod.uk/DefenceInternet/DefenceNews/DefencePolicyAndBusiness/HumanRightsConventionDoesNotApplyToMilitaryOnOverseasOperations.htm, accessed 24 May 2011.

instance. The problem is the irregularity if not illegality of UK action – and the possible human rights violation arising therefrom. A further and more particular issue surrounding the application of human rights law across borders is the remoteness of the alleged violation from the UK itself and, relatedly, the test employed in coming to a decision as to whether the law in fact applies to the situation. As will be seen below, there is a considerable body of jurisprudence surrounding this question and the courts are developing tests which condition and limit the application of human rights law abroad. From the perspective of the individual, there is again uncertainty – not in regard to a human rights violation in the first instance, but whether the UK will be responsible for it.

From the perspective of third states the application of UK human rights law across borders illustrates and engenders several issues. In the application of human rights law abroad the UK may be usurping or interfering with the ability of the territorial state to address a possible human rights violation within it – even if it is committed by the UK itself. As noted and will be discussed further below, the conditions that can lead to the application of human rights law across borders on a wholly extraterritorial basis may entail the violation of a third state's sovereignty and territorial integrity. A further possible problem is that the UK may apply an entitlement to an individual within a third state which, were it able to act itself, that state would not countenance, for example such rights as the freedom of expression and aspects of the right to family and private life. As was noted by Lord Rodger in the House of Lords in *R (Al-Skeini) v Secretary of State for Defence*,[5] the ECtHR's jurisprudence on such matters as the death penalty, sex discrimination, homosexuality and transsexuals 'may reflect the values of the contracting states, but which certainly does not reflect those in many other parts of the world'.[6] These rights can reasonably be thought to be contingent upon context and are not universal (this will be discussed further in Chapter 5). Such imposition of rights could give rise to accusations of legal imperialism, or chauvinism. In regard to the application of human rights law across borders in extradition and expulsion cases, the issue arises of the frustration of criminal justice in the extradition-seeking third state. An accused or convicted person may successfully argue that an extradition or expulsion will result in his human rights being violated in that third state, with the result that the rendition is prevented or that conditions are imposed.

From the perspective of public international law the application of human rights law across borders illustrates two problems. First, it evidences the fact that international and regional human rights law, and any existing territorial system, are not operating as they should. Ideally, where an alleged human rights violation occurs outside the UK, and the state where it occurs is unable for

5 [2007] UKHL 26 (hereinafter *Al-Skeini*). The High Court's decision in the case is reported at [2004] EWHC (Admin) 2911, [2005] 2 WLR 1401, and the Court of Appeal's decision at [2005] EWCA 1609, [2006] HRLR 7.

6 [2007] UKHL 26 at para 78.

whatever reason to act, the machinery within international law should address the situation. The application of human rights law may also interfere with or frustrate the operation of existing regimes – if not in the present then in the long term.

A second international legal issue raised by the application of UK human rights law across borders is that it can occur in a state in which the UK has effective control of territory or individuals. This is a practical and legal problem for that state, and may mean that the UK has acted in violation of international law. As noted in Chapter 2, the most fundamental tenets of public international law protect the sovereignty and territorial integrity of all states. Even in regard to extradition and expulsion cases it is possible to argue that to apply the HRA and Convention to circumstances within third states amounts to an interference with their sovereignty and territorial integrity since such an application of the law necessarily entails an appraisal of the situation within those third states. Arguably, appraisal can be tantamount to interference.

History

The history of the application of UK human rights law across borders is, compared to the criminal law, very short. The HRA fully entered into force on 2 October 2000. Human rights per se had no direct and immediate place in UK law prior to that, although, of course, they had had some effect previously in large part through the operation of the Convention, which itself entered into force in 1953, with the UK as a founding party. A history of the application of human rights abroad, therefore, must include discussion of the Convention. There is a relatively long and complex body of ECtHR jurisprudence in the area, which will be discussed below. Here it is sufficient to note the central importance of Article 1 of the Convention, limiting its application to persons 'within the jurisdiction' of state parties. The jurisprudence examining the meaning of this term and thus the scope of the Convention began with *X v Germany*[7] in 1965. The case law in this area continues to develop. The enactment of the HRA has, in a sense, heightened the relevance of the UK's membership of the Convention. There exists a close relationship between the two instruments, which will be discussed below. Here it should be noted that the jurisprudence of the ECtHR has materially and directly influenced the development of UK human rights law, in large part because UK courts must take it into account under section 2 of the HRA. A discussion of the territorial application of the Convention, therefore, is the first step in analysing the precise application of the HRA with the (very much living) history of the Convention being also a history of the application of UK human rights law across borders.

7 (1965) 8 Yb ECHR 158 (Commission).

The current law

The Convention

The Convention is a product of the Council of Europe, which is governed by the Statute of the Council of Europe 1949. Shortly after the conclusion and entry into force of the Convention the issue of its spatial application arose. Following *X v Germany*,[8] decided in 1965, a long series of decisions, discussed below, have considered the issue. It should be noted here that in spite of this jurisprudence, indeed because of it, the law remains unclear. However, the starting point of an examination of the territorial scope of the Convention is not the ECtHR's jurisprudence; rather it is the Convention itself. The Convention imposes obligations on the state parties to it and creates and governs the ECtHR. Article 1 provides that 'The High Contracting Parties shall secure to everyone within their jurisdiction the rights and freedoms defined in Section I of the Convention'.[9] The precise meaning of the word 'jurisdiction' is therefore critical. Possible meanings include 'territory', 'residence' and 'control'. The drafting history of Article 1 is illuminating. As discussed in *Bankovic v Belgium et al*,[10] the provision in draft form referred to persons residing within the territory of state parties. This was thought to be too narrow and a suggestion was made to change it to 'living in' the territory.[11] 'Living in' was not adopted, as the *travaux préparatoires* state:

> The Assembly draft had extended the benefits of the Convention to 'all persons residing within the territories of the signatory States'. It seemed to the Committee that the term 'residing' might be considered too restrictive. It was felt that there were good grounds for extending the benefits of the Convention to all persons in the territories of the signatory States, even those who could not be considered as residing there in the legal sense of the word. The Committee therefore replaced the term 'residing' by the words 'within their jurisdiction' which are also contained in Article 2 of the Draft Covenant of the United Nations Commission.[12]

Apart from one comment by a representative in the drafting process to the effect that the obligations arising under the Convention apply to all persons within the territory of state parties, the *travaux préparatoires* fail to refer to the issue in

8 Ibid.
9 See, generally for the extraterritorial application of human rights, Coomans, F. and Kamminga, M.T. (eds), *Extraterritorial Application of Human Rights Treaties*, Intersentia, Mortsel, 2004.
10 (2001) 11 BHRC 435 (hereinafter *Bankovic*).
11 As stated in *Smith* at para 303, per Lord Collins.
12 Council of Europe, *Collected Edition of the* Travaux Préparatoires *of the European Convention on Human Rights*, Vol III, Nijhoff, The Hague, 1975, at p 260.

any more depth.[13] Therefore, whilst the meaning of 'within their jurisdiction' is wider than residence, it is necessary to turn to the case law under the Convention for greater clarity.[14]

Three preliminary points

Prior to discussing the jurisprudence of the ECtHR, three preliminary points need to be made. The first is in regard to the nature of Article 1 itself; the second relates to the unity of the rights under the Convention; and the third concerns the two forms of human rights law applied across borders.

Article 1 is a provision unlike those containing substantive rights in the sense that it is fixed in its meaning. It is well known that the Convention has been held to be a 'living instrument'.[15] The Court has held that 'the Convention is a living instrument which, as the Commission rightly stressed, must be interpreted in the light of present-day conditions'.[16] The Court has also held that the Convention can evolve over time to include, for example, protection from corporal punishment, as in *Tyrer v UK*,[17] and the rights of post-operative transsexuals, as in *Goodwin v UK*.[18] However, it has been held that Article 1 is excluded from this evolutionary process. As stated in *Smith*, '*Bankovic* made it clear that article 1 was not to be interpreted as a "living instrument" in accordance with changing conditions'.[19] The position relating to the territorial application of the Convention in 1953, then, is that which applies today.

The second preliminary point is that the rights within the Convention apply either *in toto* or not at all. Suggestions that a certain right may apply to an event or circumstance but not the whole Convention will not be countenanced. As Lord Browne stated in *Al-Skeini*:

> There is one other central objection to the creation of the wide basis of jurisdiction here contended for by the appellants under the rubric 'control and authority', going beyond that arising in any of the narrowly recognised categories already discussed and yet short of that arising from the effective control of territory within the Council of Europe area. *Bankovic* (and later

13 *Bankovic*, at paras 20 and 21.

14 Article 56 of the Convention also relates to its spatial application in that it entitles a state party to declare that the Convention is to extend to a territory over which it is responsible. This was at issue in *R (Quark Fishing Ltd) v Foreign Secretary* [2005] UKHL 57. Interestingly, for our purposes, it was held in the case that ss 6 and 7 of the HRA do not extend to territories where such a declaration has been made.

15 The 'living instrument' approach has its roots in *Tyrer v UK* (1979–80) 2 EHRR 1. See, generally, Mowbray, A., 'The Creativity of the European Court of Human Rights' [2005] 5 *Human Rights Law Review* 1.

16 *Tyrer v UK* (1979–80) 2 EHRR 1 at para 31.

17 Ibid.

18 (2002) 35 EHRR 18.

19 *Smith*, at para 303, citing *Bankovic*, at paras 64–4, per Lord Collins.

Assanidze) stands, as stated, for the indivisible nature of article 1 jurisdiction: it cannot be 'divided and tailored.[20]

This has the effect of significantly limiting the possibility of the Convention applying across borders. It follows from the impossibility of ensuring the application of all rights – and especially positive obligations under the Convention – in areas outside the regular territory of state parties.

The third preliminary point is that the application of UK human rights law across borders takes two forms – termed here as 'extradition and expulsion' and 'wholly extraterritorial'. Both of these applications have arisen in the consideration of the scope of the Convention.[21] The first is more long-standing and occurs where an individual within the territory of a state party argues that his or her extradition or expulsion may lead to a violation of his or her human rights in the requesting or receiving state. This type of case is termed 'extradition and expulsion' for the obvious reason that it arises in the course of forcibly removing a person from a state by one of these means. It has also been called a 'foreign case'.[22] The law is applied in a pre-emptive sense, in that an alleged human rights violation has not yet occurred. The second form of application arises when an individual is affected by the actions of a state occurring outside its territory, and consideration is taken in the courts of that state of possible human rights violations arising as a consequence. This application is termed 'wholly extraterritorial' in that both the alleged victim and *situs* of violation are outside the territory of the state at the relevant time. Here the law is generally applied in an *ex post facto* sense – arguments are made that one's human rights have been infringed, not that they could be in the future. Of the two types of application the second finds considerably more support in academic writings as a 'true' form of the extraterritorial application of the law. However, it is clear that the first also entails the application of law outside borders. The applicant or putative victim is within the territory of the state applying human rights law, not abroad, but the law is applied across borders nonetheless. The original and still leading

20 *Al-Skeini*, at para. 128, as cited by Lord Phillips in *Smith* at para. 27.

21 It must be noted that certain writers believe that 'extradition and expulsion cases' are not properly included as a part of the law applied across borders, or of the corpus of extraterritorially applicable human rights law. Agreeing with the present author is Miller, S., 'Revisiting extraterritorial jurisdiction: a territorial justification for extraterritorial jurisdiction under the European Convention' (2009) *European Journal of International Law* 1223 at p 1242, mentioned in Chapter 5. Disagreeing with this view are Coomans and Kamminga, *Extraterritorial Application of Human Rights Treaties* (n 9 above), at pp 3–4, who suggest three types: where a state has effective control over an area, where a state exercises power and authority over persons by abducting or detaining them, and 'perhaps in certain other extraterritorial situations such as extraterritorial killings not preceded by arrest'.

22 By Lord Bingham in *R (Ullah) v Special Adjudicator* [2004] UKHL 26 at para 9 (hereinafter *Ullah*). The case is discussed below. Extradition and expulsion have not been differentiated in the case law of the ECtHR for the purposes of jurisdiction. This was accepted by Lord Steyn in *Ullah*, at para 33.

ECtHR extradition and expulsion authority is *Soering v United Kingdom*.[23] Here it was held that Soering's extradition from the UK to West Virginia in the United States would breach Article 3 of the Convention in that he would probably spend a considerable time on death row. The judgment considered the question of the applicability of the law because the possible future human rights violation would occur outside the UK and in a non-state party to the Convention. The case (and all similar cases) entails an application of law across borders in that it inevitably and necessarily involves an '*assessment of conditions in the requesting country*'.[24] The human rights standards under the Convention and HRA are used to measure or test those conditions. The extraditing or expelling state party may be complicit in a human rights violation because of the conditions in the destination state in the sense that, but for the extradition or expulsion, it would not occur. The Court in *Soering* stated that 'It would hardly be compatible with the underlying values of the Convention . . . were a contracting state knowingly to surrender a fugitive to another state where there were substantial grounds for believing that he would be in danger of being subjected to torture . . . Extradition in such circumstances . . . would plainly be contrary to the spirit and intendment of [Article 3]'.[25] It should be noted that not all the arguments made in extradition and expulsion cases relate to conditions in the destination state. Some cases argue that, for example, the removal of a person from the UK will interfere with his or her Article 8 rights in that he or she is separated from his or her family in the UK. In such cases, no assessment of foreign conditions is made, and thus the law is not applied across borders to the facts in the third state. Cases such as these may, however, discuss the germane law and will to some extent be examined below. Generally, however, cases that involve the application of the HRA and the Convention within third states (in the form of the assessment of conditions outside UK territory) will comprise the subject of discussion as one of the two forms of the application of human rights law across borders.

ECtHR jurisprudence – extradition and expulsion cases[26]

Since 1989 ECtHR jurisprudence has built upon the principle set down in *Soering* that an extradition or expulsion may entail a violation of human rights on account of the conditions within the requesting or receiving state. A number

23 (1989) 11 EHRR 439.

24 Ibid at para 91 (emphasis added). See also *Chahal v UK* (1997) 23 EHRR 413. Article 3(2) of the Convention against Torture and Other Cruel, Inhuman or Degrading Treatment or Punishment 1984, 1465 UNTS 85, specifically mandates the consideration of circumstances in a foreign state where there are allegations that torture may result from an extradition or expulsion.

25 (1989) 11 EHRR 439 at para 89.

26 Sections of this chapter have their basis in an article by the present author, Arnell, P., 'Human Rights Abroad' (2007) 16(2) *Nottingham Law Journal* 1.

of the leading cases have originated from the UK. A non-UK case containing a clear statement of the law in regard to Article 3 and one which explicitly makes the point that in extradition and expulsion cases human rights law is applied across borders to situations in third states, is *Kaboulov v Ukraine*.[27] It is worth citing the statement in full:

> Extradition by a Contracting State may engage this State's responsibility under Article 3 of the Convention, where substantial grounds have been shown for believing that the person in question would, if extradited, face a real risk of being subjected to treatment contrary to Article 3 in the receiving country. Such responsibility inevitably involves an assessment of conditions in the requesting country and their compliance with the standards of Article 3 of the Convention. To undertake such an assessment the Court examines all the material placed before it, or, if necessary, material obtained *proprio motu* from various international, domestic, governmental and NGO sources. The Court must examine the foreseeable consequences of sending the applicant to the receiving country, bearing in mind the general situation there and his personal circumstances. At the same time, where the available sources describe a general situation, an applicant's specific allegations in a particular case require corroboration by other evidence. Ill-treatment must attain a minimum level of severity, which is relative and depends on all the circumstances of the case, such as the nature and context of the treatment or punishment, the manner and method of its execution, its duration and its physical or mental effects, if it is to fall within the scope of Article 3. When assessing conditions of detention, account has to be taken of their cumulative effects as well as the applicant's specific allegations and detention duration. Furthermore, diplomatic assurances do not absolve the Court from the obligation to examine whether they in practice provided a sufficient guarantee that the applicant would be protected against the risk of ill-treatment prohibited by the Convention.[28]

In addition to Article 3, other articles of the Convention are capable of forming an argument against extradition or expulsion. Indeed, the evolution of the law in this area has led to an increase in the number of articles being relied upon by applicants in extradition and expulsion cases and the acceptance by the ECtHR of the possibility that such arguments may be successful.

In *Soering* itself, an argument was made on the basis of Article 6 – protecting the right to a fair trial – as well as Article 3. The Court held that the lack of legal aid in certain circumstances may affect a person's Article 6 rights in the United States: 'The Court does not exclude that an issue might exceptionally be raised under Article 6 by an extradition decision in circumstances where the

27 *Kaboulov v Ukraine* (2010) 50 EHRR 39.
28 Ibid at paras 107–8 (references omitted).

fugitive has suffered or risks suffering a flagrant denial of a fair trial in the requesting country'.[29] The Court held that in this case no such exceptional circumstances existed. Twenty years after *Soering* was the case of *Saadi v Italy*.[30] Saadi alleged that his deportation would expose him to the risk of being subjected to treatment contrary to Article 3, a flagrant denial of justice under Article 6, and an infringement of his right to respect for his family life protected by Article 8. He also argued that it would entail a violation of the safeguards protecting the expulsion of aliens under Article 1 of the Seventh Protocol to the Convention. However, the ECtHR did not make a decision on articles other than Article 3 because it held that the article would be violated if Saadi's deportation order was enforced.[31] The case is notable, however, for the UK's intervention in an attempt to have the jurisprudence in this area change direction. The UK argued, *inter alia*, that the ECtHR's decision in the previous case of *Chahal v UK*[32] required to be re-visited. The decision-making process, the UK argued, should take account of the threat presented by the person to be deported and a weighing up of Article 3 rights of the applicant against the Article 2 rights of the wider community. The UK also emphasised that state parties may obtain diplomatic assurances that an applicant would not be subjected to treatment contrary to the Convention.[33] These arguments were rejected by the ECtHR, and the principle that the prohibition of extradition and expulsion where there are substantial grounds for believing there is a real risk of treatment contrary to Article 3 was confirmed.

An ECtHR case that did entertain arguments against expulsion on an article additional to Article 3 was *Boultif v Switzerland*,[34] where Article 8 was considered. *Boultif* is interesting because it is both 'foreign' and 'domestic', containing arguments based on conditions within Switzerland, the deporting country, and the putative destination, Algeria. After discussing the facts and law, the Court stated: 'the Convention does not guarantee the right of an alien to enter or to reside in a particular country. However, the removal of a person from a country where close members of his family are living may amount to an infringement of the right to respect for family life as guaranteed in Article 8 § 1 of the Convention'.[35] This was the domestic aspect of the case and did not, therefore, entail the application of law across borders. In regard to the foreign aspect, the ECtHR went on to hold that the refusal of Switzerland to grant a

29 *Soering*, at para 113.
30 (2009) 49 EHRR 30.
31 Ibid at para 160.
32 (1997) 23 EHRR 413.
33 (2009) 49 EHRR 30 at paras 122–3. See Moeckli, D., '*Saadi v Italy*: The Rules of the Game Have *Not* Changed' [2008] 8 HRLR 534. See below on the question of non-torture assurances.
34 (2001) 33 EHRR 50.
35 Ibid, at para 39, citing *Moustaquim v Belgium*, 18 February 1991 (Series A, no 193), at p 18, para 36.

residence permit to Boultif, an Algerian, gave rise to a breach of his Article 8 rights (he was married to a Swiss national). Amongst the reasons for this was the fact that the applicant's wife would find herself in Algeria. The court stated that it would: 'also consider the seriousness of the difficulties which the spouse would be likely to encounter in the applicant's country of origin, although the mere fact that a person might face certain difficulties in accompanying her or his spouse cannot in itself preclude expulsion'.[36]

In *Bader v Sweden*,[37] the ECtHR considered Articles 2, 3 and 6 in an extradition and expulsion case. Here deportation from Sweden to Syria was opposed by a family of applicants. Amongst the arguments against deportation was one based on Articles 2 and 3 on account of one applicant having been tried and convicted *in absentia* for a crime for which the death penalty was applicable. The ECtHR held, citing *Öcalan v Turkey*,[38] that 'it also follows from the requirement in Article 2 § 1 that the deprivation of life be pursuant to the "execution of a sentence of a court", . . . and that the most rigorous standards of fairness are observed in the criminal proceedings both at first instance and on appeal'.[39] The Court continued:

> to impose a death sentence on a person after an unfair trial would generate, in circumstances where there exists a real possibility that the sentence will be enforced, a significant degree of human anguish and fear, bringing the treatment within the scope of Art.3 of the Convention. In this connection it should also be noted that the Court has acknowledged that an issue might exceptionally be raised under Art.6 of the Convention by an extradition decision in circumstances where the fugitive has suffered or risks suffering a flagrant denial of a fair trial in the requesting country. It follows that an issue may arise under Arts 2 and 3 of the Convention if a contracting state deports an alien who has suffered or risks suffering a flagrant denial of a fair trial in the receiving State, the outcome of which was or is likely to be the death penalty.[40]

It should be noted that the position of extradition and expulsion and capital punishment has evolved since *Bader*. In *Al Saadoon and Mufdhi v UK*,[41] the ECtHR held that an interpretation of Article 3 as prohibiting capital punishment was no longer incorrect even though it is permissible under Article 2(1).

The judgment in *Al Saadoon*[42] on its merits is relevant for our present purpose of describing the evolution of the law in the area. The admissibility decision[43]

36 (2001) 33 EHRR 50 at para 48.
37 (2008) 46 EHRR 13.
38 (2005) 41 EHRR 45.
39 (2008) 46 EHRR 13 at para 43.
40 Ibid.
41 (2010) 51 EHRR 9 (hereinafter *Al Saadoon*).
42 Ibid.

in the case is also germane – being an instance whether the ECtHR applied the Convention on a wholly extraterritorial basis, which will be discussed below. The facts giving rise to *Al Saadoon* were that the applicants were arrested and held by UK forces in Iraq following the 2003 invasion. In May 2006 they were reclassified from 'security' detainees to 'criminal' detainees by the British authorities. The Iraqi High Tribunal, set up under Iraqi law to try Iraqi nationals and residents accused of war crimes, crimes against humanity and genocide, sought the transfer of the applicants. The decision to transfer the applicants from UK custody to the Iraqi authorities was challenged by way of judicial review in the Divisional Court. It held the transfer lawful[44] and the Court of Appeal[45] dismissed the applicants' appeal. The applicants were refused leave to appeal to the House of Lords, and subsequently complained to the ECtHR. They argued that their transfer to Iraqi custody gave rise to breaches of Articles 2, 3 and 6, and Article 1 of the Thirteenth Protocol (abolishing capital punishment). As they had been transferred to Iraqi custody in spite of an interim measure under rule 39 of the ECtHR's Rules of Court, the applicants also argued that there had been a breach of Articles 13 and 34 (right to a remedy and right of individual petition).

The ECtHR held that there had been a violation of Article 3. It stated that there was a real risk of the applicants being subjected to the death penalty and executed if transferred. This, together with the evolution of the position in regard to capital punishment, gave rise to a violation of Article 3. Further, the Court noted that the UK was obliged under Article 2 and Article 1 of the Thirteenth Protocol not to enter into any arrangement or agreement which involved it detaining persons with a view to transferring them to stand trial on capital charges. The ECtHR held that the UK had failed to take proper account of its obligations under these articles, but that there was no need to decide whether there had been a violation of them. In regard to Article 6 the Court reiterated the point that a violation may exceptionally arise through an extradition or expulsion decision where there was a risk of a flagrant breach, and then accepted the views of the Divisional Court and the Court of Appeal that this had not been established. Finally, the ECtHR held that there had been a violation of Articles 13 and 34. Overall, *Al Saadoon* is notable for being the first time the ECtHR had become seized of a question arising out of the actions of the British forces in Iraq. Further, the decision in regard to the transfer of the applicants from British custody to that of the Iraqi authorities is noteworthy for its extension of Article 3 to capital punishment, and perhaps even more so for its application of the law relating to extraditions and expulsions to an area itself outside the UK.

43 *Al Saadoon v United Kingdom (Admissibility)* (2009) 49 EHRR SE11.

44 *R (Al-Saadoon) v Secretary of State for Defence* [2008] EWHC Civ 3098.

45 [2009] EWCA Civ 7.

A final case to be noted builds upon aspects of the accepted arguments based on Article 3, *Ahmad v United Kingdom (Admissibility)*.[46] In *Ahmad*, several arguments were advanced by four applicants (one being Abu Hamza, mentioned in Chapter 3) in this conjoined case against extradition to the United States to face terrorist-related charges. The arguments included that the applicants could be designated 'enemy-combatants' by the American authorities and thus tried outside the regular criminal court structure, that they may be at risk of rendition to a third country, that the diplomatic assurances given by the United States could be broken, that evidence used against them could have been secured with the use of torture, and that the length and conditions of their possible imprisonment were in violation of human rights. The applicants also raised the issue of plea-bargaining in the United States – something that will be discussed below in relation to the case of Gary McKinnon. In support of their arguments against extradition the applicants relied on Articles 2, 3, 5, 6, 8 and 14. The ECtHR accepted certain of their arguments and declared the case partially admissible, in particular in regard to the condition of post-trial detention and the possible length and nature of sentences imposed upon the applicants if convicted. In regard to the former the ECtHR stated in regard to three of the applicants who were at real risk of being detained in the ADX Florence 'supermax' prison that:

> the Court considers that these complaints raise serious questions of fact and law which are of such complexity that their determination should depend on an examination on the merits. They cannot, therefore, be considered manifestly ill-founded within the meaning of art.35(3) of the Convention. The Court therefore declares admissible the applicants' complaints based on art. 3 in respect of their possible detention at ADX Florence.[47]

Amongst the considerations highlighted by the applicants was the length of solitary confinement, spartan prison cells and the nature of the 'step-down' programme under which the conditions in which prisoners were held would be relaxed over time and with good behaviour. In regard to the length of the sentences the applicants argued that if convicted they would be given life or consecutive sentences approaching 75 years. Whilst the Court accepted that a life sentence did not in itself give rise to a breach of Article 3 (referring to *Kafkaris v Cyprus*[48]) it did alight on the issue of the reducibility of sentence. The applicants argued that the mechanisms stated to exist by the US Government under which a sentence could be reduced could not, in fact, be met by, or would

46 (2010) 51 EHRR SE6. See Foster, S., '*Ahmad v United Kingdom (Admissibility)* (24027/07): extradition, prison conditions and the European Convention on Human Rights 1950' (2010) 16 *Coventry Law Journal* 30.
47 (2010) 51 EHRR SE6 at para 146. The Court held that the argument was not admissible under Arts 6 and 8.
48 (2009) 49 EHRR 35.

not be applied to, the applicants. The Court accepted that the applicants' case was admissible on this point. A decision on the merits is pending.

ECtHR jurisprudence – wholly extraterritorial cases

The second form of human rights law applied across borders is termed wholly extraterritorial. As with extradition and expulsion cases there is a considerable body of ECtHR jurisprudence concerning it. Unfortunately, this case law is generally opaque.[49] Further, the law is still evolving – a case discussed below, *R (Al-Skeini) v Secretary of State for Defence*,[50] is presently pending decision by the ECtHR. The first clear statements by Convention organs on the application of the Convention across borders were made in cases and admissibility decisions concerning northern Cyprus. These arose following Turkey's invasion in 1974 and, *inter alia*, relate to the treatment of Greek Cypriots in the north of the island. In the *Cyprus v Turkey* ruling in May 1975, the Commission held that state agents 'bring any other persons or property within the jurisdiction of that State, to the extent that they exercise authority over such persons or property'.[51] In the first case in which the ECtHR itself was concerned with northern Cyprus, *Loizidou v Turkey (Preliminary Objections)*,[52] three sets of circumstances were held to fall within the jurisdiction of a state party even though they occurred outside its territory. These were a pending extradition and expulsion, the production of effects outside a state's territory by actions of its agents, and the exercise of effective control over an area outside its territory by agents of a state.[53] It was held in *Loizidou* that the acts of the northern Cypriot authorities could be attributed to Turkey in light of Turkey's control over them and its military presence on the island. It was largely against the background of the northern Cyprus decisions that the ECtHR decided the leading and controversial case of *Bankovic*.

Bankovic, a decision of the Grand Chamber of the ECtHR, has engendered much debate and criticism. Highlighting the disagreement surrounding the decision were the arguments put before the High Court in *Al-Skeini*, where Singh QC for the claimants suggested that the case was 'just one among a long line of Strasbourg authorities', whilst Greenwood QC for the Secretary of State averred that it was a watershed and that 'Even if earlier cases were not doubted

49 Discussion includes Loucaides, L., 'Determining the Extra-Territorial Effect of the European Convention: Facts, Jurisprudence and the *Bankovic* case' (2006) 4 EHRLR 391; Lawson, R., 'Life after *Bankovic*: on the Extraterritorial Application of the European Convention on Human Rights', in Coomans and Kamminga (n 9 above), at p 83; and Gondek, M., 'Extraterritorial Application of the European Convention on Human Rights: Territorial Focus in the Age of Globalization?' (2005) 52 NILR 349.

50 [2007] UKHL 26.

51 (1976) 4 EHRR 482 at para 8.

52 (1995) 29 EHRR 99.

53 Ibid at para. 62.

in their outcomes, they were subject to a fresh rationalisation, so that what at an earlier stage may have seemed a matter of broad principle, had to be re-evaluated as narrow exceptions'.[54] Further, Loukis Loucaides, Cypriot judge in the ECtHR, has called the decision 'an example of bad law influenced by the considerations relating to the factual situation'.[55] Conversely, McGoldrick calls *Bankovic* a 'hard case which made good law. That good law is consistent with the previous jurisprudence'.[56]

Giving rise to *Bankovic* was a NATO-led bombing within the former Yugoslavia. The applicants were survivors and relatives of the deceased of that mission. They argued that their or their relative's human rights had been violated and that they came within the jurisdiction of several state parties to the Convention. The ECtHR held, in essence, that the Convention's application is normally limited to the territory of state parties, but it is exceptionally applicable outwith that territory where a state 'through the effective control of the relevant territory and its inhabitants abroad as a consequence of military occupation or through the consent, invitation or acquiescence of the Government of that territory, exercises all or some of the public powers normally to be exercised by that Government'.[57] Significantly, the Court stated that it must 'take into account any relevant rules of international law when examining questions concerning its jurisdiction . . . The Convention should be interpreted as far as possible in harmony with other principles of international law of which it forms a part'.[58] The ECtHR then discussed extraterritorial jurisdiction generally and stated that whilst it is not excluded by international law, the application of law across borders is 'as a general rule defined and limited by the sovereign territorial rights of the other relevant states'.[59] It continued: 'a State may not actually exercise jurisdiction on the territory of another without the latter's consent, invitation or acquiescence, unless the former is an occupying State in which case it can be found to exercise jurisdiction in that territory, at least in certain respects'.[60] Following this emphasis upon extant rules of general international law the ECtHR held that 'jurisdiction' 'must be considered to reflect [the] ordinary and essentially territorial notion of jurisdiction, other bases of jurisdiction being exceptional and requiring special justification in the particular circumstances of each case'.[61] It found confirmation of the essentially

54 *Al-Skeini*, at paras 114 and 115.
55 Loucaides (n 49 above), at p 393.
56 McGoldrick, D., 'Extraterritorial Application of the International Covenant on Civil and Political Rights', in Commans and Kamminga (n 9 above), at p 41.
57 *Bankovic*, at para 71.
58 Ibid at para 57.
59 Ibid at para 59.
60 Ibid at para 60.
61 Ibid at para 61. In line with this general proposition that the exercise and assumption of extraterritorial jurisdiction needs justification is the *Case of the SS Lotus, (France v Turkey)* (1927) PCIJ Rep, Series A, No 10. See, generally, Arnell, P., 'Criminal Jurisdiction in International Law' [2000] *Juridical Review* 179.

territorial notion of jurisdiction in the *travaux préparatories*,[62] noted above. The ECtHR summarised its view in regard to the application of the Convention by stating that 'the Convention is a multi-lateral treaty operating . . . in an essentially regional context and notably in the legal space (espace juridique) of the Contracting States . . . The Convention was not designed to be applied throughout the world, even in respect of the conduct of Contracting States'.[63]

Following *Bankovic*, a number of ECtHR decisions have re-visited the question of the precise scope of the Convention in wholly extraterritorial cases. In summary, these have suggested that there are two sets of circumstances that can give rise to the wholly extraterritorial application of the Convention: where the armed forces or agents of a state have effective control over a spatial area outside its territory and where they have a degree of personal authority over an alleged victim. These have been termed 'effective control of an area' and 'state agent authority' respectively.[64] An example from 2005 is the ECtHR case of *Issa v Turkey*.[65] Here both tests of personal authority and effective control of an area were considered in examining possible Turkish jurisdiction outside the territory of the Council of Europe, namely Iraq. The Court held:

> The Court does not exclude the possibility that, as a consequence of this military action, the respondent State could be considered to have exercised, temporarily, effective overall control of a particular portion of the territory of northern Iraq. Accordingly, if there is a sufficient factual basis for holding that, at the relevant time, the victims were within that specific area, it would follow logically that they were within the jurisdiction of Turkey (and not that of Iraq, which is not a Contracting State and clearly does not fall within the legal space (*éspace juridique*) of the Contracting States (see the above-cited *Bankovic* decision, § 80).[66]

On the facts the ECtHR held that the applicants had not proved that their relatives, allegedly killed by Turkish soldiers in northern Iraq, were under the personal authority of Turkish soldiers or the overall effective control of Turkey.[67] It should be noted that this decision has been criticised by the House of Lords and the Supreme Court in *Al-Skeini* and *Smith* respectively. These cases will be discussed below.

A final ECtHR case highlighting the application of the Convention in a wholly extraterritorial sense is the admissibility decision in *Al Saadoon*.[68] The

62 *Bancovic*, at para 63.
63 Ibid at para 80.
64 By the Court of Appeal in *Al-Skeini*, at para 50.
65 (2005) 41 EHHR 27. This case is also authority for the position that the Convention can apply outside the territory of state parties to the Convention: see Wilde, R., 'The "Legal Space" or "Espace Juridique" of the European Convention on Human Rights: Is it Relevant to Extraterritorial State Action' [2005] EHRLR 115.
66 (2005) 41 EHHR at para 74.

substantive aspect of this decision has been noted above, where the ECtHR held that the transfer of the two applicants gave rise to a violation of Article 3. Prior to that decision on the merits the Court was seized with the question of whether the applicants were within the jurisdiction of the UK for the purposes of Article 1. As it will be recalled, the applicants had been arrested by UK forces following the invasion of Iraq in March 2003 and detained in a British-run detention facility. The UK, relying on *Bankovic*, argued that the applicants were not within its jurisdiction, averring that 'the United Kingdom was not exercising any public powers through the effective control of any part of the territory or the inhabitants of Iraq, such as would exceptionally justify the extra-territorial application of the Convention'.[69] In coming to this conclusion, the UK referred to various UN Security Council resolutions and the fact that Iraqi courts had been operating and applying Iraqi law in the case and had requested the transfer of the applicants in May 2006. The ECtHR disagreed. It held:

> The Court considers that, given the total and exclusive *de facto*, and subsequently also *de jure*, control exercised by the United Kingdom authorities over the premises in question, the individuals detained there, including the applicants, were within the United Kingdom's jurisdiction. This conclusion is, moreover, consistent with the dicta of the House of Lords in *Al-Skeini* and the position adopted by the Government in that case before the Court of Appeal and House of Lords.[70]

As will be seen below, this case has a number of similarities with *Al-Skeini*. Generally, however, it provides authority for the proposition that where a state exercises effective control over an area outwith its territory, and indeed outwith the Council of Europe, instances of human rights violations occurring there may engender the responsibility of that state under the Convention.

The Human Rights Act 1998

The range and particular application of the HRA is greatly affected by the Convention and ECtHR jurisprudence. This follows from the basic fact that the HRA gives 'further effect to the Convention'.[71] As noted above, the meaning

67 Further relevant cases include *Öcalan v Turkey* (2003) 37 EHRR 10 and *Ilascu v Moldova* (2005) 40 EHRR 46.

68 See, for a discussion of the case, and the law generally on the application of the Convention across borders: Janik, C. and Kleinein, K., 'When Soering went to Iraq . . . : problems of jurisdiction, extraterritorial effect and norm conflicts in light of the European Court of Human Rights' *Al-Saadoon* case' (2009) 1 *Gottingen Journal of International Law* 459.

69 *Al Saadoon*, at para 79.

70 Ibid at para 88, references omitted.

71 The Long Title of the HRA provides that it is 'An Act to give further effect to rights and freedoms guaranteed under the European Convention on Human Rights'.

of 'within their jurisdiction' in Article 1 of the Convention, as interpreted and applied by the ECtHR, is relatively clear. The Convention appears to apply in three extraterritorial circumstances: where a state party has effective extraterritorial control of the *situs* of the particular act or person, where a state party's agents exercise extraterritorial authority over a putative victim and, perhaps more obviously, where a person is within the territory of a state party and subject to extradition or expulsion to a state where a future human rights violation may occur. When considering the spatial application of the HRA the question is whether, and if so to what extent, the position under the Convention affects its applicability across borders. Two arguments can be made. On the one hand, since section 2(1) of the HRA obliges UK courts to take into account *inter alia* jurisprudence of the ECtHR, the application of the HRA is governed by the rules found in the cases discussed above. On the other hand, the Convention is a multilateral treaty and not part of municipal UK law, and the HRA itself is silent on the issue of its general extent. Article 1 is not included within the HRA.[72] The existing rules of law governing in such circumstances – rules of statutory interpretation – largely militate against its application across borders. Together these factors suggest that the spatial application of the Convention and the HRA are not co-terminate. Of the two possibilities, the former is correct. In applying the HRA courts in the UK have, to date, effectively adopted the ECtHR's approach to jurisdiction (not without criticism however; see below). Prior to analysing the germane jurisprudence it is useful to examine the precise relationship between the HRA and the Convention. This is relevant in part because it sheds light on whether courts in the UK were, and are, obliged to adopt the ECtHR's approach as a matter of law. Or instead, whether there was, and is, scope for divergence in the approach taken to the extent of the HRA by UK courts.

The precise nature of the relationship between the Convention and the HRA is not clearly defined or explained academically or judicially. Academic commentary on the point is generally concerned with whether the HRA 'incorporated' the Convention or gave it 'further effect'. 'Incorporation' implies that a single set of rules govern the geographic application of both the HRA and the Convention. It suggests the transplantation of the Convention (or parts of the Convention) together with its attendant jurisdictional rules into UK law. Given 'further effect', on the other hand, appears to open the door for the possibility of distinct rules governing the scope of the HRA. It can be understood to mean that (certain) rights guaranteed under the Convention have been adopted and are now guaranteed by the HRA and conditioned by the rules (or absence of

72 Lord Drummond Young stated that the reason for the absence of Art 1 'is obvious; article 1 is the provision that renders the Convention binding on the High Contracting Parties, but it does not of itself confer any specific rights on persons who find themselves within the jurisdiction of any High Contracting Party. Thus it has no place in domestic law', in *Al Fayed, Petitioner* [2004] SLT 319 at para 5.

rules) within the Act itself. An illustration of the academic debate is made by Fenwick:

> The HRA does *not* 'incorporate' the Convention rights into substantive domestic law, since it does not provide that they are to have the 'force of law', the usual form of words used when international treaties are incorporated into domestic law . . . the rights *are* in a sense incorporated into domestic law when asserted against public authorities or when the issue in question, which relates to a Convention right, falls within the scope of EC law.[73]

Seemingly in agreement with Fenwick is Himsworth, who states that the HRA does not 'in a strong sense' incorporate the Convention and make it part of UK law.[74] In contrast is this judicial *dictum* of Lord Scott, who stated that 'The ECHR is not part of domestic law except to the extent that it has become so under the 1998 Act. The 1998 Act did not entrench the articles of the ECHR so as to bar Parliament from subsequently enacting legislation inconsistent with those articles. Parliament can, if it wishes to do so, enact such legislation'.[75] Further case law discussing the relationship between the Convention and the HRA will be discussed below. Here, it is sufficient to note that divergent terminology is used to describe the relationship between the instruments, and this fact does not assist in understanding.

In addition to judicial and academic commentary being of use in coming to an understanding of the relationship between the HRA and the Convention are the rules of statutory interpretation and, of course, the terms of the HRA itself. The rules of statutory interpretation include the presumption that legislation will be limited to the territory of the UK unless the statute itself specifies otherwise.[76] In *R v West Yorkshire ex p Smith*, Donaldson LJ stated that 'every parliamentary draftsman writes on paper which bears the legend, albeit in invisible ink, 'this Act shall not have an extra-territorial effect, save to the extent that it expressly so provides".[77] The HRA does not contain a provision which

73 Fenwick, H., *Civil Liberties and Human Rights*, Cavendish, London, 2002, at pp 134–5 (emphasis in original).

74 Himsworth, C., 'Devolving Rights Seriously', in Boyle, A. (ed.), *Human Rights and Scots Law*, Hart Publishing, Oxford, 2002, at p 22. Miller writes: 'Strictly speaking . . . the Human Rights Act does not "incorporate" the ECHR but is an Act to give further effect to rights and freedoms guaranteed under the European Convention on Human Rights', in Miller, A. (ed.), *Human Rights a Modern Agenda*, T and T Clark Publishing, Edinburgh, 2000, at p 8.

75 *A (FC) and others (FC) v Secretary of State for the Home Department* [2004] UKHL 56 at para 144.

76 Bennion has written: 'Unless the contrary intention appears, Parliament is taken to intend an Act to extend to each territory of the United Kingdom but not to any territory outside the United Kingdom', in Bennion, F., *Statutory Interpretation: A Code*, 4th edn, Butterworths, London, 2002, at p 82. Of course this is just a presumption, and one that is increasingly explicitly overcome.

77 [1983] QB 335 at 358.

expressly stipulates that it is to apply outwith the UK. Indeed, it does not contain a general provision on either its spatial or personal application. Certain terms of the HRA militate against its application across borders. The two references to its application, or extent, are section 22(6), which states that the Act extends to Northern Ireland, and section 22(7), which provides that 'Section 21(5), so far as it relates to any provision contained in the Army Act 1955, the Air Force Act 1955 or the Naval Discipline Act 1957, extends to any place to which that provision extends'. Also relevant is section 11, which states, *inter alia*, that '(a) A person's reliance on a Convention rights does not restrict – (a) any other right or freedom conferred on him by or under any law having effect in any part of the United Kingdom'.[78] From this specific provision, and in light of the rule of interpretation above, it is reasonable to conclude that the HRA applies on an intra-territorial basis only. However, the presumption in favour of the territorial application of the HRA has been rebutted.

Four factors have led to this rebuttal. First, courts are bound to take into account the jurisprudence of the ECtHR and Commission in interpreting Convention rights. As was explicitly noted in *R (Ullah) v Special Adjudicator* by Lord Bingham: 'the House is required by section 2(1) of the Human Rights Act 1998 to take into account any relevant Strasbourg case law'.[79] Second, section 3(1) of the HRA provides that 'So far as it is possible to do so, primary legislation and subordinate legislation must be read and given effect in a way which is compatible with the Convention rights'. This includes the HRA itself. In *Al-Skeini* the Divisional Court could 'see no reason why section 3(1) should not apply to the Act itself and to the question of its scope'.[80] Third, there is a presumption that legislation giving effect to a treaty will be compatible with the obligations within it.[81] Fourth, the rule of statutory interpretation provides that the object and purpose of an Act should be taken into account in determining its meaning.[82] Together, these factors have led to similar rules governing the scope of both the HRA and the Convention. Lord Nicholls has stated: 'the

78 Sections 11 and 22 were referred to by counsel for the Secretary of State as evidence against the application of the HRA to the facts in *R v Secretary of State for the Foreign and Commonwealth Office ex p B and others* [2004] EWCA 1344, [2005] QB 643 at para 69 (hereinafter *B and others*).

79 [2004] UKHL 26 at para 20.

80 *Al-Skeini*, at para 291.

81 *Solomon v Commissioners of Customs and Excise* [1966] 3 All ER 871; and, with specific reference to the Convention itself, see *T, Petitioner* [1996] SCCR 897.

82 *Murray v Inland Revenue* 1918 SC (HL) 111. Indeed, there are 'special considerations' in regard to the interpretation of statutes incorporating or giving effect to conventions in UK law, resulting in it being 'absurd to interpret [conventions] differently from the courts of other countries which are also parties to the treaty or convention' and 'the court should adopt the European method of looking at the design and purpose of the legislation and interpreting the legislation to have the desired effect or in a manner less constrained by technical rules of English or Scottish law or by legal precedent but on broad principles of general application': Walker, D.M., *The Scottish Legal System*, 8th edn, W Green, Edinburgh, 2001, at p 431, footnotes omitted.

territorial scope of the obligations and rights created by sections 6 and 7 of the Act was intended to be co-extensive with the territorial scope of the obligations of the United Kingdom and the rights of victims under the Convention. The Act was intended to provide a domestic remedy where a remedy would have been available in Strasbourg'.[83] As will be seen in the analysis of UK jurisprudence below, the rules governing the application of the HRA have been accepted by UK courts to be those developed by the ECtHR.

UK jurisprudence

Extradition and expulsion cases

A number of cases have been heard in UK courts relating to the application of the HRA to persons and circumstances across borders. They have included both extradition and expulsion and wholly extraterritorial cases. In regard to extradition and expulsion cases the rule established in *Soering* has been considered and applied in cases including, in the Supreme Court, *Norris v Government of the United States*;[84] in the House of Lords, *R (Ullah) v Special Adjudicator*,[85] *R (Razgar) v Secretary of State for the Home Department (No 2)*[86] and *McKinnon v United States*;[87] in the Divisional Court, *McKinnon v Government of the USA, Secretary of State for the Home Department*[88] and *R (Gary McKinnon) v Secretary of State for Home Affairs*;[89] and in the High Court of Justiciary, *Wright v Scottish Ministers (No 2)*.[90] In all these cases the court was seized with the question of whether human rights considerations gave rise to a bar to the extradition or expulsion of the individual concerned. This jurisprudence is notable for one of three, at times related, reasons. It affects a widening of the law, such as in *Norris*, *Razgar* and *Ullah*, it provides an example of the application of the law to somewhat unusual facts, such as in the *McKinnon* cases, and it represents a common argument and situation, such as in *Wright v Scottish Ministers.*

The facts giving rise to *Norris* were charges made in the United States against Ian Norris, former chief executive officer of the engineering company Morgan Crucible. The company had previously entered into a plea bargain with the US

83 *R (Quark Fishing Ltd) v Foreign Secretary* [2005] UKHL 57 at para 34. Lord Justice Sedley in the Court of Appeal stated in this regard: 'I consider the Act to be not only presumptively but designedly coextensive with the Convention': *Al-Skeini*, at para 189.
84 [2010] UKSC 9.
85 [2004] UKHL 26.
86 [2004] UKHL 27.
87 [2008] UKHL 59.
88 [2007] EWHC 762 (Admin).
89 [2009] EWHC 2021 (Admin).
90 2004 SLT 823. There are numerous other authorities. Amongst them are *R (Wellington) v Secretary of State for the Home Department* [2008] UKHL 72; *Dudko v The Government of the Russian Federation* [2010] EWHC 1125 (Admin); and *Khan v Government of the United States of America* [2010] EWHC 1127 (Admin).

authorities, and various persons were granted immunity from prosecution – excluding Norris. Norris was charged by the Grand Jury in Pennsylvania in 2004 with one charge of price-fixing and three charges of obstructing justice. The House of Lords in a previous case[91] held that since at the relevant time price-fixing was not a crime in English law, Norris could not be extradited in regard to it. However, the case proceeded and Norris challenged his extradition on the obstruction of justice charges on the basis that it would engender a violation of his Article 8 rights. The evidence was that if he were convicted on the charges Norris would probably spend 21–27 months in prison, and perhaps significantly longer. It was also stated that his trial might not take place for a year or more after his extradition.[92] It was in regard to the period of time that Norris would be in the United States – as well as his forced relocation – that formed the crux of the case. In fact, apart from the custody abroad, the case did not consider foreign factors; as such, it is a domestic case. In part referring to his wife, Norris argued that his:

> poor health, together with the length and closeness of their marriage, has made them highly dependent on each other. This and their advancing years, make them less resilient to the separation that Mr Norris' extradition would involve. It was originally Mrs Norris' intention to accompany her husband to the United States should he be extradited, but in a witness statement that she made last year she says that she cannot now contemplate going to the US to live on her own there without friends and family support. Because Mrs Norris will not accompany her husband to the United States, the interruption to their family life should he be remanded in custody, and during his imprisonment, should he be convicted, will be total.[93]

Lord Phillips, in a judgment with which the bench of nine judges agreed, concluded:

> One has to consider the effect on the public interest in the prevention of crime if any defendant with family ties and dependencies such as those which bind Mr Norris and his wife was thereby rendered immune from being extradited to be tried for serious wrongdoing. The answer is that the public interest would be seriously damaged. It is for this reason that only the gravest effects of interference with family life will be capable of rendering extradition disproportionate to the public interest that it serves. This is not such a case.[94]

Norris' appeal was dismissed.

91 *Norris v Government of the United States of America* [2008] UKHL 16.
92 [2010] UKSC 9 at paras 72–3.
93 Ibid at para 80.
94 Ibid at para 82.

More relevant than the decision on the facts in *Norris*, are the judgments on the law, in particular in Lord Phillips' speech. Amongst the salient points is the reiteration of the distinction between foreign and domestic cases. As was first explicitly discussed in *Ullah* and *Razgar*, below, two types of case can be identified in which human rights are argued in extradition and expulsion cases. One relates to the circumstances within the UK that may be engendered by the extradition and expulsion of an individual; the other concerns the circumstances in which a person may find himself in the state to which he is sent. The first of these has been termed a domestic case, and the second a foreign case. Lord Phillips summarised ECtHR jurisprudence on foreign cases to provide:

> that it will only be in exceptional circumstances that a foreign case will involve an infringement of the Convention and that the Convention will only prove a bar to extradition or deportation where there is a real risk of a *flagrant* breach of the Convention. It is not any anticipated breach that will suffice.[95]

Lord Phillips notes that in foreign cases the law does not distinguish between extradition and expulsion cases, unlike in domestic cases. Finally, it is of note that Lord Phillips suggested an appropriate approach for judges to take in extradition hearings:

> The judge . . . has to consider a considerable number of possible statutory barriers to extradition. These include the matters that might violate human rights . . . This is a fact-specific exercise, and the judge must have regard to the relevant features of the individual case. It is at this point that it is legitimate for the judge to consider whether there are any relevant features that are unusually or exceptionally compelling. In the absence of such features, the consideration is likely to be relatively brief. If, however, the nature or extent of the interference with article 8 rights is exceptionally serious, careful consideration must be given to whether such interference is justified. In such a situation the gravity, or lack of gravity, of the offence may be material.[96]

In coming to a decision on whether interference is justified, a proportionality test should be applied. Lord Phillips stated that 'it is more helpful, when considering proportionality, to consider whether the consequences of interference with article 8 rights are exceptionally serious rather than simply whether the circumstances are exceptional'.[97] Whilst this case usefully demonstrates a number of relevant facets of the law, it was a domestic case. It is, of course,

95 Ibid at para 29 (emphasis in original).
96 Ibid at para 62.
97 Ibid at para 95.

foreign cases that are of greater relevance for the purposes of this discussion in that they necessarily entail an application of the law across borders through consideration of circumstances outwith the UK.

The leading foreign cases in UK jurisprudence are *Razgar* and *Ullah*,[98] jointly heard in the House of Lords. The central question in these cases was whether articles additional to Article 3 could be relied upon to prevent an extradition or expulsion. In *Ullah* Article 9, protecting the freedom of thought, conscience and religion, was considered. The applicants argued that their right to practice their religions would be infringed in the countries to which the UK was proposing to send them. In the leading judgment Lord Bingham first examined the possibility that any article other than Article 3 could found the basis of an argument in such cases. He accepted the importance of the right to life, stating: 'Given the special importance attached to the right to life by modern human rights instruments it would perhaps be surprising if article 3 could be relied on and article 2 could not'.[99] Lord Bingham after referring to ECtHR case law, then accepted the possibility of Articles 4, 5, 6 and 8 applying in extradition and expulsion cases.[100] He concluded in regard to Article 9:

> I find it hard to think that a person could successfully resist expulsion in reliance on article 9 without being entitled either to asylum on the ground of a well-founded fear of being persecuted for reasons of religion or personal opinion or to resist expulsion in reliance on article 3. But I would not rule out such a possibility in principle unless the Strasbourg court has clearly done so, and I am not sure it has.[101]

A similar threshold test as that used in cases based on Article 3 was held to be applicable here. This is that a 'stringent test' should be adopted by courts requiring the applicant to show strong grounds for believing that, if returned, he or she faced a real risk of being subjected to a violation of the right in question.[102] Referring to the facts, Lord Bingham held the appellants fell far short of satisfying this test. Lord Steyn agreed, holding that the arguments based upon Ullah's religious preaching (Ahmadhi) and Do's observance of Catholicism did not meet the requisite standard, and indeed were 'wholly unmeritorious'.[103]

98 *Do v Immigration Appeal Tribunal* was reported together with *Ullah* [2004] UKHL 26.

99 [2004] UKHL 26 at para 15. As was noted above, the position in regard to capital punishment has evolved.

100 Ibid at paras 16–18. The opinion of the Court on Art 8 was split, with Lord Walker and Baroness Hale disagreeing with the view that it could be invoked in extradition and expulsion cases. This was the issue in *Razgar*, discussed below.

101 Ibid at para 21.

102 Ibid at para 24. Lord Carswell stated that the law provides that the breach must be 'flagrant', which denotes the right being completely denied or nullified in the requesting state, at para 69.

103 Ibid at para 26.

In *Razgar*, the House of Lords was faced with the question of whether Article 8 could form the basis of an argument in an extradition and expulsion case where the removal did not also violate Article 3. Razgar was an Iraqi asylum-seeker. The Secretary of State was attempting to send him to Germany, the state from which he entered the UK. The House of Lords, by 3 to 2, held that Article 8 could be invoked on its own. Lord Bingham stated:

> the rights protected by article 8 can be engaged by the foreseeable consequences for health of removal from the United Kingdom pursuant to an immigration decision, even where such removal does not violate article 3, if the facts relied on by the applicant are sufficiently strong . . . an applicant could never hope to resist an expulsion decision without showing something very much more extreme than relative disadvantage as compared with the expelling state.[104]

Following the decision on principle the court held by a majority that it was not possible to hold as manifestly unfounded the argument that Razgar's removal would infringe his Article 8 rights.[105] Lord Bingham usefully stated the questions that should be considered in cases such as Razgar's:

> (1) Will the proposed removal be an interference by a public authority with the exercise of the applicant's right to respect for his private or (as the case may be) family life?; (2) If so, will such interference have consequences of such gravity as potentially to engage the operation of article 8?; (3) If so, is such interference in accordance with the law?; (4) If so, is such interference necessary in a democratic society in the interests of national security, public safety or the economic well-being of the country, for the prevention of disorder or crime, for the protection of health or morals, or for the protection of the rights and freedoms of others?; (5) If so, is such interference proportionate to the legitimate public end sought to be achieved?[106]

Baroness Hale, dissenting, highlighted the fact that difficult decisions need to be made in these circumstances:

> this is a field in which harsh decisions sometimes have to be made. People have to be returned to situations which we would find appalling. The United Kingdom is not required to keep people here who have no right to be here unless to expel them would be a breach of its international

104 [2004] UKHL 27 at para 10.
105 Lord Walker dissented in part due to the 'wide and imprecise' language used in interpreting Art 8, ibid at para 34.
106 Ibid at para 17.

> obligations. It does the cause of human rights no favours to stretch those obligations further than they can properly go.[107]

Clearly, then, whilst Article 8 has been held to apply in cases of extradition and expulsion, the test that has been developed to resist extradition and expulsion is not easy to meet.

A series of cases that illustrate the unusual circumstances that may arise in the area of extradition and expulsion are those pertaining to Gary McKinnon.[108] Three decisions are relevant for our present purposes: the first Divisional Court decision, the decision of the House of Lords and the second Divisional Court case. The legal saga involving McKinnon has its origins in the October 2004 US extradition request following US Grand Jury indictments charging McKinnon with a number of offences arising from his hacking activities. The first High Court decision followed McKinnon's opposition to extradition at Bow Street Magistrates' Court and the subsequent decision of the Secretary of State ordering his extradition.[109] Having failed in his arguments the case was argued again, unsuccessfully, in the House of Lords.[110] McKinnon's fight against extradition has been, exceptionally, continued on account of arguments being made as to his medical situation. The Divisional Court again heard representations on his behalf in *R (McKinnon) v Secretary of State for Home Affairs*[111] on 31 July 2009. In the first Divisional Court case McKinnon challenged his extradition on four grounds. One of these was on the basis of Article 8. It was held that there were not the 'exceptional' circumstances necessary in his case to have human rights concerns bar his extradition.[112] The court held that there was nothing exceptional in his personal, domestic and family circumstances, that the fact that a longer sentence could be imposed by a US court did not in itself assist McKinnon, and that the fact that he could be tried in the UK did not lead to his extradition being disproportionate. All the other grounds of appeal were also rejected. McKinnon appealed to the House of Lords. It addressed one question, whether:

> it was an abuse of process of extradition proceedings, such that the proceedings be stayed, and/or an unjustified interference with the defendant's

107 Ibid at para 65. Baroness Hale termed this a 'health case' in that the arguments centred upon the possible disparity in treatment available between the UK and the putative destination state.

108 See, generally, Arnell, P. and Reid, A., 'Hackers Beware – The Cautionary Story of Gary McKinnon' (2009) 18 *Information and Communications Technology Law* 1.

109 [2007] EWHC 762 (Admin).

110 [2008] UKHL 59. Following this case McKinnon unsuccessfully petitioned the ECtHR seeking an injunction against extradition, see Press Release 601, 28 August 2008,

111 [2009] EWHC (Admin) 2021. See, further, Taylor, N., 'Case Comment – *R. (on the application of McKinnon) v DPP*: prosecution – claimant's extradition sought by the US for computer hacking offences' [2010] 5 *Criminal Law Review* 421.

112 The court cited *Launder v United Kingdom* (1997) 25 EHRR CD 67 at para 3 in support of the 'exceptional circumstances' threshold.

> human rights, for the requesting state to engage in plea bargaining, including a threat to the defendant that, unless he agrees to be extradited, reparation to the United Kingdom to serve any sentence imposed, in the requesting state will not be supported by the prosecuting authorities in the requesting state.[113]

The House of Lords held that it was 'common ground' that any rights that he may have had under Articles 5(4) and 6 added nothing to the abuse of process claim.[114] In doing so, it refused to entertain the possibility of applying Article 5 or 6 to the system of plea-bargaining in the United States. Instead, it focused on McKinnon's core argument that the plea bargain offer by the US authorities entailed such a disparity in possible sentence (three to four years, with only six months to be served in a low security US prison, as against eight to ten years in a US high security prison) that 'disproportionate' and 'impermissible pressure' to surrender his legal rights was placed upon him.[115] In support of this argument McKinnon relied on *US v Cobb*,[116] a decision of the Supreme Court of Canada, where an abuse of process argument was upheld in the face of US plea-bargaining. McKinnon's reliance on *Cobb* was to no avail, as the case was distinguished by the House of Lords. Lord Brown emphasised the very high hurdle that must be met to successfully resist extradition, stating:

> It is difficult, indeed, to think of anything other than the threat of unlawful action which could fairly be said so to imperil the integrity of the extradition process as to require the accused, notwithstanding his having resisted the undue pressure, to be discharged irrespective of the strength of the case against him.[117]

The House of Lords unanimously dismissed McKinnon's appeal.

The second Divisional Court case in which McKinnon fought extradition arose, exceptionally, on account of a diagnosis that he was suffering from a form of autism, called Asperger Syndrome. It was argued on McKinnon's behalf that extradition would give rise to a violation of Article 3 and Article 8 on the basis of the prison conditions in which he would be held (in conjunction with his medical condition). It was also argued that McKinnon should be prosecuted in England. The court held in regard to Article 3:

> It is well recognised that Article 3 applies to conduct of the most serious and severe kind. It is particularly difficult for a person to establish a breach of his Article 3 rights where the conduct that is envisaged is, as in the

113 [2008] UKHL 59 at para 7.
114 Ibid at para 9.
115 Ibid at para 28.
116 [2001] 1 SCR 587.
117 [2008] UKHL 59 at para 41.

> present case, not the deliberate infliction of harm by agents of a foreign state but neglect or a lack of resources on the part of that state.[118]

Lord Justice Burnton concluded:

> Ultimately, I have to weigh the impressive medical evidence adduced by the Claimant against the severity involved in Article 3. I have no doubt that he will find extradition to, and trial and sentence and detention in the USA, very difficult indeed. His mental health will suffer. There are risks of worse, including suicide. But if I compare his condition with those considered in the authorities to which I have referred above, even taking full account of the (in my view undesirable) possibility of his being prosecuted in this country, his case does not approach Article 3 severity.[119]

The Court rejected McKinnon's arguments.

The final case to be noted is the Scottish case of *Wright v Scottish Ministers (No 2)*.[120] Here, Wright's argument against extradition to Estonia on the basis of Article 8 was dismissed. It was held that whilst his case was tenable in law it was not established in fact. As with a number of the other authorities, the high threshold needed to establish such an argument was emphasised, with the High Court of Justiciary citing with approval passages in both *Ullah* and *Razgar*.[121] Significantly, the court, in discussing the proportionality of the interference with Wright's Article 8 rights as against the interests served by extradition, stressed the need to liberally construe extradition treaties: 'the court should not, unless constrained by the language used, interpret any extradition treaty in a way which would "hinder the working and narrow the operation of most salutary international arrangements"'.[122] The court later discussed the purpose of extradition:

> The object of extradition is to return a person who is properly accused or has been convicted of an extradition crime in a foreign country to face trial or to serve his sentence there . . . The extradition process is only available for return to friendly foreign states with whom this country has entered into either a multi or a bilateral treaty obligation involving mutually agreed and reciprocal commitments. Mr. Perry, on behalf of the claimant, accepts that there is a strong public interest in our respecting such treaty obligations. Such international co-operation is all the more important in modern times,

118 [2009] EWHC 2021 (Admin) at para 67.
119 Ibid at para 89.
120 2004 SLT 823.
121 Ibid at paras 53–4.
122 Ibid at para 59; citing *R v Ashford Remand Centre ex p Postlethwaite* [1988] 1 AC 924 at 946, per Lord Bridge.

> when cross-border problems are becoming ever more common, and the need to provide international solutions for them is ever clearer.[123]

The court concluded in regard to the proportionality argument that:

> we have not been persuaded that the mere possibility of prosecution of the reclaimer in Scotland, presumably under sec 20 of the 1971 Act, can be seen as rendering the reclaimer's extradition, with the consequent interference with his Art 8 rights, as not 'necessary in a democratic society . . . for the prevention of disorder or crime', within the meaning of Art 8(2) of the European Convention on Human Rights.[124]

As with McKinnon, the possibility of a prosecution in the UK did not affect the decision to order extradition.

Wholly extraterritorial cases

As with extradition and expulsion cases, the Supreme Court and the House of Lords, amongst other UK courts, have been seized of the question of whether the HRA applies on a wholly extraterritorial basis, and, if so, in what circumstances. One of the leading cases is *R (Smith) v Oxfordshire Assistant Deputy Coroner*.[125] The facts giving rise to this case was the death of Private Smith in Iraq of hyperthermia. Following his death his mother sought an order stating that the inquest into his death had to meet the procedural requirements under Article 2 of the Convention guaranteeing the right to life. The Secretary of State conceded this point; but two issues of public importance were raised, which the Supreme Court agreed to consider: 'Is a soldier on military service abroad in Iraq subject to the protection of the Human Rights Act 1998 when outside his base?'; and, if so, 'must the death of such a soldier be the subject of an inquest that satisfies the procedures that article 2 of the European Convention on Human Rights implicitly requires where there is reason to believe that a death may be attributable to default on the part of a public authority?'[126] The Court of Appeal had answered the point that concerns us most, the first, in the affirmative. The Supreme Court, by six justices to three, overturned the decision on that point and allowed the appeal. It held that the HRA did not apply to soldiers when outside their base. In the leading judgment, Lord Phillips began by laying the groundwork for the application of the HRA to wholly extraterritorial situations. He noted, first, the public authority obligation in section 6(1) of the HRA. He then stated that 'It is common ground that the HRA is

123 2004 SLT 823 at para 64; citing *R v Secretary of State for the Home Department ex p Warren* [2003] EWHC 1177 (Admin) at para 40, per Hale LJ.

124 Ibid at para 70.

125 [2010] UKSC 29.

126 Ibid at para 2.

capable of applying outside the territorial jurisdiction of the United Kingdom, but that section 6(1) will only be infringed by conduct that the Strasbourg Court would hold to have violated a Convention right'.[127] Therefore, the scope of HRA is co-terminate with that of the Convention. Lord Phillips then proceeded to examine the leading cases both under the Convention and the HRA, including *Bankovic*, *Issa* and *Al-Skeini*. In doing so he emphasised a number of core principles, including the 'original meaning principle', the 'effective territorial control principle' and the 'whole-package principle'. He also brought to the fore the issue of 'state agent authority'.[128] This last point is of particular importance in that, if it exists, it may operate to apply the law to soldiers outside their bases. This argument is that if persons who are subjected to state agent authority are within the jurisdiction of the particular state party, *a fortiori* are the state agents themselves.[129] Rose QC for Smith argued that since Smith was, as a matter of both domestic and international law, subject to the jurisdiction of the UK, the HRA should apply to him.[130]

After reviewing the authorities and discussing the various forms of state authority – judicial, executive and legislative – Lord Phillips stated that the central question was 'whether, applying the original meaning principle, it is right to include a State's armed forces abroad as falling within the jurisdiction of the State for purposes of article 1 by reason of the special status that they enjoy'. In regard to which, he stated: 'that is the proposition that Miss Rose advances and it is one that is, as the Grand Chamber pointed out in *Bankovic*, not reflected by State practice. It is, furthermore, almost wholly unsupported by Strasbourg jurisprudence'.[131] He used the word 'almost' in that some support for the notion can be found in the admissibility decision of *Cyprus v Turkey*[132] in 1975. Lord Phillips concluded on the jurisdiction point that:

> [T]he contention that a State's armed forces, by reason of their personal status, fall within the jurisdiction of the State for the purposes of article 1 is novel. I do not believe that the principles to be derived from the Strasbourg jurisprudence, conflicting as some of them are, clearly demonstrate that the contention is correct. The proper tribunal to resolve this issue is the Strasbourg Court itself.[133]

127 Ibid at para 5.
128 Ibid at para 17.
129 Lord Phillips, at para 52, stated in this regard: 'I have some difficulty with the logic of the proposition that State agents whose acts bring those affected by them within article 1 jurisdiction must, in consequence, themselves also be within the article 1 jurisdiction of the State whose agents they are'.
130 Ibid at para 33.
131 Ibid at para 48.
132 (1976) 4 EHRR 482.
133 [2010] UKSC 29 at para 60.

He held that Smith was not within the jurisdiction of the UK whilst he was outside premises under the effective control of the British army in Iraq. Lord Collins agreed with Lord Phillips. After a thorough examination of the relevant authorities, he concluded:

> article 1 reflects the territorial notion of jurisdiction, and that other bases of jurisdiction are exceptional and require special justification. In practice the exceptions recognised by the Court have either consisted of (1) territorial jurisdiction by a state over the territory of another contracting state; (2) extensions of territorial jurisdiction by analogy; and (3) commonsense extensions of the notion of jurisdiction to fit cases which plainly should be within the scope of the Convention.[134]

Lord Collins held that the first exception was manifest where a state had effective control over territory outwith its borders, and the second covered the application of the law to prisons and military bases. An example of the third exception, Lord Collins noted, was *Öcalan v Turkey*.[135] A final point to be taken from *Smith* is that it considers, but largely rejects, the notion of a 'jurisdictional link' playing a role in decisions as to the existence of jurisdiction.[136]

A second UK authority is *R (Gentle) v Prime Minister*.[137] The case is noteworthy, in part, because it contains both wholly extraterritorial and extradition and expulsion-related arguments. The facts leading to this judgment were the deaths of two soldiers in Iraq, Gordon Gentle and David Clark. Following inquests in the UK, the mothers of the two men instituted proceedings, arguing that sections 1 and 2 of the HRA in conjunction with Article 2 of the Convention gave them the right to insist on a public enquiry into the circumstances leading to the invasion of Iraq and more specifically the provision of advice to the Government as to the legality of the invasion. Particularly, the 'parasitic' right implicit in Article 2 requiring an independent and effective investigation into a death where the substantive article may have been infringed provided the basis of the appellants' case. Both the judge at first instance and the Court of Appeal dismissed the arguments of the deceaseds' mothers. The House of Lords refused the appeal. In a relatively brief leading judgment Lord Bingham held that in order successfully to found an argument on the procedural element of Article 2, the substantive right itself must exist; the parasitic right cannot exist independently. He held that the right under Article 2 was not 'a generalised provision protective of life, irrespective of any specific death or threat'.[138] Article 2 had never been applied in the manner the appellants argued,

134 Ibid at para 305.
135 (2005) 41 EHRR 45; the example was given by Lord Collins at para 306.
136 This is of relevance to the proper law approach theme of this book, and as such will be addressed in Chapter 5.
137 [2008] UKHL 20.
138 Ibid at para 7.

Lord Bingham noted, for three reasons, including that the deaths of the appellants were not 'within the jurisdiction' of the UK as required by Article 1. The appellants also relied upon '*Soering*-type' arguments in that the decision-making process was within the UK, albeit the effects of the decision in the form of military action were outwith the jurisdiction. Lord Bingham stated that there was an obvious distinction between the *Soering* line of jurisprudence and the present case on the basis that in those cases the action of the UK on UK territory relating to the person in question was 'likely to have an immediate and direct impact on that individual elsewhere'.[139] The decision was unanimous, with all nine Lords refusing the appeal.[140]

R (Al-Skeini) v Secretary of State for Defence[141] is the third case to be heard by the House of Lords or Supreme Court since mid-2005 in the area of the wholly extraterritorial application of the HRA. Like *Smith* and *Gentle*, the facts arose from the UK invasion of Iraq in 2003. Subsequent to the decision of the House of Lords the case has been taken to the ECtHR and a decision is pending. The House of Lords case is significant for its detailed analysis of both ECtHR and domestic case law. *Al-Skeini* in the House of Lords was an appeal from a Court of Appeal decision,[142] where it was held that the HRA applied to a prison in Iraq under UK control during the period between the cessation of combat operations and the assumption of power by the Iraqi interim government. It had been conceded by the Crown that the UK was exercising extraterritorial jurisdiction for the purposes of the Convention in regard to the prison, the central issue for the Court of Appeal being whether the HRA itself applied.[143] Specifically, the Court of Appeal had overturned the High Court's ruling that the failure sufficiently to investigate the death of the applicant's son, Baha Mousa, in prison contravened Article 2 of the Convention on the basis of new evidence of ongoing investigations. However, like the High Court, the Court of Appeal dismissed the claims of five other applicants because it did not accept that the UK was exercising Article 1 jurisdiction over the Iraqi territory outside the prison where they died. A distinction was drawn between the wider territory, where an 'effective control of an area' test was applied, and the prison.[144] The

139 Ibid at para 9.

140 See, further, Palmer, S., 'Military Intervention, Public Inquiries and the Right to Life' (2009) *Cambridge Law Journal* 17; and Slapper, G., 'The Right to Life on the Battlefield' (2010) 74 *Journal of Criminal Law* 383.

141 [2007] UKHL 26.

142 [2005] EWCA Civ 1609.

143 As Lord Justice Sedley stated: 'the Crown accepts that such an establishment is analogous to a diplomatic legation: not an extension of British territory but a United Kingdom enclave within another state, and so within the *éspace juridique* of the Convention', ibid at para 185.

144 A related case is that of *R (Al-Jedda) v Secretary of State for Defence* [2007] UKHL 58, where it was held, following *Al-Skeini*, that whilst the HRA and Convention could apply to persons detained by British forces in Iraq (as the claimant was), the operation of Security Council Resolution 1546, S/Res/1546 (2004), *inter alia* endorsing the formation of an interim Iraqi government, qualified the application of the law and therefore limited the applicant's human rights.

House of Lords agreed with the conclusion of the Court of Appeal. The appeal by the five unsuccessful appellants was rejected as was the cross-appeal by the Secretary of State in regard to the sixth appellant, Baha Mousa. The question that faced the House of Lords, like the Court of Appeal, was whether section 6 of the HRA was intended to apply outside the UK.[145] Lord Rodger held, applying a purposive approach to the interpretation of the HRA:

> The purpose of the1988 Act is to provide remedies in our domestic law to those whose human rights are violated by a United Kingdom public authority. Making such remedies available for acts of a United Kingdom authority on the territory of another state would not be offensive to the sovereignty of the other state. There is therefore nothing in the wider context of international law which points to the need to confine sections 6 and 7 of the 1988 Act to the territory of the United Kingdom.[146]

He continued that the crucial argument in favour of wider interpretation of section 6 was that, as the Secretary of State accepted, the central purpose of sections 6 and 7 of the HRA was 'to provide a remedial structure in domestic law for the rights guaranteed by the Convention'.[147] Lord Brown also adopted a purposive approach to the interpretation of section 6, stating the HRA's 'very purpose being to ensure that, from the date it took effect, it would no longer be necessary for victims to complain about alleged violations of the Convention internationally in Strasbourg instead of domestically in the UK'.[148] Lord Rodger stated that the speech of Lord Nicholls in *R (Quark Fishing) Ltd v Secretary of State for Foreign and Commonwealth Affairs*[149] provided powerful support for this approach – that the obligations under sections 6 and 7 mirror the UK's treaty obligations under the Convention, with the term 'co-extensive' being used.[150]

Subsequent to accepting that the application of the HRA and the Convention are co-extensive Lord Rodger and Lord Brown in *Al-Skeini* discussed the specific applicability of the Convention itself. Lord Rodger noted that the problem faced by the House of Lords was that the judgments and decisions of the ECtHR were contradictory. He examined the conflict between *Bankovic* and *Issa*, referred to above. In essence this concerned the importance of the requirement that a victim be within the effective control of the state party as opposed to the particular activity of its agents. Lord Rodger held that no assistance could be reaped from *Issa* and refused the appeal. Applying the principles of *Bankovic* as

145 [2007] UKHL 26 at para 42, per Lord Rodger.
146 Ibid at para 54. The question of whether a violation of the sovereignty of a third state in such circumstances is engendered is discussed in Chapter 5.
147 Ibid at para 56, citing *Aston Cantloe and Wilmcote with Billesley Parochial Church Council v Wallbank* [2003] UKHL 37, [2004] 1 AC 546 at para 44, per Lord Hope.
148 [2007] UKHL 26 at para 138.
149 [2005] UKHL 57.
150 [2007] UKHL 26 at para 58.

he interpreted them, he held that the five appellants were not within the jurisdiction of the UK when they were killed. Because the Secretary of State had conceded that Mousa had been within the jurisdiction of the UK, the House of Lords generally eschewed the question. Lord Brown, however, did comment generally, stating that the ECtHR had accepted the applicability of the Convention in four sets of circumstances: where a state party exercised effective control over territory and its inhabitants abroad; where its diplomatic and consular agents acted abroad (as well as on board aircraft and vessels flying that state's flag); where a state's responsibility could be engaged because of acts which produced effects or were performed outside their territory; and where a person is within a state party and extradition or expulsion is being considered.[151] Lord Brown held that the effective control was limited to the territory of the Council of Europe state parties, and that the UK's jurisdiction over Mousa was founded on the 'narrow basis found established by the Divisional Court, by analogy with the extraterritorial exception made for embassies'.[152]

Related to the basis upon which *Al-Skeini* was decided in the House of Lords in that it concerned the application of the HRA to diplomatic premises abroad is *R (B and others) v Secretary of State for Foreign and Commonwealth Affairs*.[153] Here the Court of Appeal held that the actions of UK consular officials in their offices in Melbourne did not breach the Convention, assuming that it did apply there. The facts in this case were that two children who had been detained in the Woomera detention centre had found their way into the consulate. They argued that if handed back to the Australian authorities their rights would be infringed. On the facts, the court held against the applicants, stating that the treatment they would receive if returned was not serious enough to warrant the UK to disregard its obligation under the Vienna Convention on Consular Relations 1963 to return them to the Australian authorities. Significantly, the court analysed the case acting under the assumption that the situation in the consulate was within the jurisdiction of the UK under Article 1. The Court stated that 'We are content to assume (without reaching a positive conclusion on the point) that while in the Consulate the applicants were sufficiently within the authority of the consular staff to be subject to the jurisdiction of the United Kingdom for the purpose of Article 1'.[154] The court commented on the relationship between the Convention and the HRA. It cited with approval Lord Hoffmann in *In re McKerr*:[155]

> Although people sometimes speak of the Convention having been incorporated into domestic law, that is a misleading metaphor. What the Act has done is to create domestic rights expressed in the same terms as those

151 Ibid at para 109.
152 Ibid at para 132.
153 [2004] EWCA 1344, [2005] QB 643.
154 Ibid at para 66.
155 [2004] 1 UKHL 12.

> contained in the Convention. But they are domestic rights, not international rights. Their source is the statute, not the Convention. They are available against specific public authorities, not the United Kingdom as a state. And their meaning and application is a matter for domestic courts, not the court in Strasbourg.[156]

As noted above, the domestic courts have held that the particular application of the HRA and Convention are co-terminate.

The final UK wholly extraterritorial authority to be noted is the Scottish case of *Al Fayed, Petitioner*.[157] In this case an argument to apply the HRA on a wholly extraterritorial basis was considered and rejected. In particular, Lord Drummond Young in the Outer House of the Court of Session dismissed a petition for judicial review of the Lord Advocate's refusal to hold a public inquiry into the circumstances of Dodi Al Fayed's death in Paris in August 1997. The petition was made on the basis of Mohamed Al Fayed's residence in Scotland. Lord Drummond Young held that the Convention normally only extends to events that occur within a state party's territory and that there was no reason why Al Fayed's right to a public investigation under Article 2 should be enforceable in any other jurisdiction than France. He stated: 'The death of the petitioner's son occurred in France. It follows that any obligations under the Convention in relation to that death are primarily those of France, and the obligations of the United Kingdom under the Convention do not extend to the investigation of such a death'.[158] In emphasising the importance of territory, Lord Drummond Young stated:

> The European Convention on Human Rights was concluded against a background of customary international law, and the obligations that it imposes on High Contracting Parties must be construed in the light of that background. Under international law, the jurisdiction exercised by a state is primarily territorial. While exceptions exist, notably in relation to ships and aircraft and diplomatic and consular premises, the primary rule is that a state is entitled to exercise jurisdiction over all persons and things within its own territory.[159]

While *Al Fayed* is distinguishable from *Al-Skeini* and *B and others inter alia* because the locus of the alleged violation was within the territory of another party to the Convention, it is relevant for its emphasis on the importance of international law and territorial jurisdiction.

156 Ibid at para 74, from *In re McKerr*, at para 63.
157 [2004] SLT 319.
158 Ibid at para 4.
159 Ibid at para8. Lord Drummond Young also stated that practical difficulties stood in the way of the application of human rights across borders; these are noted in Chapter 5.

Enforcement

Enforcement is a material part of an examination of the general subject of the application of human rights law across borders, as it was in regard to the criminal law. A description of enforcement leads to greater insight into the nature of the concerns motivating the application of law across borders as well the procedural mechanisms that allow that application. It also highlights the differences between human rights law and criminal law in this area. For example, the distinction between the application of law by the executive, legislature and judiciary rightfully drawn in the criminal sphere has significantly less relevance in regard to human rights. Further, whereas the executive plays a central role in the enforcement of the criminal law in regard to human rights, the role of the executive is reversed. As is clear, the executive, in the form of the various emanations of the state including the Home Office, the civil service more generally and the military and diplomatic service does not enforce human rights law. It is, rather, the subject of that enforcement. This is a fundamental difference. It is one of the main factors that affects and shapes the discussion below. An examination of the enforcement of human rights law, then, must focus more upon the legislative but especially the judicial activity in this area as opposed to the executive. It must also treat the two forms of the extraterritorial application of human rights separately. Whilst there are, of course, similarities between extradition and expulsion and wholly extraterritorial cases – both entailing the process of measuring circumstances abroad as against UK law – there are also differences. These make separate analyses appropriate.

The first point to be made in a description of the enforcement of human rights law across borders is that the subjects of that enforcement are, today, exclusively emanations of the UK itself. These take the form of 'public authorities'. As was noted above, human rights law in the UK applies most directly and immediately to public authorities by virtue of the obligation placed upon them by section 6 of the HRA. This is not to suggest that human rights obligations do not or cannot affect private persons; they do and can because courts are public authorities and so are bound to act compatibly with the HRA when applying the law as between private persons. The definition of 'public authority' itself is very wide, including bodies which are not prima facie 'public'.[160] However, to the author's knowledge there have been no cases where a private person outside the UK was held to be under an obligation to act compatibly with human rights under the HRA. This basic fact – that the subjects of the application of human rights

160 There is a wealth of writing and jurisprudence on the question of horizontal human rights and 'public authorities', including Williams, A., 'A Fresh Perspective on Hybrid Public Authorities under the Human Rights Act 1998: Private Contractors, Rights-stripping and "Chameleonic" Horizontal Effect' [2010] *Public Law* 139; Beatson, J., *et al*, *Human Rights: Judicial Protection in the United Kingdom*, Sweet and Maxwell, London, 2008, esp. Ch 4; and Elliot, M., '"Public" and "private": Defining the Scope of the Human Rights Act' (2007) 66 *Cambridge Law Journal* 485.

abroad are UK public authorities – greatly affects the nature of enforcement. On the opposite side of the coin, the nature of enforcement follows not only from the subjects of that enforcement being public authorities but also the private nature of those seeking to enforce it – victims of human rights violations. Section 7(1) restricts the ability to bring proceedings under the HRA to victims of the unlawful act. Thus, the enforcement of human rights law is the opposite of the criminal law, with private persons instigating the application of the law as against the state. In the criminal sphere, the state instigates the application of the law against private legal persons. A second point is the meaning of 'enforcement' within human rights law. It is reasonable to hold that it denotes the process through which an entity is held to be responsible for actions that violated the human rights of an individual. If a public authority is held to be responsible the victim is entitled to a remedy. Under the HRA, there is no limit on the remedies that can be sought. Section 8(1) of the HRA states: 'In relation to any act (or proposed act) of a public authority which the court finds is (or would be) unlawful, it may grant such relief or remedy, or make such order, within its powers as it considers just and appropriate'. Specifically in relation to the application of human rights law across borders, the remedy sought through the enforcement of the law has been, in the main, a bar on an extradition or expulsion or an enquiry into an unlawful death.

Extradition and expulsion cases

The enforcement of the law clearly differs according to whether extradition and expulsion or wholly extraterritorial cases are being examined. Enforcement is distinct in process and remedy sought. In regard to process, the question of the enforcement of the law arises in the course of extradition proceedings or in challenges to asylum and deportation decisions by way of judicial review. As noted in *McKinnon* and *Norris* above, attempts were made to enforce human rights law with a view to overturning a decision of the Secretary of State agreeing an extradition request from the United States. The Extradition Act 2003 explicitly requires consideration of human rights as a possible bar to extradition. Section 11 of the 2003 Act mandates human rights as one of the possible bars to extradition that a judge must consider in regard to extradition requests from Category 1 states. Section 21(1) provides that the judge 'must decide whether the person's extradition would be compatible with the Convention rights within the meaning of the Human Rights Act 1998'. Decisions rejecting arguments on the basis of human rights were appealed and led to the final judgments in both *McKinnon* and *Norris*. In expulsion cases such as *Razgar* and *Ullah*, on the other hand, attempts were made to enforce human rights law across borders by way of judicial review.[161] The procedural basis for Razgar's case was both judicial

161 There is a large body of interwoven law (international, EU and domestic) governing the substance and procedure of immigration and asylum cases. See, generally, in regard to

review and section 65 of the Immigration and Asylum Act 1999.[162] He challenged the Secretary of State's decision to remove him under the terms of the Dublin Convention.[163] In *Ullah*, the appellant sought to challenge the decisions of the Secretary of State and special immigration adjudicator to reject his claim for asylum. In regard to the vast majority of both extradition and expulsion cases, the person seeking to have the law enforced is within the territory of the UK itself. As has been seen above, there are some exceptional cases where the applicant has been outside the UK, either under the effective control of the UK abroad or within diplomatic premises; *B and others* is such as case. In the past there was a further possibility that allowed persons to appeal a decision to expel from outside the UK following the expulsion.[164] Generally, however, the majority of cases where human rights law is measured against situations outside the territory of the UK, under the law of extradition or asylum and immigration, take place under a procedure occurring within the UK itself.

Perhaps even more germane than the process through which cases arise is the particular remedy sought in extradition and expulsion cases. This is that the Secretary of State desist from his or her planned course of action – the extradition or expulsion of the individual concerned. Decisions of the Secretary of State are challenged directly or indirectly. A direct challenge can arise in extradition proceedings. An indirect challenge is one that arises from an appeal against

the enforcement of asylum law in the UK, Clayton, G., *Immigration and Asylum Law*, 4th edn, Oxford University Press, Oxford, 2010, esp. Chs 12 *et seq*.

162 Section 65 is no longer in force. It has been replaced by, *inter alia*, s 84(g) of the Nationality, Immigration and Asylum Act 2002, which states that a ground of appeal against an immigration decision includes 'that removal of the appellant from the United Kingdom in consequence of the immigration decision would breach the United Kingdom's obligations under the Refugee Convention or would be unlawful under section 6 of the Human Rights Act 1998 as being incompatible with the appellant's Convention rights'.

163 The Dublin Convention for Determining the State Responsible for Examining applications for Asylum Lodged in one of the Member States of the European Communities 1990 has now been replaced by the so-called 'Dublin Regulation' (Council Regulation Establishing the Criteria and Mechanisms for Determining the Member State Responsible for Examining an Asylum Application Lodged in one of the Member States by a Third-country National, Council Regulation (EC) No 343/2003, 18 February 2003. This regulation mandates, in general, that asylum seekers arriving in the EU make their claims for asylum in the first state they enter. Interestingly, the ECtHR has ruled that the application of the Regulation by Belgium in returning an asylum-seeker to Greece was in violation of the Convention on account of Greece's inadequate refugee processing arrangements, in *MSS v Belgium and Greece* (30696/09), unreported, 21 January 2011.

164 This was one of the issues in *Razgar*, in that the decision of the Secretary of State that the claim was manifestly unfounded under s 72(2)(a) of the Immigration and Asylum Act 1999 (now repealed) had the consequence of allowing removal prior to appeal. Therefore, were Razgar to appeal it would have to have occurred whilst he was abroad. The ability to expel an individual whilst an appeal of an immigration decision under s 82(1) of the Nationality, Immigration and Asylum Act 2002 is pending is presently forbidden by s 78 of that Act. The rules governing who can appeal from within the UK are found in s 92 of the 2002 Act. See further below on the rules governing 'safe countries'.

a decision relating to the grant of leave to remain within the UK. In both instances, the remedy ultimately sought is negative – the applicant or appellant is seeking to stop or overturn a decision relating to an extradition, expulsion or decision detrimental to his or her immigration status. This type of remedy is distinct from that normally sought where human rights law is applied on a wholly extraterritorial basis. An example of an extradition and expulsion case is *R (Daley-Murdock) v Secretary of State for the Home Department*.[165] Here, the Secretary of State had refused to grant leave to remain and stated that the applicant was liable to removal to Jamaica. Justice Williams held in regard to a challenge on the basis of Article 8:

> I am persuaded that the Defendant's assessment of the Claimant's children's educational needs, their links to Jamaica, the likely impact of their removal to that country and the ease or difficulty, as the case may be, of family relocation within that country was flawed to the extent that the Defendant's decision in relation to Article 8 is unreasonable or irrational.[166]

The Secretary of State was thereby obliged to reconsider his decision on these points in a lawful manner. A second illustration of the particular remedy sought is *QJ (Algeria) v Secretary of State for the Home Department*.[167] This was an appeal against the dismissal of an appeal of a decision to order the appellant's deportation under section 32(5) of the Borders Act 2007. This section introduced the compulsory deportation of 'foreign criminals', subject to certain exceptions, through, in part, amendment of the Nationality, Immigration and Asylum Act 2002. The appellant argued, *inter alia*, that his deportation to Algeria would give rise to a violation of his Article 8 rights. He had a wife and two children in the UK, and one of the children was suffering from a serious medical condition. What had given rise to the section 32(5) order was his conviction for terrorist-related offences, in regard to which he was sentenced to 11 years' imprisonment. The Court of Appeal had, as had the Special Immigration Appeals Commissioner, applied the test as laid down by Lord Bingham in *Razgar* and concluded that it was not disproportionate to deport the appellant. The remedy sought – the quashing of the deportation order – was refused and the appeal was denied.

Under the heading of enforcement it is necessary to note the attempts made by the UK to circumvent the law by obtaining assurances, in agreements or otherwise, that the receiving country will comply with international human rights law. Related to these, in a sense, is the list of 'safe countries' found in Schedule 3 to the Asylum and Immigration (Treatment of Claimants, etc.) Act

165 [2010] EWHC (Admin) 1488.

166 Ibid at para 32. These factors were both domestic and foreign, in that they concerned the situation within the UK as well as that in Jamaica.

167 [2010] EWCA (Civ) 1478.

2004. The agreements concluded by the UK are designed to address the issue of human rights abuses in third countries by securing the agreement of those countries that they will act in compliance with certain human rights in the event of the deportation of an individual to them. The list of safe countries deems certain states as places from where an asylum seeker would not be sent to another state in contravention of his human rights. Both merit discussion. The UK has secured assurances from Ethiopia, the Lebanon, Jordan, Libya and Algeria in regard to the treatment of persons deported to those countries. These are known as 'deportation with assurances' arrangements, or DWAs. The Memorandum of Understanding (MOU) between the Government of the United Kingdom and Northern Ireland and the Government of the Hashemite Kingdom of Jordan Regulating the Provision of Undertakings in Respect of Specified Persons Prior to Deportation[168] is one example. It provides that 'It is understood that the authorities of the United Kingdom and of Jordan will comply with their human rights obligations under international law regarding a person returned under this arrangement'. The MOU details eight specific undertakings, including that a returned person will be treated in a humane and proper manner. This agreement, and as well as a set of assurances given by Algeria, was at issue in the House of Lords case of *RB (Algeria) v Secretary of State for the Home Department*.[169] In this conjoined appeal, the appellants in effect argued that the assurances were insufficient to enable their lawful deportation to Algeria and Jordan. The argument was based upon the fact that Algeria had not been prepared to agree to independent monitoring and that the assurances did not in fact promise that the appellants would not be subjected to inhuman treatment. Counsel for Othman argued that the assurances could not be relied upon as a matter of principle where there were systemic human rights violations in the receiving state and a culture of impunity for those allegedly responsible. In both cases, the Special Immigration Appeals Commission (SIAC) had held that there were no substantial grounds for believing that the claimants would be exposed to treatment contrary to Article 3 if returned. The Court of Appeal upheld the decisions on the Article 3 point, stating that the issue was one of fact from which no appeal lay. The House of Lords agreed with the Court of Appeal and the SIAC on this aspect of the cases. Lord Phillips, in the leading judgment, referred to several ECtHR decisions, including *Saadi v Italy* referred to above, and held that the law did not require that assurances must eliminate all risk of inhuman treatment before they can be relied upon. He held that assurances form one part of the matrix of information that must be considered, stating: 'If . . . after consideration of all the relevant circumstances of which assurances form part, there are no substantial grounds for believing that a

168 Cited at http://news.bbc.co.uk/1/hi/uk/4143214.stm, accessed 25 May 2011.

169 [2009] UKHL 10. The case had been taken to the ECtHR with a hearing in December 2010; judgment is pending. Omar Othman, one of the appellants, is also known as Abu Qatata.

deportee will be at real risk of inhuman treatment, there will be no basis for holding that deportation will violate article 3'.[170] Lord Phillips held further that the application of the matrix of information by the SIAC could not be found to be irrational, and he dismissed the appeal on this point. Lord Hoffmann agreed that the decision of the SIAC was not irrational.[171]

A second mechanism that the UK Government has adopted which can and does affect the enforcement of human rights law abroad applies in asylum and immigration cases and operates through declarations that certain countries are 'safe' for the purpose of human rights and the Refugee Convention. The law is found in the Asylum and Immigration (Treatment of Claimants, etc.) Act 2004, section 33 and Schedule 3. The Schedule contains three lists of safe third countries. The first are those states party to the Dublin Convention referred to above. There are presently 29, to which the Schedule provides that they shall be deemed to be, *inter alia*, a place 'from which a person will not be sent to another State in contravention of his Convention rights'.[172] The second and third lists relate to states deemed safe for removal for the purposes of the Refugee Convention. In regard to the states within the first and second lists Schedule 3 places an obligation on the Secretary of State to certify that human rights claims against removal are clearly unfounded unless he or she is satisfied that they are not. A certification by the Secretary of State has the effect of preventing an appeal within the UK. The leading case relating to Schedule 3 is the House of Lords decision in *Secretary of State v Nasseri*.[173] In this case Nasseri, an Afghan national, had entered the EU in Greece and made an unsuccessful asylum application there. He travelled to the UK where he again made an asylum claim. Following the Dublin Convention the UK sought and received Grecian responsibility for the determination of the case. Nasseri was notified that he would be removed to Greece. He objected on the basis that there was a real risk that if sent to Greece he would be returned to Afghanistan where he would face inhuman or degrading treatment in contravention of Article 3. Nasseri applied by way of judicial review to quash the decision of the Secretary of State or, in the alternative, for a declaration that paragraph 3(2)(b) of Schedule 3 was incompatible with the HRA. It was held that the decision of the Secretary of State was lawful according to the terms of paragraph 3(2)(b). The question that

170 Ibid at para 114. A conflicting decision is *AS (Libya) v Secretary of State for the Home Department* [2008] EWCA Civ 289, where the Court of Appeal upheld SIAC's decision to allow the appeals of two Libyans against their deportation on the ground that a memorandum of understanding reached with Libya could not adequately guarantee their human rights.

171 Ibid at para 192. He stated: 'far from being irrational, [the decision] seems an entirely reasonable conclusion which SIAC was entitled to draw from the basic facts it had found to exist about the situation in Algeria'. See, further, Elliot, M., 'The "War on Terror", UK Style: the Detention and Deportation of Suspected Terrorists' (2010) 8 *International Journal of Constitutional Law* 131.

172 Schedule 3, para 3(2)(b).

173 [2009] UKHL 23.

faced the House of Lords was whether it should make a declaration of incompatibility. The Secretary of State argued that whilst the conclusive presumption in paragraph 3(2)(b) might be incompatible with Convention rights in another instance it was not incompatible in the present case because 'the presumption coincided with reality. Greece was a place from which he would not be sent to another State in contravention of his Convention rights'.[174] The House of Lords largely agreed with this conclusion. There was no real risk of a human rights violation in Greece through the deportation of the applicant to a third state, and, in light of the fact that there was not a free-standing duty to investigate possible treatment, there was no incompatibility. Lord Hoffmann stated in regard to the list system 'that unless the Secretary of State chooses to keep an eye on what is happening in listed countries and, if appropriate, invited Parliament to amend the list, she runs the risk of a declaration of incompatibility if the presumption produces the wrong result'.[175] As the law stands, then, the list system has little influence to affect the enforcement of human rights law across borders to 'safe countries', only operating where it is accepted that there is no real risk. Of course the law would not be applied across borders in such circumstances in any event.

Wholly extraterritorial cases

The enforcement of human rights law across borders in wholly extraterritorial cases arises in completely different circumstances than in extradition and expulsion cases. The remedy sought through enforcement also differs. Procedurally, however, the cases that have arisen have done so under the law of judicial review, which is similar to a number of the authorities referred to above. A leading wholly extraterritorial case is *Smith*,[176] substantively discussed above. It will be recalled that the applicant, the mother of the deceased Private Smith, sought judicial review of the coroner's original decision on the grounds, *inter alia*, that he had erred in holding that Article 2 did not apply and that he had no power to provide disclosure of documentation. The coroner subsequently consented to the quashing of his verdict and the ordering of a fresh inquest on the basis that he had erred on the disclosure point, and the Secretary of State conceded that since the deceased had died on a British base he was within the jurisdiction of the UK. Both the claimant and the Secretary of State, however, requested that the court deal with the remaining grounds of the claim and provide guidance for the fresh inquest. By the time the case had reached the House of Lords the issues were distilled into two questions of public importance: is a soldier on military service abroad in Iraq subject to the protection of the HRA when outside his base and, if so, must the death of such a soldier be the subject

174 Ibid at para 9.
175 Ibid at para 23.
176 [2010] UKSC 29.

of an inquest that satisfies the procedures demanded by Article 2 of the Convention? From the point of view of enforcement and procedure, then, *Smith* began as a judicial review of decisions made within a coroner's inquest. In *R (Gentle) v Prime Minister*,[177] the circumstances giving rise to the case were, sadly, similar to *Smith*, i.e. the death of British soldiers in Iraq. As in *Smith*, an inquest was held in the UK following the deaths of the two soldiers. Unlike *Smith*, however, no question as to the propriety of the inquest arose. Instead, the mothers of the two soldiers applied for permission to claim judicial review of the refusal to hold an inquiry into the circumstances which led to the invasion of Iraq. They argued that sections 1 and 2 of the HRA, in conjunction with Article 2 of the Convention, gave them the right to insist on a public enquiry into the circumstances leading to the invasion of Iraq and, in particular, the provision of advice to the Government as to the legality of the invasion. The issue in the High Court was whether the claim was arguable. Justice Collins held that even though the threshold for deciding on arguability is a relatively low one, it was not met.

Judicial review was also the procedural basis for *Al-Skeini*.[178] Here claims were made for judicial review on the basis of Articles 2 and 3 of the Convention. At the hearing, Collins J granted the claimants permission to apply in relation to two preliminary issues, to be determined prior to issues in the remainder of the application. These were, as noted above, whether the Convention and HRA applied to the circumstances of this case and, if so, whether the procedural duty under Article 2 had been violated by the UK. The substantive issues in *Al-Skeini* have yet to be definitively settled, with decision pending from the ECtHR relating to the two preliminary issues. In *B and others*,[179] an application for judicial review was made against the removal of the applicants from the British Consulate in Melbourne. The applicants had argued that the refusal engaged the responsibility of the UK. In particular, it was argued that the Secretary of State and his Consular officials were in breach of the Convention and the HRA in refusing to permit the applicants to remain in the Consulate, rather than, as they should have done, initiating a process with the object of preventing the return of the applicants to the Australian detention centre.

The final case highlighting the procedure leading to the possible enforcement of wholly extraterritorial cases is *Al Fayed, Petitioner*.[180] As noted above the case arose from the death of the applicant's son and Princess Diana in Paris. Al Fayed had presented a petition for judicial review in the Court of Session seeking reduction of the decision of the Lord Advocate to refuse to hold public inquiry in Scotland into the death of Dodi Fayed in France. The petition was served on the Lord Advocate and the Advocate General making out two grounds of

177 [2008] UKHL 20.
178 [2007] UKHL 26.
179 [2004] EWCA 1344, [2005] QB 643.
180 [2004] SLT 319.

incompatibility with Article 2 of the Convention and unreasonableness. The petition was dismissed.[181]

The remedy sought through the enforcement of wholly extraterritorial cases has to date generally been related to an inquest or inquiry or lack thereof following the death outside of the UK of its nationals, in particular soldiers. In *Smith*, the remedy sought originally was a new inquest that took into the specific requirements laid down by Article 2. As noted, this was conceded by the Coroner and Secretary of State early on in the judicial process. In *Al-Skeini*, the claimants sought judicial review of the Secretary of State's alleged failure and/or refusal to conduct independent inquiries into the deaths of the deceased, to accept liability for those deaths and to pay just satisfaction. Again, it was conceded that the death of the sixth claimant, Baha Mousa, occurred within the jurisdiction of the UK. In a sense similar, but with a different result, was *Al Fayed, Petitioner*. Al Fayed sought an inquiry into his son's death in Paris on the basis that the Scottish Ministers were obliged to instruct and he had a right to require such because of his Scottish residence and his being next-of-kin to the deceased. The remedies sought in the other two wholly extraterritorial authorities discussed above were, in contrast, unusual. In *Gentle*, the appellants sought a mandatory order requiring the defendants (the Prime Minister, the Secretary of State for Defence and the Attorney General) to establish an independent inquiry to examine all the circumstances of the deaths of their sons. The inquiry was to include the question of whether the decision to use force against Iraq was lawful. In *B and others*, the remedies initially sought by the applicants were fivefold, namely:

> A Declaration that the Secretary of State for the Foreign and Commonwealth Office, through his consular officers, acted unlawfully, a mandatory order obliging the Secretary of State for the Foreign and Commonwealth Office to make available British Consular offices and/or other premises in Australia falling within UK jurisdiction to the claimants should they be able to return, a mandatory order requiring the Secretary of State for the Foreign and Commonwealth Office to facilitate the claimants' journey to the British consular and/or other premises falling within UK jurisdiction, a mandatory order requiring the relevant UK authority to consider the claimants' asylum applications, and damages.[182]

The remedies sought in *B and others* were unusual and specific to the circumstances giving rise to the case. Indeed, the circumstances behind wholly extraterritorial cases are generally uncommon.

181 Al Fayed's case against France directly was also unsuccessful. In *Al Fayed v France* (2008) 46 EHRR SE7 the ECtHR held that his argument that the investigation in France was a violation of Arts 2, 6(1) and 13 was unmeritorious and inadmissible.

182 [2004] EWCA 1344, [2005] QB 643 at para. 23.

Overall, the extent and nature of the enforcement of human rights law on a wholly extraterritorial basis hinges on the rarity of such cases, the practical difficulties attendant to it and the legal complexity of the still-evolving tests triggering the application of law outwith the UK. In regard to the first point there have been relatively few cases where the law has been applied on a wholly extraterritorial basis – certainly in comparison to extradition and expulsion cases. This mirrors the practice in the criminal sphere where there have been relatively few convictions of persons for crimes committed on a wholly extraterritorial basis as compared to those with a territorial connection of some kind. This factor is circumstantial. It is simply that the UK relatively rarely exercises effective control over persons outside its borders in circumstances where human rights violations might arise. Practically, a number of factors militate against the application of human rights law on a wholly extraterritorial basis. These were iterated by Lord Drummond in *Al Fayed, Petitioner*:

> the process of collecting evidence would inevitably be difficult. The witnesses are most likely to be present in the country where the death occurred. Any real evidence, such as the car in which the deceased was travelling in the present case, is likely to be situated there, and any tests carried out on such evidence are likely to have occurred there. Any documentary evidence is likely to be found there. The initial police investigation, which is clearly of the utmost importance when a death is investigated, will inevitably have taken place in the country where the death occurred. Any post-mortem is also likely to have taken place there. In short, the evidence relating to the death will nearly always be situated predominantly in the country where the death took place. In these circumstances an investigation by any other state will face formidable difficulties; indeed, unless the state where the death occurred is willing to co-operate, the difficulties in recovering evidence are likely to be insuperable.[183]

The practical difficulties described by Lord Drummond Young themselves give rise to another issue – that an investigation in such circumstances would not be 'effective'. As Lord Drummond Young notes:

> Both the European Court of Human Rights, in *Jordan v United Kingdom*[[184]] and other cases, and the House of Lords, in *R (Amin) v Secretary of State for the Home Department*[[185]] have held that, if it is to satisfy the requirements of article 2 of the Convention, any investigation of a death must be effective. If one state is obliged to examine a death that occurred in territory of another, the likelihood of achieving an effective investigation is clearly low.[186]

183 [2004] SLT 319 at 578.
184 (2001) 32 EHHR 6 at paras 105 and 107.
185 [2003] UKHL 51 at paras 18 and 20(6).
186 [2004] SLT 319 at 578.

The final factor affecting the enforcement of human rights law on a wholly extraterritorial basis is the uncertainty in the law itself. As seen, whilst there is a degree of clarity around the fact that the law applies to areas where a state exercises effective control, such as a detention centre in a third country or diplomatic premises (and even here the (UK) law applies in large part on the basis of concession by the Secretary of State on the question not a judicial determination), there remains the question of state agent authority as a basis for the law to apply. Indeed, the absence of a body of clear and consistent judicial pronouncements on the nature of the effective control requirement itself affects the enforcement of the law.

5 Synthesis

Extra-legal context, criticisms, themes and conclusion

Introduction

The application of UK criminal law and human rights law across borders has been described above. In order to further aid understanding, a synthesis and analysis of the law is necessary. This has three parts: discussion of the extra-legal context of the application of law across borders, a critique of the law so applied and the development of the two themes introduced in Chapter 1. Linking all three elements of this synthesis is the premise that the application of law across borders is largely unnecessary and deficient. It is largely unnecessary because ideally it would be applied and enforced in only the most exceptional of circumstances. As has been seen, there is an ever-increasing amount of law in this area. It is deficient for a number of reasons including that it is applied on an *ad hoc* basis which lacks coherence and consistency. Cumulatively these facts lead to the conclusion that the present law and practice of the UK in the area is untenable in the long term.

Extra-legal context – fundamental differences

The legal context surrounding the application of UK law across borders has been described in Chapter 2. In coming to a complete understanding of the subject, however, one must also take note of extra-legal considerations. Put simply, it is important to recognise the material diversity in economic, political and cultural beliefs between, and within, states. Whilst this diversity has many manifestations for our purposes, it is variations in the understanding of, and approaches to, criminal and human rights law that are the most relevant. Consideration of global differences is necessary because the application of law across borders will almost certainly engage, to some extent at least, the legal system of a third state. 'Engage' in this sense denotes an intersection or overlap of regulation. This engagement may cause concern in third states because of the high regard that states place on the aims of the criminal law and human rights law. These aims can include the security of the state and its citizens, the imposition of an official or societal approach to morality and the position of the individual within the community and state. Actual or perceived UK interference with these interests in third states will not-unreasonably engender objection. Two points must be made in noting the extra-legal economic, political and cultural context of the application of law across borders: first, there is material diversity in views held as to the correct or optimal arrangement and nature of a state's economic, political and cultural systems; second, and in essence inimical to the first, there is a body of opinion to the effect that this diversity should not exist.

It is obvious that states take divergent views of the most desirable manner in which to organise their economic, political and cultural systems. Whilst this variety is perhaps less than in the past[1] approaches to, and stages of, economic, political and cultural development vary considerably. Whilst this point is axiomatic, there is value in laying down authority highlighting economic, political and cultural differences between states. This value stems from the substance of authority and its standing. A useful body of authority evidencing this diversity are the constitutions of various states. Article 1 of the Constitution of the People's Republic of China, adopted in 1982, provides:

> The People's Republic of China is a socialist state under the people's democratic dictatorship led by the working class and based on the alliance of workers and peasants. The socialist system is the basic system of the People's Republic of China. Disruption of the socialist system by any organization or individual is prohibited.[2]

Chapter 1, article 1 of the Russian Constitution 1993 states, 'The Russian Federation – Russia is a democratic federal law-bound State with a republican form of government'.[3] It goes on to provide protection for the labour and health of people (article 7), a 'free flow of goods, services and financial resources, support for competition, and the freedom of economic activity' (article 8) and ideological diversity (article 13). Article 4, section 4 of the US Constitution provides that 'The United States shall guarantee to every State in this Union a Republican Form of Government, and shall protect each of them against Invasion; and on Application of the Legislature, or of the Executive (when the Legislature cannot be convened) against domestic Violence'.[4] The First Amendment to the US Constitution states that 'Congress shall make no law respecting an establishment of religion, or prohibiting the free exercise thereof; or abridging the freedom of speech, or of the press; or the right of the people peaceably to assemble, and to petition the Government for a redress of grievances'.[5] Clearly, the essence of the core beliefs of these states is discernable by reference to their

1 A thesis largely adopted by Fukyama, F., *The End of History and The Last Man*, Avon Books Inc., New York, 1992.

2 Cited at http://www.npc.gov.cn/englishnpc/Constitution/2007-11/15/content_1372963.htm, accessed 26 May 2011.

3 Cited at http://www.constitution.ru/en/10003000-02.htm, accessed 26 May 2011.

4 Cited at http://www.gpoaccess.gov/constitution/index.html, accessed 26 May 2011.

5 Ibid.

constitutions. It is not difficult to conceive of the umbrage any one of them may take were a third state to act in a way that could be seen to interfere with anything it deemed so important to merit constitutional protection.

Germane cultural differences between states are readily seen in well-known and controversial cases relating to freedom of expression, speech and artistic license. Leading examples include the controversy following the publication of particular cartoons in a Danish publication[6] and in the reaction to Salman Rushdie's novel *The Satanic Verses*.[7] Here, views towards the freedom of expression and the protection that ought to be afforded religion have directly clashed – human rights law being the 'frontline', so to speak, between the two considerations. More particularly for our present purposes the possibility of an application of law across borders in this area may give rise to conflict. The cartoons and novel emanating from a Danish newspaper and a UK national respectively had effects within third countries in that they were, or could be, available there. Attempts were made to apply foreign law to Danish and UK nationals and concerns which in turn led to protest from those states. Indeed, because of the internet, 'publication' can 'occur' in any number of places instantaneously. The growth in the immediacy of communications and the volume of the international movement of ideas and publications has not been accompanied with a homogenisation of cultural belief. Cultural differences are, of course, also manifest in divergent views as to substantive and indeed procedural and evidential criminal law. As just mentioned Denmark, the UK and indeed the Council of Europe were legitimately able to object on account of the application of foreign criminal law to persons, corporations or circumstances within their borders – particularly the 'fatwa' against Salmon Rushdie issued by Ayatollah Khomeini.[8] Of course, there are a multitude of further, less high-profile differences in substantive criminal law and procedure. Subjects that have engendered particular debate and controversy include the age of criminal responsibility,[9] marital rape,[10] drug usage[11] and homosexuality.[12] Each of these

6 See http://news.bbc.co.uk/1/hi/world/europe/6037597.stm, accessed 26 May 2011. See further Nathwani, N., 'Religious cartoons and human rights – a critical legal analysis of the case law of the European Court of Human Rights on the protection of religious feelings and its implications in the Danish affair concerning cartoons of the Prophet Muhammad' (2008) 4 *European Human Rights Law Review* 488; and, more generally, Parmar, S., 'The Challenge of "Defamation of Religions" to Freedom of Expression and the International Human Rights' (2009) 3 *European Human Rights Law Review* 353.

7 See http://news.bbc.co.uk/1/hi/world/middle_east/185778.stm, accessed 26 May 2011.

8 See Munro, C., 'Prophets, Presbyters and Profanity' [1989] *Public Law* 369.

9 Article 40(3)(a) of the United Nations Convention on the Rights of the Child provides that 'States Parties shall seek to promote the establishment of laws, procedures, authorities and institutions specifically applicable to children alleged as, accused of, or recognized as having infringed the penal law, and, in particular: (a) The establishment of a minimum age below which children shall be presumed not to have the capacity to infringe the penal law'.

10 See Fomenky, C., 'Cultural Practices and Violence Against Women' (2008) 17(4) *Commonwealth Judicial Journal* 15, describing the position in Cameroon and the United Nations Declaration on the Elimination of Violence against Women.

subjects illustrates variety in criminal law and therefore contains the seeds of conflict where law is applied across borders. For example, a prosecution for rape within marriage committed outside the UK may be brought within the UK even where the law of the state where the act took place does not recognise the crime.[13] In such an eventuality, the *lex loci delicti* may well object to any interference within an area that it governs, although the nationality and domicile of the parties may be critical here for both states. The relevant UK law is section 1 of the Sexual Offences 2003 Act, which defines rape in England and Wales, and section 72, which provides for its application outside the UK in certain circumstances. Its application across borders is dependent upon, in part, the particular relationship the accused has with the UK – a national, resident or neither. A modern example of cultural differences affecting the application of criminal law came to international attention following the criminal prosecutions of Pitcairn islanders.[14] Views as to sexual promiscuity, age of consent and degrees of appropriate separation in sexual relations were all in question. It is in regard to these unsettled areas and subjects in particular that the application of UK law – criminal and human rights law – can give rise to controversy.[15]

Extra-legal context – universalist authorities

States' variety in approach to economic, political and cultural arrangements is an indisputable fact, as is the view that, in essence, this diversity exists on account of misapprehension. Such a view largely falls under the head of universalism. It criticises variation in certain core beliefs or practices – by holding that there is only one correct view. Consequently, it opposes the position that approaches or beliefs can legitimately vary according to the context in which they arise. Adherents to universalist beliefs espouse the correctness or appropriateness of certain views and state that these views should, and eventually will, apply globally. Context, history, geography, economics and political arrangement all fail to overcome this universalist dogma. Whilst it is beyond the scope of this book to engage materially in this discussion it is critical to note

11 See Downes, D. *Contrasts in Tolerance: Post-War Penal Policy in The Netherlands and England and Wales*, Clarendon Press, Oxford, 1988.

12 Kirby, M., 'Legal Discrimination Against Homosexuals – A Blind Spot of the Commonwealth of Nations?' [2009] *European Human Rights Law Review* 21.

13 The marital exception to rape was rejected in Scotland in *S v HMA* 1989 SLT 469 and in England and Wales in *R v R (Rape: Marital Exemption)* [1992] 1 AC 599.

14 Power, H., 'Pitcairn Island: sexual offending, cultural difference and ignorance of the law' [2007] *Criminal Law Review* 609.

15 See, further, Unsworth, C., 'Blasphemy, Cultural Divergence and Legal Relativism' (1995) 58 MLR 658, and, in an international context, Bostain, I., 'Cultural Relativism in International War Crimes Prosecutions: the International Criminal Tribunal for Rwanda' (2005) Berkley Electronic Press, Working Paper 656, cited at http://law.bepress.com/expresso/eps/656, accessed 26 May 2011.

the debate and profess a position.[16] This is because the view taken towards universalism necessarily and fundamentally conditions one's view of the application of law across borders. On the one hand, universalists could legitimately argue that the application of law across borders is appropriate, and a positive and useful tool to be employed. They could argue that it be used to attempt to engender change through the imposition of the 'correct', universally applicable rules. On the other hand, one disinclined towards universalism could object to the application of law across borders on precisely this basis – that it amounts to an interference with state sovereignty by attempting to apply or enforce foreign norms not accepted by the territorial authority and where the view towards universality is not shared. A vivid description of the sense of universalism that may give rise to controversy avers that:

> A universalist approach to international law . . . expresses the conviction that it is possible, desirable, indeed urgently necessary (and for many, a process already under way), to establish a public order on a global scale, a common legal order for mankind as a whole. International law, according to this understanding, is not merely a tool-box of rules and principles destined to govern inter-state coordination and cooperation; rather it constitutes a 'comprehensive blueprint for social life', as Christian Tomuschat has called it.[17]

Clearly, this is an aggressive version of the concept, and one, it is submitted, that is not practical to espouse or desirable to seek. It is tantamount to economic, cultural and political imperialism through the application of law (although in the passage, international law, not municipal law, was referred to). Practically, it cannot succeed purely on the basis of the consensual nature of international law. However, this does not mean that some states, academics and NGOs do not continue to impose their universalist concepts.

It is in regard to human rights that the greatest amount of writing and most strident arguments have been made in favour of universality – of a single set of norms applying to every state. Indeed, there exist international instruments supporting the position. The Vienna Declaration and Programme of Action adopted by the World Conference of Human Rights under the auspices of the United Nations states in paragraph 1:

16 From a human rights perspective, a useful introductory source relating to universality is found in Steiner, H., Alston, P. and Goodman, R., *International Human Rights in Context*, 3rd edn, Oxford University Press, Oxford, 2007. See also Donnelly, J., *Universal Human Rights in Theory and Practise*, Cornell University Press, Princeton, 1989 and Brems, E., *Human Rights: Universality and Diversity*, Kluwer Law International, London, 2001.

17 Simma, B., 'Universality of International Law from the Point of View of the Practitioner' [2009] EJIL 265 at p 267, footnotes omitted. See also Jouannet, E., 'Universalism and imperialism: the true-false paradox of international law?' (2007) 18 EJIL 379.

> The World Conference on Human Rights reaffirms the solemn commitment of all States to fulfil their obligations to promote universal respect for, and observance and protection of, all human rights and fundamental freedoms for all in accordance with the Charter of the United Nations, other instruments relating to human rights, and international law. The universal nature of these rights and freedoms is beyond question.[18]

Notably the Declaration goes on to accept, or concede, a degree of variation. Recognising variety in human rights, and political, economic and cultural systems, paragraph 5 states:

> All human rights are universal, indivisible and interdependent and interrelated. The international community must treat human rights globally in a fair and equal manner, on the same footing, and with the same emphasis. While the significance of national and regional particularities and various historical, cultural and religious backgrounds must be borne in mind, it is the duty of States, regardless of their political, economic and cultural systems, to promote and protect all human rights and fundamental freedoms.[19]

The Vienna Declaration is only one authority amongst a number of international statements and copious academic comment on the nature of human rights. Many of these argue for the desirability (or perhaps, more accurately, the unapplied actuality) of universal human rights. It is clear that these authorities and statements exist in the face of material variance in state practice.[20] As seen above in regard to the freedom of expression, for example, pronounced disagreements exist over the permissibility of criticising or discussing religion and religious figures.

Whilst less evident than in regard to human rights, there is a view that substantive criminal law should be, or is, universal in scope. The most obvious authority here is the relatively large number of conventions that mandate the criminalisation of certain acts. Several of these treaties are particularly widespread. The United Nations Convention against Torture and other Cruel, Inhuman or Degrading Treatment or Punishment, for example, has nearly 150 state parties, with Rwanda becoming a party in December 2008. With approximately three-quarters of all states party to the Convention, and the existence of torture as a crime within customary international law, it is perhaps untenable to argue that acts of torture should escape criminal sanction –

18 Cited at http://www.unhchr.ch/huridocda/huridoca.nsf/(symbol)/a.conf.157.23.en, accessed 30 May 2011.

19 Ibid.

20 Thienel, T., 'The ECHR in Iraq: the judgment of the House of Lords in *R (Al-Skeini) v Secretary of State for Defence*' (2008) 6 *Journal of International Criminal Justice* 115, criticises the House of Lords decision and the view that human rights law is culturally inappropriate in Iraq.

ignoring the non-legal arguments. There are, of course, many other criminally related conventions. A number of these have been mentioned in Chapter 3. For present purposes, however, the existence of conventions mandating the criminalisation of certain acts lends support to the argument that certain activity should be universally criminal. On the other hand, the need for such treaties in the first instance militates against the fact that states generally criminalise certain acts. A second cogent factor weighing in favour of the universal criminality of certain acts is simply that they are forbidden by all states. Murder and treason, for example, have a place in the substantive criminal law of every state. Of course, the exact definition, punishment and context of these acts can and do differ widely. For example there is considerable variation in approach to abortion, euthanasia and capital punishment – subjects that can be seen to be at the margins of criminal homicide. Notably and importantly these are also amongst the subjects that have come to the fore in the application of UK law across borders.[21] This fact lends weight to the cautionary stance presently advocated in relation to universality – both as regards the criminal law and human rights law.

Related to the universality of the criminal law is legal homogenisation on a regional basis – here, geography, history and politics have led to a form of quasi-universalism. In some areas of the world, Europe in particular, there has been a movement to homogenise substantive criminal law and procedures tangential thereto. The Council of Europe, discussed in Chapter 2, has concluded a large number of conventions in this regard. The EU, under the European arrest warrant scheme and more generally, has also been working in this area. The Lisbon Treaty takes some considerable steps in this direction with the Third Pillar of the EU, containing co-operation on justice and home affairs, being brought within the EU proper.[22] In essence, the Lisbon Treaty 'abolishes the . . . largely intergovernmental system of the . . . Third Pillar, and 'communitarises' policy co-operation and judicial co-operation in criminal matters'.[23] The European arrest warrant is based upon the European Council Framework Decision of 13 June 2002 on the European arrest warrant and the surrender procedures between Member States.[24] Recital 6 of the Preamble to the Decision states that 'The European arrest warrant provided for in this Framework Decision is the first concrete measure in the field of criminal law implementing the principle of mutual recognition which the European Council referred to as the "cornerstone" of judicial cooperation'. This mutual recognition assumes

21 Capital punishment and issues surrounding its application were at issue at the seminal ECtHR case *Soering v United Kingdom* (1989) 11 EHRR 439, discussed in Chapter 4.

22 The United Kingdom has secured an opt-out in regard to the Area of Security, Freedom and Justice, under Protocol 21 of the TFEU. See Ladenburger, C., 'Police and Criminal Law in the Treaty of Lisbon: A New Dimension for the Community Method' (2008) 4 *European Constitutional Law Review* 20.

23 Ibid at p 29.

24 2002/584/JHA.

not only that the criminal justice systems within each Member State of the EU forego the need for scrutiny of extradition requests, but also that the substantive law within states is largely similar, allowing for a list of framework offences to provide the basis of the surrender arrangements. Paragraph 2 of Article 2 of the Framework Decision contains a list of offences, or rather 'kinds of criminal conduct, described in very general terms'.[25] As the House of Lords has noted:

> Some of these, such as murder and armed robbery, are likely to feature, expressed in rather similar terms, in any developed criminal code. Others, such as corruption, racism, xenophobia, swindling and extortion, may find different expression in different codes. Included in the list, and relevant to this case, are the offences of trafficking in human beings, facilitation of unauthorised entry and residence and forgery of administrative documents. Underlying the list is an unstated assumption that offences of this character will feature in the criminal codes of all Member States.[26]

Underlying the arrest warrant system, therefore, is the assumption that all EU states criminalise these behaviours, that they should be criminalised and that the will to co-operate internationally to prosecute them exists. Clearly, arguments against the application of law across borders based upon universalism are weaker in the European context than globally. Europe is often conceived as an *éspace juridique*.[27] However, there is no doubt that universalism can form the basis of a legitimate criticism of the application of the law across borders on a global scale. As such, it is discussed further below.

Jurisdictional conflict and approaches thereto

In light of the application of UK criminal law and human rights law across borders and the fact that many third states act similarly, jurisdictional conflict is seemingly inevitable. This follows from the law being applied across borders, the importance attached to state sovereignty and territorial integrity, an almost infinite degree of inter-state interaction in the form of commerce, criminality, travel, diplomacy and military missions, and the largely permissive and liberal international jurisdictional regime. Perhaps surprisingly, then, conflict is relatively rare. Whilst there have been disagreements, several of which are discussed below, in light of the multiple applicability of law and the level of interaction between states there have been relatively few serious or high-profile incidents between states. Indeed, it is not with regard to the criminal law strictly speaking or human rights law that have given rise to the most acrimonious disputes between states, including the UK, but competition law. The most

25 *Office of the King's Prosecutor, Brussels v Armas and others* [2005] UKHL 67 at para 5.
26 Ibid.
27 As referred to in, e.g. *Bankovic v Belgium* (2001) 11 BHRC 435.

high-profile incident arose from Iran's issuance of a fatwa against Salman Rushdie over his authorship of the *Satanic Verses* – discussed above. A controversial case in which there was an attempt to exercise criminal jurisdiction involved Augusto Pinochet. Here, the controversy arose not so much as a result of the application of Spanish law to crimes of torture, but instead Pinochet's position as former head of state.[28]

Cases that have given rise to considerable discussion and controversy involve the application of both the criminal law and human rights law – in a wide sense. They entail the 'long-arm' application of the law by the United States and, in turn, a consideration of human rights by the UK, and as such fall within the area of extradition and expulsion. The leading ECtHR case is *Soering v UK*[29] – discussed in Chapter 4. More recently have been the so-called *Nat West Three* case and the *Gary McKinnon* case, where the United States applied its criminal law to circumstances which, to a greater or lesser extent, occurred in the UK. The UK, in turn, has applied its human rights law to circumstances in the United States in adjudging whether a violation would be engendered through an extradition.[30] These cases have given rise to a degree of controversy in both the United States and UK. The United States, on the one hand, felt that its interests were affected to such an extent that an application of its criminal law was merited. It was of the view that the accused has been/would be rightfully tried in the United States under its law. Certain groups within the UK, on the other hand, are of the view that in both these cases an application of the territorial criminal law was/is more appropriate. In the case of *McKinnon*, the UK itself appeared to be wavering, having failed to extradite McKinnon when there were no immediate legal hurdles in the way of doing so. On the other hand, the application by the UK of its human rights law across borders in these circumstances – considering the possible treatment of the accused persons on their extradition to the United States under the *Soering* principle – discomfited certain groups of people there in that it suggested that the US criminal justice system was deficient.

In accordance with the relatively small number of disagreements between states following the application of criminal law and human rights law across borders is the muted response in the form of a system to mitigate conflicts. There is no, one central agreement in either area of law governing the allocation of competencies or adjudging jurisdictional disputes where international or transnational criminal behaviour or human rights violations have occurred.[31]

28 It should be noted that although Spain sought to apply its criminal law in this case, English criminal law was considered in order to satisfy the double criminality extradition requirement. The cases arising in regard to Pinochet were noted in Chapter 3.

29 (1989) 11 EHRR 439.

30 As in the Pinochet proceedings, the UK also 'applied' its criminal law in these cases in a notional sense to satisfy the double criminality extradition requirement.

31 The Harvard Research in International Law, Draft Convention on Jurisdiction with Respect to Crime (1935) 29 AJIL 435, forms the basis of an attempt to codify criminal jurisdiction which, of course, did not evolve into a treaty.

As noted in Chapter 2, customary international law has developed categories of jurisdiction which exist alongside the general rules of international law protecting the sovereignty and territorial integrity of states. Additionally, and forming one of the themes of this book, a considerable body of specific conventions has been concluded in the area of the criminal law, and to a lesser extent human rights law, which allocate competencies. The only notable agreement here is bilateral and exists between the UK and the United States. This is the Attorney General and Lord Advocate's Guidance for Handling Criminal Cases with Concurrent Jurisdiction between the United Kingdom and the United States of America and corresponding Domestic Guidance, mentioned in Chapter 3. It addresses the possibility of jurisdictional conflicts and governs problems arising from the competing desires to apply the law, and acts to co-ordinate criminal prosecution – as opposed to limiting competency. Admittedly, it does contain provision in regard to minimisation of conflict and deferral of prosecutions. Generally, in the application of substantive criminal law and human rights law across borders, there is very little directly applicable regulation governing conflicts or limiting competencies. Both with regards to criminal and human rights law, their application is legally conditioned and limited only by the general conventional rules of public international law *inter alia* protecting state sovereignty and territorial integrity, specific treaties governing extradition, various inimical acts and general or specific human rights protection, and the rules of customary international law arising from state practice and *opinio juris*.

Criticisms of UK law applied across borders

The criminal law

The application of UK criminal and human rights law across borders can be criticised on a number of grounds. In some cases, these criticisms apply to a particular form of law applied across borders – executive, legislative and judicial – whilst in others they apply generally. These criticisms should be borne in mind when it is argued below that the law is developing, and should continue to develop, a proper law approach. This is because the proper law approach both feeds off and addresses many of the criticisms. Criticisms can be categorised under the following heads: lack of unifying principle, state sovereignty, neo-imperialism, universalism, extant mechanisms and fora, effectiveness and politics and realpolitik issues. Whilst some criticisms transcend single categories, classification is useful in describing and understanding their range. One criticism, which is focused on the nature of the law itself as opposed to something extrinsic to it, is that the application of the criminal law across borders lacks a unifying core principle. Such a principle could focus on the strength of the connection between the UK and the crime, for example, with or without reference to the nationality or allegiance of the accused, or could relate to the harm actually or possibly inflicted on UK state interests. Instead of developing a coherent single focus the law has grappled with maintaining and expanding its scope whilst at the same time abiding to its historical affinity to territory. The result has been a relatively complicated picture that has taken different approaches to crimes commencing or terminating within the UK – substantively and in regard to inchoate crimes. This extension of the territorially applicable criminal law has developed in a piecemeal and *ad hoc* manner resulting in inconsistency – in both statute and common law. Perhaps the pre-eminent example of this can be seen in the statutory and common law relating to conspiracy.

A similar evolutionary history, and resultant criticism, exists in relation to the criminal law applied across borders on a relationship basis. Again, no clear and consistent principle can be discerned that underlies the extension of law. This is seen in the variety of approaches to the particular relationship, with the law referring to nationals, subjects and residents, amongst others. Interestingly, and usefully for the purposes of developing the proper law approach, is use of the term 'close connection' in the Bribery Act 2010.

The extension of the law on a crime-centric basis is also *ad hoc* and unprincipled. In contrast with the extension of the law on a territorial and relationship basis, however, this is perhaps more understandable – and acceptable – in light of the fact that the law is particularly driven by international legal obligation. The 2010 House of Commons Briefing Paper on Universal Jurisdiction stated in this regard:

> In the UK, because each extension of universal jurisdiction has been in response to specific treaties rather than the result of a general assessment of the appropriate approach and scope, the UK courts do not have jurisdiction to try everything that might be considered a serious international crime.[32]

The nature of the criminal law as it stands can be defended and explained. Relevant here are the facts that it is based in both the common law and statute and the great complexity of society and criminality. Further, it is not suggested that the identification of an appropriate unifying principle, let alone its introduction and application, would be a simple task. This difficulty, however, should not prevent an attempt to do so. Indeed, it is argued below that the proper law approach can come into play here. The main point is that the lack of a central or unifying principle in the application of the criminal law is legitimately criticised. It is based on the desire for conceptual clarity – in response to the need for the criminal law to apply in a predictable and consistent way – as well as allowing persons and foreign states to determine and predict whether certain conduct is subject to the application of UK criminal law. A unifying principle

32 Thorp, A., 'Universal Jurisdiction, International Affairs and Defence Section', House of Commons Briefing Papers, SN/1A/5422, 25 March 2010, at p 7.

would also assist prosecutorial authorities in reaching to decisions to prosecute in a coherent and open way based on public and objective criteria.

Interference with the sovereignty and territorial integrity of third states forms the basis of one of the most cogent criticisms of the application of UK criminal law across borders. This is founded on the fact that in almost all cases part of the criminal conduct, or an effect of it, takes place or is felt within a third state. This entitles the third state to apply its own law. As seen in Chapter 2, the international law governing criminal jurisdiction is generous in its allocation of competencies. The application of UK criminal law to a third state which is also entitled to apply its law does not in itself give rise to an infringement of that state's sovereign rights. Concurrent competence often exists legitimately. However, questions are raised where the connection between a crime or criminal is objectively greater in the third state, and especially so where the conduct at issue is lawful in that state. Admittedly, the principle of double criminality in the law of extradition can militate against this – although there may be circumstances where the accused is already in the UK having acted abroad. More specifically and apart from extradition law, certain enactments condition the application of the law to circumstances where conduct is also criminal in the *lex loci delicti* – in particular where it is extended to apply to UK residents – an example being section 72 of the Sexual Offences Act 2003. These factors noted, the possibility that the UK will apply its law to an individual or circumstance which has a greater connection or link with a third state than itself does exist. In such circumstances it could be argued that the UK is violating the rules protecting state sovereignty. In practical terms, however, this is unlikely. In modern cases, for example the *Nat West Three* and *Gary McKinnon* cases, the UK chose not to prosecute – in spite of attempts to force UK prosecutions by those concerned – and instead deferred to the United States. Further, 'application' in this discussion has been taken to be synonymous with its enforcement. As described above, the application of the criminal law across borders is, in the vast majority of cases, legislative, and thus in a material sense latent. Third states may object only to the executive or judicial enforcement of the law, not its enactment to circumstances that may arise within or against its territory. If the third state does not object, however, this does not mean that the legislative extension of the law is acceptable. Rather, the state would not be sufficiently affected to object to a UK legislative enactment extending its law. Overall, the fact remains that the world is demarcated into sovereign territorial states that generally have exclusive competence to regulate the persons and events within them. It is clear that in certain circumstances the application of UK criminal law across borders can interfere with the rules of law protecting state sovereignty and territorial integrity. As such, it can be criticised.

The application of UK criminal law across borders can also be perceived as a neo-imperialist tool imposing the UK's version of 'universal' criminal law.[33] The

33 The debate over the position of torture (specifically inhuman and degrading treatment) as acceptable in certain circumstances is ongoing. Lord Hoffmann in *R (Wellington) (FC) v*

universality point has been discussed above. Here it sufficient to note that there are differences amongst states as to what is thought appropriate and necessary to criminalise. It cannot and should not be assumed by the UK Parliament or prosecution services that the substantive criminal law of third states is akin to that in the UK. In regard to neo-imperialism, it is not unreasonable to equate the application of UK criminal law to an individual or circumstance in a third country with the imposition or attempted imposition of the values and beliefs present in the UK as manifest in its legislation and common law. This perception arises whether or not the act is criminal in the third state, but applies with particular vigour if it is not criminal there. As with the criticism based on state sovereignty, however, this argument is perhaps more theoretical than real. This follows the relative rarity of the enforcement of the criminal law across borders, together with the fact that the crimes applied and enforced are usually those found in the law of most states. In other words, the UK does not apply what can be thought of as politically motivated or otherwise controversial crimes in this way. This is not to suggest that such crimes will not be applied across borders. A more general point in regard to the application of UK criminal law across borders and neo-imperialism is that only states with the requisite resources and a developed legal system can apply their law in other states. It has been noted in this regard that '[P]rosecutions may be vulnerable to accusations of double standards on the grounds that universal jurisdiction only serves to prosecute those from third world states, whilst no cases have been brought successfully against the leaders of western states'.[34] This double standard can give rise to suggestions of legal neo-imperialism, where western states, through the legislative – and judicial – application of their law, interfere and affect events in less-developed states.

A more tangible yet perhaps equivocal criticism of the application of UK criminal law across borders is that it can conflict with, or even defeat, extant mechanisms or fora designed to facilitate the prosecution of international and transnational criminality. As seen in Chapter 2, there is a large body of international and regional law governing criminal co-operation and the prosecution of crime.[35] Mutual legal assistance treaties, bilateral and multilateral extradition agreements, substantive international criminal conventions and international criminal tribunals all act to foster multilateralism and co-operation. Unilateral action, which is not uncommonly the form in which the criminal law is applied

Secretary of State for the Home Department [2008] UKHL 72 at para 31 suggested that it is relative. This was criticised by Milanovic, M., in 'Extradition and Life Imprisonment' (2009) *Cambridge Law Journal* 248. If inhuman and degrading treatment is acceptable then the UK's moral responsibility to prosecute (if it indeed has one) is absolved. For an analysis of the debate, see Ginbar, Y., *Why Not Torture Terrorists? Moral Practical and Legal Aspects of the 'Ticking Bomb' Justification for Torture*, Oxford University Press, Oxford, 2008.

34 Thorp, 'Universal Jurisdiction' (n 32 above), at p 9.

35 See also Rackow, P. and Birr, C. 'Recent Developments in Legal Assistance in Criminal Matters' (2010) 2 *Göttingen Journal of International Law* 1087.

and enforced across borders, can be seen to be antithetical to international criminal justice. Admittedly, a proportion of this international regulation is explicitly designed to facilitate the application of UK criminal law across borders – criminal conventions mandating the extension of UK criminal law being the paradigmatic example. That noted, the role of territory is central within international law generally and international criminal law more specifically. The vast majority of international agreements and mechanisms that exist to facilitate the operation of criminal justice across borders refer and rely on territory. Where the territorial state is unwilling or unable to act in regard to an alleged crime then any action on its part may be subject to trial by an international criminal tribunal – although existing tribunals and courts try only the most serious crimes. It is reasonable to expect that only where the territorial state (normally being the state with the closest connection to the crime) is unwilling and unable to try the offence at the time and for a reasonable period afterwards, and its does not fall within the competence of an international tribunal, that the UK should apply its criminal law across borders. It may be preferable in such situations to provide assistance to the territorial state to facilitate prosecution. Crimes of so-called sex tourism, for example, may not be prosecuted where they occur due to a lack of resources, expertise or evidence. In such circumstances, the UK could assist where the accused is a UK national, and extradite the individual back to the state concerned if the accused has returned to the UK.

Arguably of greatest weight is criticism that the application of UK criminal law across borders is ineffective. There are two elements to this criticism: that it does not appear to deter extraterritorial and transnational criminal behaviour and that it has not led to a material number of prosecutions and convictions of guilty persons. This brings us back to the discussion in Chapter 1 in regard to the purposes of the criminal law. If it can be assumed that the purposes of the criminal law include deterrence and the punishment of offenders – which is reasonable – then it appears that cross-border application of criminal law does not achieve these aims. If, on the other hand, the central purpose of the law is to provide a public code of unacceptable behaviour then its effectiveness is not affected by deterrence and enforcement issues. Indeed, in this the law is relatively effective in that it is clear that the commission of certain acts across borders by UK nationals and residents is illegal and that persons may be prosecuted and punished when they return to the UK. Clearly, however, the purpose of the criminal law is wider than the provision of a code of unacceptable behaviour – deterrence and punishment are also core to its aims. As such, the fact that the volume of extraterritorial and transnational crime is increasing but that the law is not being enforced can lead one reasonably to conclude that it is largely ineffective.

Part of the reason behind the ineffectiveness criticism is that there are almost insuperable evidential and procedural difficulties affecting the practice. Indeed, these integral elements of the criminal justice system were behind the 1996 Policy Review of Extraterritorial Jurisdiction, which concluded that it was inadvisable to extend the law. It stated:

> There are difficulties in mounting effective prosecutions or offences committed abroad which are common to all jurisdictions, including civil law jurisdictions, since extra-territorial jurisdiction is, by its nature, an exception or complement to normal territorial jurisdiction . . . Thus, it is possible to say, in general terms, that exercising extra-territorial jurisdiction is not a simple matter, although it can be done on the basis of a high level of co-operation and input of resources. For the United Kingdom there are additional difficulties arising from its common law heritage which post particular challenges to the successful exercise of extra-territorial jurisdiction.[36]

In regard to the enforcement of the law on a crime-centric basis the 2010 House of Commons Briefing Paper on Universal Jurisdiction stated: 'It is inherently more difficult for a prosecution to gather evidence when the crime was allegedly committed in another country by a non-national against other non-nationals'.[37] Following the 1996 Policy Review, Baroness Blatch stated: 'The review advised against any general extension of extra territorial jurisdiction because of the implications which so substantial an extension of jurisdiction would have for the procedures and rules of evidence of the United Kingdom courts'.[38] Underlying these statements is the fact that the criminal law has evolved in the light of a strong attachment to territory. The demands made by the law of evidence and procedure, now supplemented by the requirements of Article 6 of the Convention guaranteeing the right to a fair trial, lead to considerable difficulties in successfully prosecuting international and transnational criminality.

The final head under which the application of UK criminal law across borders can be criticised is politics and realpolitik issues. Two criticisms may be levied. The first is that the application of law may transgress the purely legal and enter the realm of the political. The criminal law generally is closely related to politics – for example, a decision to protect certain interests over others is inevitably a political one. However, when applied across borders the danger that the law is politicised – immediately and explicitly – is magnified. Relevant here is that an arrest and prosecution may be motivated, at least in part, by extra-legal reasons. This danger is particularly prevalent where private prosecution or other input into the prosecution process is possible. Countering this possibility in England and Wales is the fact, as noted above, that the Attorney General's consent is required prior to prosecutions taking place for a number of crimes applied across borders on a crime-centric basis. This consent applies to prosecutions, not arrest. A relevant development is the attempt to arrest the former Israeli Foreign Minister, Tzipi Livni. An arrest warrant was sought at the request

36 Home Office, *Review of Extraterritorial Jurisdiction. Steering Committee Report*, July 1996, at p 20.

37 Thorp, 'Universal Jurisdiction' (n 32 above), at p 8.

38 *Hansard*, HL, 23 July 1996, col WA117.

of private individuals. Whilst her eventual prosecution was almost certainly doomed to fail on account of the Attorney General not consenting to the request, the possible issuance of an arrest warrant did affect Livni's behaviour.[39] The requirement of consent to prosecute, however, is relevant to the criticism that the application of criminal law across borders may be overly political, in two ways. First, whilst it tempers politically motivated attempts to prosecute (and arrest) made by an individual, it is itself a political filter ensuring that prosecutions for certain crimes such as torture and war crimes proceed only if palatable to the government of the day. Second, crimes prosecuted on a crime-centric basis are themselves inherently political. Torture, genocide and war crimes, for example, contain within their definitions reference to a political motive or context.[40] Whilst it is not suggested that such crimes should not be prosecuted, there is a danger that political considerations will affect the decision where an individual state prosecutes, as opposed to an international or regional tribunal.

The second criticism under the head 'politics and realpolitik issues' follows on from the evidential and procedural difficulties mentioned above. This relates to the cost of undertaking such prosecutions, and the benefit to the national interest that result from them. In most cases, the costs of prosecuting a transnational or extraterritorial crime are considerably greater than a domestic prosecution. This follows from the *situs* of witnesses and evidence and the resulting complexity. As noted above in the prosecution of Zardad for torture and hostage-taking, he underwent two trials with the second entailing the attendance of Afghani witnesses.[41]

The question of the benefit to the national or public interest resulting from the application of the criminal law across borders is difficult. The cost in terms of money and resources must be weighed against the demands of the victim(s) for retribution, the statement by the state that certain conduct will not be tolerated, the deterrence of future crimes, etc. There is, it must be accepted, a point where it is no longer in the interests of the UK to apply its law in the circumstances. For example, the domestic UK public interest is, at best, only tangentially affected by the prosecution of a non-national for crimes committed

39 The law is in the process of being changed in order to limit the ability of private citizens to play a role in the issuance of arrest warrants. Clause 152 of the Police Reform and Social Responsibility Bill requires the consent of the Director of Public Prosecutions prior to the issuance of an arrest warrant for a number of crimes, including torture, piracy and hostage-taking.

40 This criticism clearly applies with less force to crimes applied on a relationship or territorial basis.

41 For the procedural and evidential difficulties arising from the application of the criminal law across borders, in the UK and the Netherlands, see, further, Corns, C., 'Interrogating nationals abroad: jurisdictional issues from *R. v Thomas*' [2008] *Criminal Law Review* 121 and Van den Herik, L., 'The difficulties of exercising extraterritorial criminal jurisdiction: the acquittal of a Dutch businessman for crimes committed in Liberia' (2009) 9 *International Criminal Law Review* 211.

outside the UK against other non-nationals especially if the possibility of deportation exists (assuming that the accused is present in the UK). Indeed, the UK's public interest dictates that prosecution is eschewed in almost all cases where the law is applied on a crime-centric basis.

Human rights law

UK human rights law applied across borders is deserving of criticism on a number of grounds. These largely mirror those levelled at the criminal law, but vary in their weight and emphasis. The fact that the criticisms of human rights and criminal law are similar is itself noteworthy. As discussed in Chapter 1, the nature and purpose of human rights and criminal law are very different – indeed, in several senses opposite. On the other hand, what is being examined is the application of law across borders. The application of law, be it the criminal law or human rights law, takes place within the context of international law and sovereign states. A degree of similarity in criticism therefore is to be expected. Generally, a description of the criticisms of the application of UK human rights law across borders provides insight into the similarities and differences between it and the criminal law as well as into the contextual points that apply equally to both.

As with the criminal law, the lack of a unifying principle or overall coherence behind human rights law is criticised. Further grounds of criticism, mirroring those applying to the criminal law, are state sovereignty and territorial integrity, neo-imperialism, extant fora, effectiveness and political and realpolitik issues.

The lack of a unifying principle underlying the application of human rights law across borders is its principle defect. The law is applied largely on an *ad hoc* and reactionary basis. The fact that human rights law when applied across borders is in the form either of extradition and expulsion or wholly extra-territorial makes it difficult to discern a single coherent principle governing or underlying the law.[42] A further factor is the nature and influence of the Convention and ECtHR on the law – criticisms here must generally be directed at the Convention and the Court rather than at the HRA and UK courts and jurisprudence. Indeed, a number of UK judicial *dicta* criticise the state of the ECtHR jurisprudence on this point. An example is Lord Phillips in *R (Smith) (FC) v Secretary of State for Defence* in regard to the application of human rights law on the basis of the personal status of the armed forces:

> [T]he contention that a State's armed forces, by reason of their personal status, fall within the jurisdiction of the State for the purposes of article 1 is novel. I do not believe that the principles to be derived from the

42 This may be fodder for those who believe that extradition and expulsion cases are not properly conceived as apart of the law applied extraterritorially.
43 [2010] UKSC 29 at para 60.

> Strasbourg jurisprudence, conflicting as some of them are, clearly demonstrate that the contention is correct . . .[43]

Conflicting cases and judicial *dicta* frustrate the development of a unifying principle. More generally, the strength of this criticism turns on the possible existence of such a principle. The two forms of human rights law applied across borders and myriad circumstances in which each can occur may make identification or development of a principle extremely difficult. The proper law approach, however, may contain the seeds of a unifying principle. As with the criminal law, there are factors linking the actual or future possible human rights violation to the UK, including territory and nationality. These factors, construed to include areas that are quasi-territorial (through the exercise of effective control), a form of subjective territoriality where persons are subject to extradition or expulsion and something akin to active personality (where those responsible for a human rights violation have a relationship with the UK) are suited to form the basis of a proper law approach, or at least the development of a central unifying principle underlying the application of all UK human rights law across borders. As the law stands, however, it is rightfully criticised for lacking a single or central unifying principle.

The rules of international law protecting state sovereignty and territorial integrity provide the basis of a second criticism of the application of human rights law across borders. As was seen in Chapter 4, some of the main authorities such as *Bankovic* and *Al Fayed, Petitioner*[44] strongly emphasise the importance of extant conventional and customary international law in relation to the protection afforded to state sovereignty and territory integrity. These rules may be violated by both forms of human rights law being applied across borders. Both encompass a UK court taking cognisance of an alleged human rights violation, past or future, that has taken place, or will take place, within the territory of another sovereign state. This may entail an intervention or interference within the internal affairs of that state. Persons and activities within the third state are subjected to the application of extraneous law. The ability of that third state to act exclusively, or not act, in regard to the situation is frustrated by the application of UK law. This in itself is not an infringement of the state's sovereignty. As seen, the rules of jurisdiction are generous and states are often entitled to act in regard to a person or circumstance in a third state. However, in regard to wholly extraterritorial cases, the precondition for the application of the law in this way of the exercise of control or, perhaps, state agent authority within the third state can be seen to exacerbate the interference. It compounds the interference by adding to the exercise of legislative and judicial regulation executive control. The extent of the interference with state sovereignty and territorial integrity through extradition and expulsion is perhaps less than wholly extraterritorial cases for this reason. The basic point is that they

44 [2004] SC 568 (hereinafter *Al Fayed*).

necessarily involve an 'assessment of conditions in the requesting country'.[45] 'Assessment' may be conceived as a form of interference. This is most clearly the case when, following an assessment, an attempt is made to affect the actions of third state by, for example, attaching conditions to the extradition or expulsion, such as the non-application of a specific punishment in the event of conviction.

Neo-imperialism forms the gist of a third criticism of human rights law applied across borders. It is founded upon the fact that human rights law may be employed as a tool, either directly or indirectly, that imposes UK policy upon or within a third state. This can occur directly, through the overt imposition of a rule such as the non-imposition of capital punishment, or indirectly, through judgment being made on the factual situation or legal system in the third state. Highlighting this rather starkly is Lord Justice Brook in a statement made in the context of a discussion of the level of effective control exercised by the UK in southern Iraq:

> And it is in any event very much open to question whether an effort by an occupying power in a predominately Muslim country to inculcate what the ECtHR has described as 'the common spiritual heritage of the member states of Europe' during its temporary sojourn in that country would have been consistent with the Coalition's goal, which was to transfer responsibility to representative Iraqi authorities as early as possible.[46]

The inculcation of the Council of Europe's (including, of course, the UK's) 'spiritual heritage' within Iraq or elsewhere is not unreasonably conflated with an act of cultural neo-imperialism. As the description of the law in Chapter 4 indicates, it is apparent that both forms of human rights law can be used and seen as tools of neo-imperialistic policy. They can be applied either with the intent to affect law or governance in a third state or occur unintentionally as a by-product of extraterritorial state action. It should be noted, however, that the weight and scope of this criticism turns, at least in part, on the human right in question and, indeed, the nature of human rights more generally. Relevant here, as discussed below, is the universal nature of human rights.

At a general level the debate surrounding universalism concerns the question of whether human rights have global application and meaning. If this is in fact correct then the arguments based on sovereignty and neo-imperialism above are clearly weakened. The point then would be how rights are protected, not their protection per se. On the other hand, if human rights are not universal but vary in application and meaning according to territory, culture, etc. then there is the real risk that the application of human rights law across borders would entail

45 *Soering v United Kingdom* (1989) 11 EHRR 439 at para 91.

46 *R (Al-Skeini) v Secretary of State for Defence* [2007] UKHL 26 at para 127 (hereinafter *Al-Skeini*).

the imposition of foreign and possibly inappropriate rules.[47] Highlighting the debate and echoing this danger, Otto has stated:

> In contemporary debates, the 'universalists', who are primarily Northern states, predict that even the slightest 'dilution' of universalism will give the green light to tyrannical governments, torturers, and mutilators of women. The universalist position completely denies that the existing universal standards may themselves be culturally specific and allied to dominant regimes of power. As political philosopher Daniel Bell observes: 'even some of the most thoughtful proponents of human rights in the West do not admit the possibility that every society need not settle on exactly the same conception of vital human interests.' At the same time, 'cultural relativist' counterarguments from Southern states entrench an intense polarization of views. The relativist position advances alternative claims to universal Truth that have their foundation in non-European cultural traditions and rejects the current human rights paradigm as oppressive for developing states with different cultures.[48]

The dangers of applying human rights law across borders are the most pronounced where there is a markedly different conception of human rights between the UK and the state where the violation occurred or which is the putative destination of an extradition or expulsion, such as between the UK and Africa and the Middle East. From an African perspective it has been noted that:

> Human rights, if they are to be truly universal must be multi-cultural . . . the European student should study the African Charter in order to better understand African perspectives and conceptions of human rights as an important constituent part of a universal concept of human rights. . . . Western and non-Western scholars should seek to overcome their gaping chauvinism and help admit other world-views into the international discourse.[49]

There is little doubt that the debate over the universality of human rights will continue. For our present purposes, however, it must be recognised that there is considerable variety in the human rights recognised and protected by states. This is an unescapable and indubitable fact. In other words, there is no practical

47 In *EM (Lebanon) v Secretary of State for the Home Department* [2008] UKHL 64 at para 42 it was stated that the UK and other Council of Europe states have 'no general mandate to impose its own values on other countries who do not share them'. Further, in *Z & T v UK* (Application No 27034/05) 28 February 2006 the ECtHR stated that a high threshold was necessary in deportation cases, 'otherwise it would be imposing an obligation on contracting states effectively to act as indirect guarantors of freedom of worship for the rest of the world'; cited in *EM (Lebanon) (FC) v Secretary of State for the Home Department* [2008] UKHL 64 at para 12.

universality. This leads to the conclusion that the UK cannot be certain that the rights protected in a state to which it is extending its law are akin to those it protects itself.

Existing with greater strength in regard to human rights law than the criminal law are the criticisms based upon the ground of extant fora. This simply follows the existence of a greater number of relevant fora and mechanisms in the area of human rights, for example the Convention, the United Nations Committee on Torture, the United Nations Human Rights Committee, the International Committee of the Red Cross, and numerous non-governmental organisations such as Amnesty International. In regard to the Council of Europe system Lord Drummond Young has stated:

> the structure of the Convention as a whole indicates that it is built around the principle of the exclusive territorial jurisdiction of each High Contracting Party. This appears from the provisions of the Convention that deal with breaches of their obligations by High Contracting Parties. The scheme of the Convention is that any complaint about such a breach must be taken not to the authorities of another state but to a supranational authority, the European Court of Human Rights.[50]

Clearly, one of the reasons for the creation of regional mechanisms generally was to address situations where territorial states were unwilling or unable to act, at all or sufficiently. In such cases, an individual within a participating state could, in certain circumstances, argue before the regional authority that that state was acting in contravention of the applicable treaty. Further, under some regional regimes there is the opportunity for inter-state complaints. Under the Convention this is governed by Article 33 (individual petition is provided for by Article 34). The possibility of inter-state complaints particularly weakens arguments in favour of the application of human rights law across borders by state parties *vis-à-vis* other state parties.

In addition to regional fora addressing the deficiencies within domestic human rights systems are international mechanisms and non-governmental organisations. An example of the former is the UN Human Rights Committee established by Article 28 of the International Covenant for the Protection of Civil and Political Rights 1966.[51] It scrutinises state reports, and where accepted by state parties, examines inter-state complaints (Article 41) and

48 Otto, D., 'Rethinking the "Universality" of Human Rights Law' [1997] *Columbia Human Rights Law Review* 1 at p 8, footnotes omitted.

49 Murray, R., 'International Human Rights: Neglect of Perspectives from African Institutions' (2006) 55 ICLQ 193 at p 197, footnotes omitted.

50 *Al Fayed*, at para 20.

51 Also relevant is the Committee Against Torture, created under Art 17 of the Torture Convention. See, generally, Dormenval, A., 'UN Committee against Torture: Practise and Perspectives' (1990) 8 NQHR 26.

individual petitions (First Optional Protocol).[52] In regard to NGOs perhaps of greatest relevance is the International Committee of the Red Cross (ICRC).[53] Germane examples of its activities are its visits to detainees in Cuba, Afghanistan and Iraq.[54] Admittedly, the ICRC does not adjudge possible human rights violations. At a 'pure' non-governmental level there are a large number of organisations that are relevant, such as Amnesty International.[55] Being non-governmental, this and similar organisations are not constrained by political or diplomatic considerations. Overall, it is reasonable to state that the existence of these various fora and mechanisms largely vitiate the need for the unilateral application of UK human rights law across borders. Indeed, it can be seen not only an unnecessary but inimical to the efficacy of the various regional, intergovernmental and non-governmental mechanisms designed to address and protect human rights – as well as the legal system of the *situs* of the violation (at the time or later).

The criticism based upon ineffectiveness has less force in regard to human rights law applied across borders than the criminal law. This is because it is largely effective in extradition and expulsion cases, albeit less so in wholly extraterritorial cases. In general terms, however, this criticism turns on the meaning of 'effective'. Simply it can be taken to mean that human rights are protected through prevention and the redress of violations. More particularly, effective human rights law results in the violation of human rights being prevented through the operation of positive obligations placed on the state as well as by an enforceable deterrent in the form of a reasonable likelihood that those responsible will be held to account and forced to provide a remedy.[56] It

52 See, generally, Joseph, S. *et al, The International Covenant on Civil and Political Rights: Cases and Material and Commentary*, Clarendon Press, London, 2000.

53 The ICRC describes itself as neither an intergovernmental organisation nor a non-governmental organisation but rather a hybrid in that it is a private association under Swiss law yet given a mandate and recognised by public international law, at http://www.icrc.org/eng, accessed 26 May 2011.

54 Wilde, R., 'Legal "Black Hole"?: Extraterritorial State Action and International Treaty Law on Civil and Political Rights' (2005) 26(3) *Michigan Journal of International Law* 739 at p 765. Wilde cites an International Committee of the Red Cross publication, *US Detention Related to the Events of 11 September and its Aftermath – the Role of the ICRC*, 14 May 2004.

55 Amnesty International's website is found at http://www.amnesty.org/, accessed 26 May 2011.

56 The interpretation of the Convention by the ECtHR to include placing positive obligations on states to ensure as far as possible that human rights are not infringed is one of the arguments used against the extraterritorial application of the Convention because of the impossibility of doing so. It has been noted that 'the prime characteristic of positive obligations is that they in practice require national authorities to take the necessary measures to safeguard a right or, more precisely, to take the necessary measures to safeguard a right or, more specifically, to adopt reasonable and suitable measures to protect the rights of the individual': Akandji-Kombe, J-F., *Positive Obligations Under the European Convention on Human Rights*, Human Rights Handbook No 7, Council of Europe, 2007, at p 7.

also leads to the provision of satisfactory and public redress to victims of violations. In regard to wholly extraterritorial cases, it is debatable whether the application of human rights abroad generally prevents or redresses violations in a meaningful way.[57] Affecting prevention is the remoteness of the law from the *situs* of the alleged violation and the context in which it is most likely to occur. Ineffective redress is in part a result of the particular tests applied giving rise to the applicability of the Convention abroad – effective control and perhaps state agent authority. These are met only in exceptional circumstances. As discussed above, the father of Baha Mousa had his human rights redressed in the House of Lords in *Al-Skeini*; the other parties to the case were not satisfied. In contrast to wholly extraterritorial cases, extradition and expulsion cases can be effective in the prevention of human rights violations. This is because, in these cases, the law is applied before a violation can take place, not subsequent thereto. The question of redress, then, generally does not arise. In regard to prevention, the law can be effective, indeed unusually so, in certain cases. In *Soering*, the law was effective in the sense that it led to assurances by the prosecuting authorities in the United States that the accused person would not be given a death sentence if convicted. However, as seen in various other authorities, such as *R (Ullah) v Special Adjudicator*[58] and *Wright v Scottish Ministers (No 2)*,[59] a 'stringent test' must be met to prevent extradition or expulsion. In these cases, as most others, the test is not met and the extradition or expulsion proceeds.

As with the effectiveness criticism, political and realpolitik issues form a ground of criticism of the application of human rights across borders which is distinct from that applying to the criminal law. This criticism relates solely to extradition and expulsion cases. It is to the effect that the application of human rights abroad may lead to the UK becoming a haven for suspected and convicted criminals. It can occur, for example, where persons migrate to the UK so as to escape the legal system of the territory where they have committed a crime. In *Soering*, the ECtHR stated in his regard:

> As movement about the world becomes easier and crime takes on a larger international dimension, it is increasingly in the interest of all nations that suspected offenders who flee abroad should be brought to justice. Conversely, the establishment of safe havens for fugitives would not only result in danger for the State obliged to harbour the protected person but also tend to undermine the foundations of extradition. These considerations must also be included among the factors to be taken into account in the interpretation

57 Wilde (n 54 above) at p 784 states: 'one should not be too sanguine as to the value of international human rights law to provide meaningful and effective review of extraterritorial state action'.

58 [2004] UKHL 26.

59 2004 SLT 823.

and application of the notions of inhuman and degrading treatment or punishment in extradition cases.[60]

Clearly, it is not in the interest of the UK to become a desired destination for those suspected of serious crimes committed outside it. Those persons may bring with them the attendant possibility of recidivism, and/or the expense of extradition proceedings when the state of the *situs* of their alleged crime discovers their whereabouts.

Themes

Two themes are discernable from the description of the application of UK law across borders. It will be recalled from Chapter 1 that these concern the increasing significance of non-UK law and practice in the area and the embryonic development of a proper law approach. The first theme is relatively simple. It is that UK law and practice increasingly operates within the context of international and foreign law. It goes further and suggests that this non-UK influence affects the application of its law across borders and does so, generally, in a way that mandates a specific and restrictive tact be taken. This theme also emphasises the importance of co-operation with foreign legal systems and international and regional legal regimes. The second theme is that a proper law approach is emerging in UK practice. There are two parts to the approach. The first suggests that a methodology is emerging which provides that the law is only applied across borders in the presence of certain links or connections between the UK and the person or circumstance. These connections include the nationality and residence of those concerned and the territorial connection to the UK. The second part of the proper law approach is that the UK may note the links between the person or circumstance and third states and, in some cases, weigh their strength relative to those existing with the UK.

Non-UK law and practice – the criminal law

The application of UK criminal law across borders is increasingly affected by European law, the law of third states and international law and practice. The description of the context of the application of law across borders in Chapter 2 and that of the criminal law itself in Chapter 3 firmly evidence the point that the time when UK criminal law existed in relative isolation from outside influence is over. Whilst it is not necessary to reiterate examples and details of the various internationally based influences on the application of UK criminal law across borders described above, it is useful here to categorise them with reference to the different forms of non-UK influence which can be identified. These are general public international law, European-based law which, of course,

60 (1989) 11 EHRR 439 at para 89.

takes the form of EU law and that emanating from the Council of Europe and foreign law, in particular judicial decisions.

The UK is party to a large number of treaties which relate to the application of its criminal law across borders. A number of these conventions have been detailed above. They affect UK criminal law and its extent in different ways. Generally, however, it can be stated that they relate to either the substantive law or what can be conceived as procedural international criminal law (comprising extradition and the provision of evidence and mutual assistance). Examples of treaties affecting UK substantive law[61] include the Convention against Torture and other Cruel, Inhuman or Degrading Treatment or Punishment 1984, the International Convention against the Taking of Hostages 1979, and the Convention for the Suppression of Unlawful Acts against the Safety of Maritime Navigation 1988. Each of these has led to the enactment of criminal prescriptions in UK law. Section 134 of the Criminal Justice Act 1988, the Taking of Hostages Act 1982 and the Aviation and Maritime Security Act 1990 respectively bring into UK law crimes which apply, in one sense or another, across borders. It is worth stating here that the UK was one of the founding members of the International Criminal Court, and in consequence the International Criminal Court Act 2001 and the International Criminal Court (Scotland) Act 2001 have been enacted. But, as noted above, the application of UK criminal law to the acts prescribed under these Acts is less expansive than it could have been. Generally, however, a large number of conventions oblige the UK to extend its criminal law across borders.[62] The number of such crimes would surely be considerably less if it were not for the influence of public international law.[63] Procedurally, the UK is party to a considerable number of bilateral extradition and mutual assistance agreements, which can act to facilitate the enforcement of the criminal law across borders. The most controversial of these is the Extradition Treaty between the Government of the United Kingdom of Great Britain and Northern Ireland and the Government of the

61 The distinction between substantive and procedural conventional law is imperfect as many of these 'substantive' conventions also contain provision in regard to prosecution, extradition, and co-operation evidentially.

62 The treaties to which the UK is party are accessible from the Foreign and Commonwealth's website, the FCO treaty service online, at http://www.fco.gov.uk/en/publications-and-documents/treaties/, accessed 26 May 2011. A unique agreement – the Agreement between the Government of the Kingdom of the Netherlands and the Government of the United Kingdom of Great Britain and Northern Ireland Concerning a Scottish Trial in the Netherlands, 18 September 1998 (1999) 38 ILM 926 – led to trial in the Netherlands of the two suspects accused of planting the bomb that resulted in the explosion over Lockerbie, Scotland.

63 Of course the UK is not obliged to become party to these conventions, and therefore the 'influence' of public international law here is a product of UK action itself. That noted, decisions to become party to such treaties in the first instance are affected by the status and standing of the agreement or proposed agreement, the nature and number of third states pre-disposed to become parties and other extraneous considerations. There may, therefore, be benefits to subscribing to a treaty outside the specific terms of that treaty itself.

United States of America 2003. Mutual assistance treaties have been discussed in Chapter 3; however, it is important to reiterate that the application, in particular the enforcement, of UK criminal law across borders is greatly affected by these treaties. Whilst the number of cases in which the criminal law is enforced across borders is relatively small – certainly in comparison with domestic prosecutions but also in relation to the number of crimes committed with an international dimension – it would be considerably smaller were it not for international agreements governing extradition and mutual assistance.

The impact of law emanating from the Council of Europe and the EU has had an even more pronounced effect on the application of UK criminal law across borders than general public international law. In contrast to international law, however, the impact is greater procedurally than substantively. That noted, the Council of Europe has concluded a number of conventions relating to substantive criminal law. Some of these oblige state parties to enact criminal prescriptions within their law. These include the Criminal Law Convention on Corruption 1999 and the Convention on Laundering, Search, Seizure, and Confiscation from the Proceeds of Crime 1990. There has also been the increasing emergence of a substantive criminal dimension to EU law.[64] Admittedly, however, the bulk of EU regulation in the area of the criminal law is procedural rather than substantive.[65] Council of Europe and EU influence on the application of UK criminal law across borders procedurally largely relates to extradition, as well as mutual legal assistance. The intra-EU extradition scheme creating a largely administrative and procedural system of extradition is governed by the Council Framework Decision of 13 June 2002 on the European Arrest Warrant and the Surrender Procedures between Member States.[66] As noted in Chapter 3, the European arrest warrant scheme has had a considerable impact in facilitating the application of law across borders, and in turn has given rise to a number of judicial authorities in which the law has been tested. The Council of Europe's main influence has been in the area of mutual assistance. It has overseen the conclusion of a number of relevant agreements including the European Convention on Mutual Assistance in Criminal Matters 1959, discussed in Chapter 3.

The domestic law of third states has no binding force on or in the UK, unlike EU and international law. This is not to say that it has not had an effect. The jurisprudence of other states has increasingly found a place in UK case law relating to the application of criminal law across borders. This has occurred largely on account of points of law arising in UK cases that are relatively novel, and courts being referred to, and considering, decisions in third state jurisdictions as aids in the decision-making process. A example of this is the

64 See, generally, Mitsilegas, V., *EU Criminal Law*, Hart Publishing, London, 2009.

65 See Fletcher, M., Lööf, R. and Gilmore, B., *EU Criminal Law and Justice*, Edward Elgar, Cheltenham, 2008, esp. Ch 6.

66 2002/584/JHA, cited at http://eur-lex.europa.eu/LexUriServ/LexUriServ.do?uri=CELEX:32002F0584:EN:NOT, accessed 26 May 2011.

Canadian case *United States v Cotroni*,[67] which was referred to in *Onwuzulike v Government of the United States of America*[68] and *Khan v United States*.[69] There are many other examples. Notable amongst them is the reference to *US v Cobb*,[70] another Canadian case, in *McKinnon v Government of the United States*[71] in the House of Lords. In *R v Bow Street Metropolitan Stipendiary Magistrate and others ex p Pinochet Ugarte (No 3)*[72] a number of decisions heard by courts outside the UK were discussed, including the Canadian case *United States of America v Swystun*.[73] In *R (Al-Fawwaz) v Governor of Brixton Prison and another*[74] the House of Lords referred to the US decision of *Demjanjuk v Petrovsky*,[75] the Israeli case of *Attorney-General v Eichmann*[76] and the Canadian case of *Kirkwood v United Kingdom*.[77] The effect of these third state decisions must not be overlooked. Whilst, of course, UK courts are free to disregard them, in most cases considerable heed is paid to the judgments. This is relevant in itself, in demonstrating the extent of non-UK legal influence in the area, and is significant in that certain third state cases add support to the emergence of a proper law of the crime approach.

Proper law – the criminal law

The second theme in this book is that a proper law approach is emerging when UK law is applied in an international or transnational sense. It the criminal sphere it acts most immediately to affect decisions of both the executive, in the form of prosecutorial authorities, and the courts. It also underlies decisions to extend the criminal law legislatively. The approach has two parts. First, it entails a process whereby the law is applied only in the presence of a material link or connection between the alleged criminal act, or human rights violation, and the UK. Second, the approach can comprise awareness on the part of the UK of the links that exist with third states and in some cases an analysis of their strength relative to those existing with the UK. This analysis, or weighing-up, can take place with a view to proceeding with the application of the law where the strength of the links justifies it, or the deferral to a third state where they do not. It is important in understanding the proper law approach as it applies to the criminal and human rights law to note the distinction between private and

67 [1989] 1 SCR 1469.
68 [2009] EWHC (Admin) 1395.
69 [2010] EWHC (Admin) 1127. These cases will be mentioned below in the discussion of the developing proper law approach.
70 [2001] 1 SCR 587.
71 [2008] UKHL 59.
72 [2000] 1 AC 147.
73 (1987) 50 Man R (2d) 129.
74 [2001] UKHL 69.
75 (1985) 603 F Supp 1468.
76 (1962) 36 ILR 5.
77 (1984) 37 DR 158.

non-private law. In the non-private sphere, the proper law approach must govern both the decision as to which body of law is applied to a person or circumstance and the legal system that applies it. This is different from the position that exists in private law. Although the UK will not apply the non-private law of a third state, it may apply its private law. This is a fundamental difference between the two spheres as far as the application of law across borders is concerned. In regard to non-private law, the questions of 'jurisdiction' (whether a court will entertain a case) and the 'applicable law' (which law governs) are not distinguished. If it is found that the law applies to a person or circumstance it is almost inevitable that a court within the UK will be competent to hear the case.

The initial point to note in outlining the argument that there is an emerging proper law approach – at least the first part or plank of the approach – is that it is, in fact, axiomatic. As the discussion above clearly demonstrates, where UK criminal law is extended it is done so on a territorial or personal basis in the vast majority of cases. The UK is beginning to conceive of territory and personal relationships as connections within a proper law approach methodology. There is an understanding that territory and relationships can be seen to be links or connections within a context where there may be other relevant connections or indeed degrees of connection. Of course, the law is not generally applied in the absence of a territorial or relationship connection between the UK and the crime or accused. This simply follows the fact the UK in general has no immediate interest in applying its law to persons or cases that have no connection with it. The criminal law serves to protect certain interests, and those interests by their very nature have a close and immediate connection to the UK. For example, the criminal law seeks to maintain the Queen's peace. Criminal behaviour on the territory of the UK is therefore subject to the criminal law. An act outwith the UK is generally only subject to the possible application of UK law if it has an impact on or in its territory. As the Home Office Steering Committee Report Review of Extra-Territorial Jurisdiction 1996 states, the exceptions to the territorial nature of jurisdiction have been in response to 'the requirements of public policy and protection of the national interest'.[78] The first part of the proper law approach, that UK criminal law is only applied in the presence of a material link between it and the alleged crime or criminal, then, is in almost all cases entirely self-evident. This conclusion can be drawn without detailed analysis of what exactly a material linkage entails because it is clear that a territorial connection and a residence or nationality link is in almost all cases sufficient.[79] Where there is a link of the requisite degree the law can be applied. Perhaps more precisely, the proper law approach stipulates that the law cannot

78 Home Office Communications Directorate, Steering Committee Report, *Review of Extra-Territorial Jurisdiction*, 1996, at p 10.

79 The presence of a territorial connection, or one of sufficient strength, is not always easy to ascertain, as the discussion of inchoate crimes in Chapter 3 demonstrates.

be applied in the absence of a sufficient link. The approach does, and must, reflect actual practice. It demonstrates that in the vast majority of cases the UK does not apply its criminal law in an egregious way. Further, it provides that where a material link is not readily evident the application must be scrutinised carefully in order to discern one. Finally, it should be noted that the first part of the proper law approach is largely self-evident because the UK generally takes a restrictive and conservative approach to the application of its criminal law across borders.

Authority in support of the first part of the proper law approach has been described in Chapter 3. As noted, the vast majority of crimes that apply across borders do so with reference to territory or the relationship of the accused to the UK. It is necessary here only to reiterate the strength of this point, as well as to highlight exceptional cases where the criminal law has been applied in the absence of such a link. The exceptional cases are discussed in order to test the strength of the rule itself. Clearly, territory has been, and remains, absolutely central to the application of UK criminal law. As demonstrated above from the developmental period of the common law to today the courts have normally sought to apply the law on a territorial basis. In 1881 Lord Young, in *HM Advocate v Hall*, stated:

> The general rule is that criminal law is strictly territorial – so that a man is subject only to the criminal law of the country where he is, and that his conduct there, whether by acting, speaking, or writing, shall be judged of as criminal or not by that law and no other.[80]

Over a century later, Lord Griffiths stated:

> Unfortunately in this century crime has ceased to be largely local in origin and effect. Crime is now established on an international scale and the common law must face this new reality. Their Lordships can find nothing in precedent, comity or good sense that should inhibit the common law from regarding as justiciable in England inchoate crimes committed abroad which are intended to result in the commission of criminal offences in England.[81]

Even here, in a case of a transnational, drug-related conspiracy, a territorial link was relied upon although it took the form of an intention alone. The second, long-standing connection between a crime and an accused and the UK is a personal one. Murder, manslaughter, culpable homicide, treason and bigamy are some of the crimes that have been applied across borders on the basis of the

80 (1881) 4 Couper 438.

81 *Somchai Liangsiriprasert v Government of the United States of America and another* [1991] 1 AC 225 at 251.

relationship between the accused and the UK alone for some considerable time. The 1996 Review of Extra-Territorial Jurisdiction commenced with the statement:

> Criminal jurisdiction in the UK generally is territorially based, in other words conduct constituting an offence must have some connection with the territory of the UK. Offences committed by British nationals abroad are not normally prosecutable in this country, unless they fall within a limited range of statutory exceptions.[82]

Even more exceptional (in terms of rarity and discordance with historical practice) are those crimes within UK criminal law that do not refer to or require either a territorial or personal connection – those termed 'crime centric' in Chapter 3. Here international law provides the impetus for the UK to act in this expansive way.

A specific type of authority supporting the argument that a proper law approach is emerging in UK law is found in the response to the problems caused by the application of the terminatory (or objective) theory. The problems led to a new and more flexible approach to the application of law with a territorial connection, known as the 'inclusionary' approach. Moving away from what was perhaps an overly stringent attachment to territory the response opens the door, as it were, to the possibility of a new methodology. This looks holistically at the links between the UK and the crime and criminal. As was discussed in Chapter 3, the practice of considering inchoate crimes as jurisdictionally *sui generis* has ceased. The more flexible approach that was previously reserved to inchoate crimes alone has come to be considered relevant in other circumstances. As noted in *R v Smith (Wallace Duncan) (No 4)*,[83] a factor underlying the development of the inclusionary approach was the desire that the law be consistent with the position in regard to conspiracy and attempts. In a sense, mirroring the common law's development of a somewhat more flexible approach are several novel legislative provisions. These include the Criminal Justice Act 1993 and the Criminal Justice (Terrorism and Conspiracy) Act 1998. The overall effect of these enactments is to expand the applicability of the law by eschewing an overly rigid or narrow approach to the extent of the law. An example here is the use of the mechanism 'any relevant event' under the Criminal Justice Act 1993. In addition, the Bribery Act 2010 employs the device of the 'close connection' in section 12(3) and (4) in extending the law to certain individuals. Whilst 'close connection' here is limited to relationship-based links, the Act utilises the term for what is believed to be the first time in a criminally related statutory provision. Overall, these disparate authorities lend implicit support for an emerging proper law approach in that they focus on the link or connection

82 Steering Committee Report, *Review of Extra-Territorial Jurisdiction* (n 78 above), at p 1.
83 [2004] EWCA (Civ) 631.

between the UK and the crime and criminal in a more holistic way than merely focusing on a specific and narrow territorial or personal attachment.

The emergence of a proper law approach does not entail a widening of the range of offences subject to being applied across borders. Indeed, the proper law approach does not lead to an expansion of circumstances and people to which the law applies, but rather greater focus upon why and how the law applies as it does. This restrictive and conservative approach is seen in the UK largely relying on territory and relationship and making very limited use of the latitude given by international law to take a broader tact, such as a crime-centric basis or one relying on the nationality of the victim. These latter links are only exceptionally utilised in UK law. As noted in Chapter 3, only one case in UK practice where the law has been enforced has been recorded to have taken place for an extraterritorial crime by a non-national or resident (at the time of trial), that of Farayadi Sawar Zardad in 2005.[84] Certain other cases which may at first glance appear to forego the requirement of a territorial or personal link in fact require a residence or nationality requirement. Even the legislative example of the International Criminal Court Act 2001, a statute one might reasonably believe would apply the law without reference to a territorial or personal link, does so. Two conclusions can be drawn here. The first is that the vast majority of crimes include (explicitly or implicitly) a requirement that there is a link to UK territory or that the accused has a certain relationship with it. Second, legislative crimes that eschew the requirement for a connection generally result from international legal obligations and are rarely enforced.

The second element of the proper law approach, perhaps unexpectedly, finds more explicit reference in UK practice than the first. In both case law and other authority is explicit or implicit reference to the proper law approach and related terminology. Judicially, there is a developing line of cases which refer to the proper law approach, and *forum non conveniens*, in extradition cases. *Forum non conveniens* is a discretionary power of courts to stay actions where the appropriate forum for trial is abroad. It has been considered in a line of cases in response to the argument that US courts are not appropriate and UK courts are. One of these line of cases, *Onwuzulike v Government of the United States of America*,[85] was referred to in Chapter 1. Following that case was *Khan v United States*.[86] Here Khan appealed a decision of Westminster Magistrates' Court which had rejected his arguments against extradition. He argued that his extradition would expose him to trial in an inappropriate forum. Whilst the High Court held that it was incompetent to raise the issue afresh on appeal, it proceeded to consider it nonetheless. Fitzgerald for Khan argued that the drugs offences with which Khan had been charged should be tried in the courts of England and Wales. He

84 See the Crown Prosecution Service's Press Release of 18 July 2005, at http://cps.gov.uk/news/press_releases/135_05/, accessed 23 May 2011.

85 [2009] EWHC (Admin) 1395.

86 [2010] EWHC (Admin) 1127.

argued that the extradition of Khan to the US would violate his Article 6 rights because trial in an inappropriate forum would be arbitrary and expose him to a flagrant denial of justice as well as violate his Article 8 rights. The Canadian case of *US v Cotroni*[87] was referred to, as it had been in *Onwuzulike*. La Forest J in *Cotroni*, citing the earlier case of *United States of America v Swystun*,[88] decided in the Court of Queen's Bench of Manitoba, held that in practice 'the decision whether to prosecute, or not to prosecute in this country and allow the authorities in another country to seek extradition, is made following consultations between the appropriate authorities in the two countries', and the factors which will usually affect such a decision include:

> where was the impact of the offence felt or likely to have been felt, which jurisdiction has the greater interest in prosecuting the offence, which police force played the major role in the development of the case, which jurisdiction has laid charges, which jurisdiction has the most comprehensive case, which jurisdiction is ready to proceed to trial, where is the evidence located, whether the evidence is mobile, the number of accused involved and whether they can be gathered together in one place for trial, in what jurisdiction were most of the acts in furtherance of the crime committed, the nationality and residence of the accused [and] the severity of the sentence the accused is likely to receive in each jurisdiction.[89]

Fitzgerald in *Khan* then cited the following passage from *R (Bermingham) v Director of the Serious Fraud Office* by Laws LJ:

> I do not accept [the US government's] submission that the possibility of a trial in the United Kingdom is legally irrelevant in a case like this. There might be an instance in which such a possibility could tip the balance of judgment in favour of a conclusion that the defendant's extradition would amount to a disproportionate interference with his Article 8 rights.[90]

The High Court rejected Fitzgerald's argument on this point. It cited *Norris v Government of the United States (No 2)*:

> Extradition proceedings should not become the occasion for a debate about the most convenient forum for criminal proceedings. Rarely, if ever, on an issue of proportionality could the possibility of bringing criminal proceedings in this jurisdiction be capable of tipping the scales against extradition in accordance with the countries treaty obligations. Unless the judge reached

87 [1989] 1 SCR 1469.
88 (1987) 50 Man R (2d) 129.
89 [1989] 1 SCR 1469 at 1498–1499.
90 [2006] EWHC (Admin) 200 at para 121.

> the conclusion that the scales are finely balanced he should not enter into an enquiry as to the possibility of prosecution in this country.[91]

The proportionality issue referred to in *Khan* arose in the context of human rights, namely when considering the qualification test found in the second paragraph of a number of articles of the Convention, such as, in this case, Article 8(2). Subject to decision here was the question of whether the interference with family life engendered by an extradition was proportionate to its legitimate aim. That aim included the public interest in honouring extradition treaties and the prosecution of transnational crime. As noted, the appeal on the point was rejected. However, *Khan* remains a case where the second part of the proper law approach was considered, even if it is not one where it had an effect in the final decision.[92]

In addition to certain judicial decisions providing support for the second plank of the proper law approach are various non-judicial sources. The annex to the 2003 Eurojust Annual Report is entitled 'Making the Decision – Which Jurisdiction Should Prosecute'. It addresses what action should be taken in the event of more that one country prosecuting similar acts.[93] The Guidelines provide that there should be a presumption that a prosecution should take place in the jurisdiction where the majority of the criminality took place or the loss was sustained.[94] They provide that some of the factors that should be considered are the location of the accused, the possibility of extradition, the division of a prosecution between states, the attendance and protection of witnesses, delay, the interests of victims and evidential problems. The Guidance defines prosecutors to include judges and other competent authorities.[95] The annex largely mirrors the Attorney General and Lord Advocate's 'Guidance for Handling Criminal Cases with Concurrent Jurisdiction between the United Kingdom and the United States of America and corresponding Domestic Guidance',[96] discussed in Chapter 3. Both, obviously, relate to the enforcement of the law, as opposed to the enactment of it.

Two final pieces of authority that provide a degree of support for the second plank of an emerging proper law approach are the Home Office Steering Committee Report Review of Extra-Territorial Jurisdiction 1996 and accom-

91 [2010] UKSC 9 at para 67.

92 A further relevant authority which supports the second part of the proper law approach is *R (Ahsan) v DPP* [2008] EWHC (Admin) 666.

93 Cited at http://www.eurojust.europa.eu/press_annual_report_2003.htm, accessed 27 May 2011, at pp 60 *et seq*.

94 Ibid at p 62.

95 Academic commentary arguing in favour of a proper law approach in the criminal law includes Arnell, P., 'The Proper Law of the Crime in International Law Revisited' (2000) 9(1) *Nottingham Law Journal* 39 and Hodgson, T.W., 'From Famine to Feast: the Prosecution of Multi-jurisdictional Financial Crime in the Electronic Age' (2008) *Journal of Financial Crime* 320.

96 The Guidance is available at http://www.publications.parliament.uk/pa/ld200607/ldlwa/70125ws1.pdf, accessed 27 May 2011.

panying guidelines and the Mutual Legal Assistance Guidelines for the United Kingdom 2010. The former provided that the application of law abroad to national and residents could be judged against a series of guidelines. The Guidelines suggested that the law could be extended:

> where the offence is serious (this might be defined, in respect of existing offences, by reference to the length of sentence currently available); where, by virtue of the nature of the offence, the witnesses and evidence necessary for the prosecution are likely to be available in the United Kingdom territory, even though the offence was committed outside the jurisdiction; where there is international consensus that certain conduct is reprehensible and that concerted action is needed involving the taking of extra territorial jurisdiction; where the vulnerability of the victim makes it particularly important to be able to tackle instances of the offence; where it appears to be in the interests of the standing and reputation of the United Kingdom in the international community [and] where there is a danger that offences would otherwise not be justiciable.[97]

Mr Howard, the then Home Secretary, and Baroness Blatch, in the House of Lords both accepted the recommendations.[98] The Guidelines were never brought into force, and were, in any event, limited to the application of the law on a personal relationship basis. That noted, they do evidence an acceptance of the need to develop a more coherent approach to the application of UK criminal law across borders in the context of international law and third states.

The final authority to be mentioned are the Mutual Legal Assistance Guidelines for the United Kingdom 2010.[99] These require that states requesting information from the UK must provide certain details in regard to the offence and its connection to the UK. Evidence will not be forthcoming without this information being provided. This fact lends supports to the view that the UK is cognisant of the importance of a connection between states and a crime or criminal and the possibility of multiple connections. For example, states requesting information from the UK must provide, *inter alia*:

> a description of the offences charged or under investigation and sentence or penalty, a copy of the legislation that criminalises the conduct in the requesting country and gives information on the offence, penalty and rights a person may be afforded and a summary of the facts giving rise to the request and connection this case has to the UK.

97 *Hansard*, HC, Written Answers, 23 July 1996, Series 6, vol 282, cols 170W–171W.

98 *Hansard*, HL, Written Answers, 23 July 1996, vol 574, Pt 131, cols WA117–WA118.

99 See http://www.homeoffice.gov.uk/publications/police/operational-policing/MLA-guidelines-8th-edition?view=Binary, accessed 27 May 2011.

Utilising a form of language not alien to the proper law approach, the Guidance requires that a:

> clear nexus (direct link) must be established between the facts of the case as detailed in the request and the evidence requested. This goes further than just stating that the requested material is relevant to the case and should specify how it is relevant and will advance the case.

Of course, the Guidance does not relate to the application of UK criminal law. It does signify, however, the UK's unwillingness to assist in the prosecution of crime where there is no material link between the state applying its law and the crime or criminal.

Non-UK law and practice – human rights law

In certain respects there are significant differences between the application of human rights law and criminal law applied across borders; in others there is a not-inconsiderable degree of similarity. An area of similarity is in regard to the external influence upon them – both are affected by non-UK law and practice. Indeed, UK human rights law is affected and conditioned by influences outwith the UK perhaps more than any other area of law. This applies in general terms – to the application of human rights law on a wholly territorial basis – and in regard to its application across borders. The influence of UK membership of the Convention is paramount here. As seen above, the Convention and the ECtHR have such a prevalent role that it is not unreasonable to conceive of them as being an integral part of UK law as opposed to existing outside it. Of course, this is not technically the case, although there is considerable literature and debate on the exact relationship between the Convention and the HRA, discussed in Chapter 4.[100] The Convention is merely an international treaty, albeit a significant one, and the ECtHR is a regional intergovernmental court, the decisions of which the UK has agreed to abide by Article 46 of the Convention. That noted, the effect of the articles themselves is direct, with the majority of them being replicated in Schedule 1 to the HRA.[101] Section 1(1) of the HRA provides that 'Convention rights' are those found in Articles 2–12 and 14 of the Convention, Articles 1–3 of the First Protocol and Article 1 of the Thirteenth Protocol. Section 1(2) provides that 'Those Articles are to have effect for the purposes of this Act'. Significantly, section 2 requires UK courts and tribunals to take into account, *inter alia*, ECtHR judgments and decisions in cases where a question arises in connection with a Convention right. Since 2 October 2000,

100 In addition to those sources cited in Chapter 4 on this point, see Ewing, K.D., 'The Human Rights Act and Parliamentary Democracy' (2003) 62 MLR 79, esp. pp 84 *et seq.*

101 A germane provision not included is Art 1, mentioned above. A further example of an excluded article is Art 13, guaranteeing a right to an effective remedy.

when the HRA fully entered into force, therefore, the relationship between UK law and international law in the form of the Convention and ECtHR jurisprudence has been extremely close.

The Convention and ECtHR jurisprudence are not alone amongst non-UK law and practice in influencing the application of UK human rights law across borders – although they are clearly pre-eminent. Other treaties and international instruments have also had an influence.[102] The leading general international convention in the field of human rights is the International Covenant on Civil and Political Rights 1966 (ICCPR). Article 2, paragraph 1 places a general obligation upon states to protect human rights. It provides:

> Each State Party to the present Covenant undertakes to respect and to ensure to all individuals within its territory and subject to its jurisdiction the rights recognized in the present Covenant, without distinction of any kind, such as race, colour, sex, language, religion, political or other opinion, national or social origin, property, birth or other status.

In regard to the applicability of the Covenant outside the territory of state parties, paragraph 10 of General Comment 31 of the Human Rights Committee 2004 provides:

> States Parties are required by article 2, paragraph 1, to respect and to ensure the Covenant rights to all persons who may be within their territory and to all persons subject to their jurisdiction. This means that a State party must respect and ensure the rights laid down in the Covenant to anyone within the power or effective control of that State Party, even if not situated within the territory of the State Party. . . . [T]his principle also applies to those within the power or effective control of the forces of a State Party acting outside its territory, regardless of the circumstances in which such power or effective control was obtained, such as forces constituting a national contingent of a State Party assigned to an international peace-keeping or peace-enforcement operation.[103]

Whilst Article 2 is binding upon the UK, and the General Comment of the Human Rights Committee is a persuasive interpretation thereof, the actual impact of these authorities is overshadowed by the Convention and ECtHR jurisprudence.[104] This is for several reasons including the date which each entered into force with a UK as a party (1953 for the Convention and 1976 for

102 See, generally, Gondek, M., *The Reach of Human Rights in a Globalizing World: Extra-territorial Application of Human Rights Treaties*, Intersentia Publishing, Mortsel, 2009.

103 CCPR/C/21/Rev.1/Add13. See, further, Coomans, F., 'The Extraterritorial Scope of the International Covenant on Economic, Social and Cultural Rights in the Work of the United Nations Committee on Economic, Social and Cultural Rights' (2011) 11 *Human Rights Law Review* 1.

104 An exception is the position and debate surrounding the application of the ICCPR to the Chagos Islands. Making the argument for the application of the Covenant there is the

the ICCPR) and the nature of dispute settlement within each – the UK allowing individual petition to the ECtHR from 1966. In addition to the ICCPR the UK is party to several human rights-related treaties that entail a degree of extraterritorial application, including the United Nations Convention Against Torture and Other Cruel, Inhuman or Degrading Treatment or Punishment 1984 and the Convention on the Rights of the Child 1989. Indeed, treaties need not address human rights explicitly and directly to affect the application of UK human rights law across borders. The Charter of the United Nations 1945 has been mentioned in this vein.[105] In contrast, a form of international instrument that is explicitly designed to have an effect on the application of human rights law across borders are the memoranda of association relating to non-torture obligations which the UK has concluded with various countries, mentioned in Chapter 4. Whilst the Council of Europe and the Convention overshadow the EU in regard to the influence upon human rights law within the UK and especially its application across borders, it has also had an effect. As noted in Chapter 4, EU rules in regard to asylum have raised questions surrounding the extent of human rights obligations, as in *Secretary of State for the Home Department v Nasseri (FC)*.[106]

In line with the Convention having the greatest non-UK treaty-based impact upon the application of UK human rights law across borders, and indeed overshadowing other international agreements, ECtHR jurisprudence is dominant as a source of non-UK case law. As has been seen above there are a number of leading precedents in regard to both extradition and expulsion and wholly extraterritorial cases emanating from the ECtHR. In light of Article 46 of the Convention and, since 2 October 2000, section 2 of the HRA, ECtHR jurisprudence is highly influential. The case law of other states and bodies, however, has also had some affect. In *RB (Algeria) v Secretary of State*,[107] for example, Lord Phillips in the House of Lords referred to decisions of the UN Committee Against Torture, *Attia v Sweden*[108] and the Federal Court of Canada case *Lai v Canada (Minister of Citizenship and Immigration)*.[109] A further example is found in *Al-Skeini* where Lord Rodger cited the ECtHR in *Issa v Turkey*,[110] which in

NGO Minority Rights Group International, Shadow report submitted to the Human Rights Committee with respect to the Sixth Periodic Report of the United Kingdom of Great Britain and Northern Ireland, July 2010, cited at http://www.ohchr.org/, accessed 27 May 2011.

105 It formed an element of the authority relied upon in *R (Gentle) v Prime Minister* [2008] UKHL 20.

106 [2009] UKHL 23. A further relevant case involving EU law, mentioned in Chapter 3, is *R (Zagorski) v Secretary of State for Business, Innovation and Skills* [2010] EWHC (Admin) 3110.

107 [2009] UKHL 10.

108 CAT/C/31/D/199/2002 (Communication No 199/2002) (unreported) at para 112.

109 [2008] 2 FCR 3 at para 116. The Canadian decision in turn mentioned Amnesty International, Human Rights Watch and the International Commission of Jurists.

110 (2005) 41 EHHR 27.

turn referred to views of the United Nations Human Rights Committee in its leading case on the extraterritorial application of Article 2(1) of the ICCPR, *López v Uruguay*.[111] This brings to light a germane point in the description of the non-UK judicial influence on human rights applied across borders. This is that whilst there is relatively little direct reference in UK law to cases other than those heard in the ECtHR, that Court itself has made reference to a wide range of sources in addition to its own jurisprudence. This is, in effect, a non-UK and non-ECtHR influence arising vicariously.

Proper law – human rights law

UK human rights law is contributing to the development of a non-private proper law approach alongside the criminal law. Its particular contribution, however, differs from the criminal law in two ways. The first is in respect of scale of the contribution. Human rights law contributes less to the approach than the criminal law. This follows one of the two types of human rights law applied in this way – extradition and expulsion cases – failing to add to the practice supporting the development of the approach. That the immediate connection with the UK in these cases is territorial leads to this conclusion. Here the UK applies human rights law to such cases as a matter of fact because the connection between it and the (future) violation is direct and territorial.[112] As the future possible victim is within UK territory there has been relatively little debate about the particular link or connection between the victim and violation and the UK. A more fundamental difference between human rights law and the criminal law in regard to the contribution they make to the emergence of the proper law approach flows from the fact that UK human rights law in essence requires and entails self-regulation. Simply, in the area of human rights law the UK and myriad public authorities are the perpetrators of human rights violation; in the area of the criminal law it is prosecutor.[113] The UK itself, in one of its many manifestations, is the pre-eminent subject of the application of human rights law.[114] The questions being addressed by the proper law approach are, first, what are the links between the UK and the crime and criminal and, second, what is the relative strength of

111 (1981) 68 ILR 29.

112 In contrast, Miller in effect argues that this fact supports the proper law approach in that the link of territory forms the basis of the application of the law across borders, in Miller, S., 'Revisiting extraterritorial jurisdiction: a territorial justification for extraterritorial jurisdiction under the European Convention' (2009) *European Journal of International Law* 1223 at pp 1242 *et seq*.

113 A result of this is that the proper law approach in the area of human rights is exclusively the concern of courts, not the executive. As was noted above, in regard to the criminal law both the judiciary and executive and, to a lesser extent, the legislature can be affected by the approach.

114 This is subject to the possible application of human rights law to private persons, discussed in Chapter 4.

those links in light of the connections with third states.[115] The questions in the field of human rights law are necessarily different – they are, first, what is the strength of the link between the UK and the victim of the past or future human rights violation and, second, what is the relative position of that link in light of the connections that may exist with third states. The point here is that in the area of human rights the UK is *ipso facto* linked to all bona fide allegations of human rights violations abroad where the UK was acting, as the perpetrator of the violation – it must be. The issue is not whether there is a link and if so what it is, but rather whether the strength of the link is sufficient to bring the violation within the jurisdiction of the UK as required by Article 1 of the Convention and so possibly engage UK responsibility. Questions relating to the particular connection between the UK and the victim of the violation (in the sense of a personal relationship, for example) lessen considerably in importance in light of this fact. An effect of the UK being necessarily linked to bona fide allegations of human rights violations abroad has been the development of the tests whereby the strength of the link is examined in the form of the 'effective control' test, possibly the 'state agent authority' test, and perhaps the developing 'jurisdictional link' test. It is somewhat paradoxical, then, that the proper law approach is of lesser relevance generally in the area of human rights law on account of the UK being necessarily and immediately linked to all human rights violations abroad properly ascribed to it and has led to it having a different type of contribution. That contribution, whilst distinct from that made by the criminal law, is no less important.

The proper law approach to the application of law across borders has two parts. As seen above the first focuses on the presence of a material connection or link between the criminal act or human rights violation and the UK. The second comprises awareness on the part of the UK of the links that exist with third states and, in some cases, an analysis of their relative strength. In regard to human rights law the first part of the approach entails examination of the link that must necessarily exist between the UK and the alleged violation. The examination considers whether the link is sufficient to enable the UK to be held responsible. Prior to discussing the nature of the link it should be noted that the UK eschews what has been termed 'universal civil jurisdiction'. The International Bar Association defines this as 'the ability of states to provide civil judicial remedies for violations of human rights and other fundamental norms of international law without requiring a link between the subject matter of the dispute or the parties on the one hand and the forum on the other'.[116] Clearly,

115 Related to the difference between the criminal law and human rights law here is the meaning of 'jurisdiction'. Milanovic notes that 'jurisdiction' under Convention jurisprudence and 'jurisdiction' in public international law are distinct, in Milanovic, M., 'From Compromise to Principle: Clarifying the Concept of State Jurisdiction in Human Rights Treaties' (2008) 8 *Human Rights Law Review* 411 at pp 417 *et seq.*

116 International Bar Association, Extraterritorial Task Force on Extraterritorial Jurisdiction, February 2009, at p 15, cited at http://tinyurl.com/taskforce-etj-pdf, accessed 27 May 2011.

the UK law does not generally provide a human rights remedy for violations on this basis.[117] It does so only where there is a link between the violation and itself, in other words where it may be responsible for the breach of human rights. This point is generally well-settled. As seen in Chapter 4, what is not settled is the nature of the link required to bring the violation within the jurisdiction of the UK. The authorities on this crucial question are mixed. The law contains concepts including 'effective control', 'state-agent authority' and 'jurisdictional link'. In the leading ECtHR case of *Bankovic v Belgium*[118] the Court concluded that that there was no 'jurisdictional link' between the persons who were victims of the act complained of and the respondent states.[119] The use of this expression by the ECtHR, however, has not continued. As noted by Lord Collins in *Smith*[120] there is only one other ECtHR decision that employs the expression, *Markovic v Italy*.[121] Lord Collins stated:

> The expression 'jurisdictional link' in the conclusion in *Banković* is plainly not intended to state or represent a separate and independent test of jurisdiction, and the same must be so of the passages in *Markovic v Italy*. Consequently, neither of those decisions suggests that there is a separate freestanding head of jurisdiction based on a jurisdictional link. . .[122]

That noted, there is reference to the 'link' between a victim and the UK in *Al-Skeini* as noted by Lord Rodger in the context of the difference between the Convention and the HRA: 'It is important therefore to recognise that, when considering the question of jurisdiction under the Convention, the focus has shifted to the victim or, more precisely, to the link between the victim and the contracting state'.[123]

In the absence of the concept of a 'jurisdictional link' being settled in either ECtHR or UK jurisprudence as establishing or justifying the application of human rights law abroad, it is necessary to look for alternatives. Most common amongst the bases establishing the application of human rights law abroad is the concept of 'effective control'. As seen above, a number of the leading authorities in the area have relied upon the effective control principle. Lawson has stated that 'the extent to which Contracting parties must secure the rights and freedoms of individuals outside their borders is commensurate with their ability to do so – that is: the scope of their obligations depend on the degree of

117 The United States under the Alien Tort Act 1789 has led the world in this regard; see, generally, Burley, A.-M., 'The Alien Tort Statute and the Judiciary Act of 1789: A Badge of Honor' (1989) 83 *American Journal of International Law* 461.

118 (2001) 11 BHRC 435.

119 Ibid at para 82.

120 [2010] UKSC 29 at para 295.

121 (2006) 44 EHRR 1045.

122 [2010] UKSC 29 at para 299.

123 *Al-Skeini*, at para 64, as it was by Lord Browne without criticism, at para 131.

control and authority that they exercise'.[124] However, the effective control principle is ill-defined and unclear within ECtHR jurisprudence; as Lawson admits, the effective control approach 'is implicit in the Strasbourg case law, even if it had not really been developed'.[125] Miller notes that effective control is tantamount to 'functional sovereignty', meaning that the state is 'in all instances, exercising functions in another state's territory which are normally associated with the acts of a sovereign state on its own territory'.[126] In other words, in wholly extraterritorial cases the link between the UK and victim and human rights violation takes the form of the control the UK exercises over the person and situation. The two accepted forms of link, then, are territory (in regard to extradition and expulsion cases) and effective control (in regard to wholly extraterritorial cases). As noted in Chapter 4, the existence of a connection based on 'state-agent authority' is questionable. Together, these links or connections are present when the UK applies its human rights law across borders. Whilst there is only tangential authority in support of the contention that conceived as links or connections they contribute towards an emerging proper law approach, the inherent logic of this conclusion, together with the occasional reference to 'jurisdictional links' or 'links' alone, lend some weight to this contention.

The second part of the proper law approach, like the first, finds relatively little explicit authority in the jurisprudence. There is indirect support, however, for the proposition that the ECtHR and UK courts are aware of the links between the victim and violation and third states and may take them into account. In both wholly extraterritorial cases and extradition and expulsion cases, the past or future human rights violation necessarily occurred or occurs in a third state. Cognisance of this fact is evident in judicial *dicta*. As noted above, forming part of the authority criticising the application of human rights across borders is this statement of Lord Justice Brook in the Divisional Court in *Al-Skeini*:

> And it is in any event very much open to question whether an effort by an occupying power in a predominately Muslim country to inculcate what the ECtHR has described as 'the common spiritual heritage of the member states of Europe' during its temporary sojourn in that country would have been consistent with the Coalition's goal, which was to transfer responsibility to representative Iraqi authorities as early as possible.[127]

Clearly in the mind of the court were the nature and culture of Iraq, and the Iraqi links to the persons and incident in question. A more general point in

124 Lawson, R., 'Life after *Bankovic*: on the Extraterritorial Application of the European Convention on Human Rights', in Coomans, F. and Kamminga, M.T. (eds), *Extraterritorial Application of Human Rights Treaties*, Intersentia, Oxford, 2004, at p 86.

125 Ibid at p 105.

126 Miller, 'Revisiting extraterritorial jurisdiction' (n 113 above), at p 1236.

127 [2004] EWHC (Admin) 2911 at para 127.

support of the awareness of UK courts and the ECtHR of the links to, and interests of, third states can be seen in the simple fact that the application of human rights law across borders is exceptional. As noted in *Bankovic*:

> the Convention is a multi-lateral treaty operating . . . in an essentially regional context and notably in the legal space (*éspace juridique*) of the Contracting States. . . . The Convention was not designed to be applied throughout the world, even in respect of the conduct of Contracting States.[128]

The restrictive approach is largely explained with reference to the nature and interests of third states. It is they, not parties to the Convention, who generally exercise control over their territories and may, or may not, apply a human rights regime within them. Indeed, an analysis of whether the UK has effective control over an area outside its territory is in some ways a process that implicitly takes into account third states and the links that they may have to a human rights violation on their territory. Only through effective control of the area in which the violation of human rights occurred is the sovereignty and ability to apply the territorial law necessarily usurped.

Conclusion

The application of UK law across borders is an important, relevant and wide-ranging subject. It is important for a number of reasons, including the impact it can have on individuals outside the state, the possible violations of international law it engenders, the affect it may have on relations with third states and the need to address international criminality and human rights violations. These have been discussed throughout this book. The cumulative weight of these factors leads to the subject being too significant to ignore. The application of law to persons and circumstances outside the UK is both long standing and relevant today. As seen, UK law, particularly the criminal law, has been applied to persons, for a considerable period of time. Treason and murder are amongst the crimes with the longest extraterritorial pedigree. The subject is also relevant, however, with an increasing number of criminal acts and human rights violations outside the UK coming to be governed by its law. Whilst the number of cases where the law is actually enforced is relatively small (the greatest number of arguments take place in extradition and expulsion cases) the cases that do arise are notable because of that rarity and because they may open the door to further cases. Indeed, in a sense, the law in regard to wholly extraterritorial human rights cases is at a critical juncture. Cases pending judgment at the ECtHR could have a significant effect on the law in the area, particularly the decision of the House of Lords in *Al-Skeini*.

128 (2001) 11 BHRC 435 at para 80.

Finally, the application of UK law across borders is a particularly wide-ranging subject. In certain ways this book has only scratched the surface. The importance of each individual topic within the subject area demands greater exploration and discussion. Whilst a thorough description of how UK criminal law and human rights law are applied to persons and circumstances outside its territory is found in Chapters 3 and 4, further coverage of specific subjects, such as the law and practice of extradition and the exact nature of the relationship between citizens and the state, beg further analysis. Further, this book has largely excluded from examination the germane subjects of the extraterritorial application of private law and competition law. Whilst these are, of course, distinct from the criminal law and human rights law, they are related in that they too are applied to persons and circumstances outside the UK. This book has described the criminal law and human rights law as applied across borders in the context in which it occurs. The nature of the law and the subject of its enforcement have been discussed, as have problems arising from the application of the law and the criticisms it engenders. In the course of this description and discussion, two themes have emerged – the considerable influence of non-UK law and practice in the area and an emerging proper law approach to the application of the law.

Final points

Three final points deserve to be made. The first is that the application of UK non-private law across borders must continue to be exceptional. There are numerous reasons for the continuation of the UK's traditional view that the ambit of the law should be limited. The arguments in favour of a more expansive tact being taken do not overcome these reasons. The UK and Scottish Parliaments should continue to exercise restraint in extending the law, and courts similarly should take a restrictive view as to the meaning of 'within their jurisdiction' in Article 1 of the Convention. Further, courts should continue to apply the rule of statutory interpretation providing that statutes are intra-territorial unless they explicitly provide otherwise. The reasons against a broad approach to the extraterritorial applicability of UK law have been mentioned throughout this book – including practicality, evidence, expense, the interests of third states and rules of international law. Further and simply, the UK should not and cannot act as a global policeman or human rights watchdog. This is just not tenable.

A second point is that the application of law across borders demands a unifying principle. This is because the law requires coherence and logic. Further, the legislative branch, courts, individuals and third states deserve to be able to understand clearly and readily why UK law applies to certain persons and circumstances outside its territory, and not to others. Related to this is possible concurrent jurisdiction and conflict with third states. It is worth iterating the International Bar Association's suggested approaches to concurrent jurisdiction. It states that there are four possible solutions:

(a) creating a legal hierarchy or other test to determine which state has priority;
(b) encouraging states to adopt discretionary doctrines to refrain from exercising jurisdiction in certain circumstances (i.e., no legal hierarchy, but consideration of doctrines such as reasonableness and comity to temper the use of extraterritorial jurisdiction);
(c) establishing methods of mutual recognition and cooperation between multiple states with jurisdiction (i.e., no legal hierarchy, but systems to encourage cooperation between states to avoid jurisdiction conflicts); and
(d) encouraging harmonisation of laws (i.e., no legal hierarchy, but encouraging convergence in the substance of laws to reduce the problems caused by jurisdictional conflicts.[129]

At the present stage of international legal development the first and fourth options appear to be unachievable. However, the second and third are, in fact, in the process of emerging. They relate to the two themes within this book.

The final point is that international co-operation is vital. The theme relating to the effect of non-UK law and practice comes to the fore here. The manner to address concerns that may arise through criminality and human rights violations occurring in an international and national legal vacuum is not through the application of UK law across borders, but instead through recourse to non-UK bodies and third states. What is preferable to a unilateral application of UK law is the provision of advice, assistance and indeed resources to third states and international bodies. The sheer volume of international and transnational criminality and human rights violations, the nature and extent of inter-personal intercourse and the complexity of crime and international relations, together with the most basic of points – the composition of the globe into territorial sovereign units – leads to no other possible conclusion.

129 International Bar Association, Extraterritorial Task Force on Extraterritorial Jurisdiction (n 116 above), at p 22.

Index